THE FORGOTTEN TRIBE
British MEPs, 1979-2020

with contributions from:

Lorin Bell-Cross
David Blackman
William Bethell
Michael Crick
Alan Donnelly
Brendan Donnelly
Duncan Enright
Tom Fieldhouse
David Gow
David Harley
Dianne Hayter
Rachel Johnson
Richard Johnson
John Kerr
Neil Kinnock
Giada Lagana
Alistair Lexden
Roger Liddle
David Lidington
Caroline Lucas
David McAllister
Giles Merritt
Claude Moraes
Tom Newton Dunn
Caroline Nokes
Rory Palmer
George Parker
Anita Pollack
George Robertson
Ivan Rogers
Michael Russell
Joshua Stratford
Christopher Tugendhat
Graham Watson
Gareth Williams

THE FORGOTTEN TRIBE

British MEPs, 1979-2020

edited by
Dianne Hayter and David Harley

The Forgotten Tribe: British MEPs, 1979-2020
Edited by Dianne Hayter and David Harley

ISBN 978-1-7391436-0-2

www.johnharperpublishing.co.uk

© John Harper Publishing 2022
Front cover photos © European Union.
Back cover photo of Dianne Hayter courtesy of and © William Knight.

Printed and bound by Severn, Gloucester

Reproduction of short extracts from this book is welcome, provided the source is acknowledged

TABLE OF CONTENTS

About the editors viii

I: THE STORY

1. Introduction, by David Harley and Dianne Hayter 3
2. The Conservative journey, from pro to anti,
   by Tom Fieldhouse 17
3. Labour's journey: from anti to pro, by Richard Johnson 39
4. The Liberal Democrats' arrival, by Graham Watson 57
5. The move to proportional representation and the rise
   of UKIP, by Lorin Bell-Cross 68

II: AS OTHERS SAW THEM

1. The view from the coalition government, by David Lidington 79
2. The view from Tony Blair's No. 10, by Roger Liddle 84
3. The view from Labour in the Thatcher and Major era,
   by George Robertson 92
4. As seen by a German MEP, by David McAllister 96
5. The view from the Commission, by Christopher Tugendhat 100
6. The view from the UK Permanent Representation
   (i) by John Kerr 104
   (ii) by Ivan Rogers..106
7. A journalist's view from Brussels, by George Parker 114

III: THE MAIN PLAYERS

1. Barbara Castle, by Anita Pollack 121
2. Ken Collins, by Anita Pollack 126
3. Basil de Ferranti, by Alistair Lexden 133
4. John Hume, by David Harley 139

5. Henry Plumb, by David Harley 144
6. Christopher Prout, by Brendan Donnelly 149
7. David Martin, by David Gow 154
8. Pauline Green, by Dianne Hayter 160
9. Graham Watson, by Giles Merritt 165
10. Glenys Kinnock, by Neil Kinnock 169
11. Richard Corbett, by David Harley 175
12. Nigel Farage, by Michael Crick 180
13. Daniel Hannan, by Dianne Hayter...185
14. Malcolm Harbour, by David Harley 189

IV: AS THEIR CHILDREN SAW THEM

1. Nicholas Bethell, by William Bethell 194
2. Bill Newton Dunn, by Tom Newton Dunn...............................199
3. Stanley Johnson, by Rachel Johnson 204
4. Derek Enright, by Duncan Enright 209
5. Roy Perry, by Caroline Nokes...216

V: THE NATIONS

1. Scotland, by Michael Russell..221
2. Wales, by Gareth Williams 230
3. Northern Ireland, by Giada Lagana...241

VI: MAKING A DIFFERENCE

1. The environment, by Caroline Lucas 251
2. Human rights and civil liberties, by Claude Moraes...............257
3. German reunification, by Alan Donnelly 263
4. Aid to democracy and human rights, by David Blackman 267

VII: FAREWELL AND CONCLUSIONS

1. The farewell, by Rory Palmer 273
2. Conclusions, by David Harley and Dianne Hayter 277

ANNEXES

1. The 351, by Joshua Stratford 285
2. List of all elected UK MEPs 1979-2020, by Joshua Stratford 296
3. Index of names 305

ABOUT THE EDITORS

Baroness Dianne Hayter was the shadow Brexit minister in the House of Lords throughout the withdrawal process, also serving as shadow deputy leader of the House and shadow consumer and Cabinet Office minister. Having helped set up the European Trade Union Confederation in 1973, Dianne later became chief executive of the European Parliamentary Labour Party. Earlier she was general secretary of the Fabian Society, director of Alcohol Concern, chair of the Labour Party and a consumer representative on the National Consumer Council, the National Patient Safety Agency and other regulatory bodies. She chaired the Legal Services Consumer Panel and is on the board of the Association of British Insurers. An historian, Dianne is the author of *Fightback: Labour's Traditional Right in the 1970s and 1980s*, co-edited *Men Who Made Labour*, and has written on Neil Kinnock, Beatrice Webb, Denis Healey, and Labour Party policy.

David Harley served as a European Parliament official from 1975 to 2010. Starting as a translator, he ended his career as deputy secretary-general of the institution and director-general of the presidency. Other senior posts held were those of secretary-general of the Socialist group, director of press and media, and spokesman of the president. From 2010 to 2020 he was chair and senior adviser in the Brussels office of the public affairs and political communications agency Burson-Marsteller, where he worked with governments, political parties and global corporations. David now divides his time between south-west London and Bordeaux. Positions currently held include that of practitioner fellow at Aston University in Birmingham and member of the advisory board of the Foreign Policy Centre. In 2011 he was awarded a CMG for "services to international diplomacy and UK-European Parliament relations". He is the author of *Matters of Record: Inside European Politics*, a transcription of the political diaries he kept during the period 1992-2010 (John Harper Publishing, 2021).

I: THE STORY

From Assembly to Parliament

When I began working for the European Parliament secretariat in Luxembourg in April 1975, it took me some time to get used to all my new colleagues constantly referring to "the Parliament". At first I thought they meant the House of Commons or another national parliament, but no: this was the rather grand term used in common parlance for my new workplace. Yet the Treaty of Rome made no mention of a Parliament, using instead the term "Assembly".

Subsequently I learned a little about the history of the name. The Treaty of Paris establishing the Coal and Steel Community on 18 April 1951 set up a "Common Assembly". Although initially a purely consultative body, the new Assembly – composed of appointed national MPs – wasted no time in formulating demands for greater legislative and budgetary powers. On 19 March 1958 it met in Strasbourg as the "European Parliamentary Assembly", and on 30 March 1962 it unilaterally changed its name to the European Parliament. From that moment onwards, irrespective of its formal legal status, the European Parliament would always refer to itself by that name.

Following the first direct elections in 1979, the acceptance in practice of the name and the gradual increase in Parliament's powers went hand in hand. This institutional persistence bore fruit, when formal recognition of the title of European Parliament was finally confirmed with the entry into force of the Single European Act on 1 July 1987.

David Harley

1. Introduction

by David Harley and Dianne Hayter

The stories in this book are for the most part written by politicians about politicians, and record from different perspectives and political standpoints the part played by the 351 women and men who represented Britain in the European Parliament from the first direct elections in 1979 to the UK's departure from the EU in 2020. Those four decades were a time of seismic change both on the European continent and in the endless ebbs and flows of the UK's relations with our European neighbours.

The contributors describe what happened behind the scenes, who these MEPs were and what they achieved, with frank assessments of how they were perceived by governments, diplomats, commissioners, other countries, the media, and by their own families. Their personal and political stories bring life and depth to this period of democratic engagement, its successes and failures, and show how these elected representatives fared in their own political parties.

In telling the story of the British presence for over 40 years in the European Parliament, the book also describes how the system within the Parliament worked, the importance of the political families and the key role of the parliamentary committees, as well as the external relationship with the Commission and the Council and the balance of power and political influence between the three institutions. It tells the major stories underwriting those four decades of continuous, close involvement: the fundamental shifts in the policy positions of the Conservative and Labour parties; the growth and blossoming of the Liberal Democrats; and the momentous impact of the change in the electoral system from first-past-the-post, which was used in elections from 1979 to 1994, to the proportional representation (PR) introduced in 1999. This change enabled the UK Independence Party (UKIP) to secure an all-important platform as well as affecting how other parties selected and managed relations with their MEPs.

All through this period, with each revision of the treaties, the European Parliament steadily amassed greater legislative powers and competences. The book provides examples of how these developments gave its political group leaders and committee chairs significant influence over the Commission and member states' ministers meeting in the Council.

The tale ends with Brexit, fought against by many of these players, championed by others, but perhaps caused in part by the failure of successive governments to explain the European project, in which these MEPs played an integral role, to the very people it was intended to serve. The EU started from the desire to end European wars, by building trade and economic cooperation in place of battlefields. By a grim irony of history, Britain's membership has ended at a time of renewed insecurity in Europe when cooperation and its benefits have never been more needed. What wider lessons can be drawn about Britain's European experience from the part played by these MEPs?

A new beginning

The UK joined the European Communities (at that time still widely referred to in Britain as the common market) in 1973 but it was only in 1979 that the former European Assembly – which had comprised nominated members (in our case MPs and peers from the British Parliament) – became a directly elected parliament, although not without some grumbling and apprehension from national parliaments. On 7-10 June elections took place across all 9 member states, to elect a total of 410 members with a combined electorate of 191,783,528 voters. In the UK, 78 Euro-constituencies were specially created for the purpose in England, Scotland and Wales, plus one constituency in Northern Ireland represented by 3 MEPs elected under PR. In mid-July, having met with their respective political groupings in Luxembourg the previous week, the 81 newly elected UK MEPs arrived in Strasbourg for their first plenary session.

It was a time of flux. Just two months earlier, the general election had seen Jim Callaghan turfed out of Number 10 by a triumphant Mrs Thatcher. Unsurprisingly the Conservative MEPs – all 60 of them – were jubilant, first by adding their European success to hers and then, alongside two Danish MEPs, forming the European Democratic Group (EDG), the third largest group in the new Parliament after the Socialists and the EPP (Christian Democrats).

These European political families mattered, and the Conservatives were in prime position. Led by James Scott-Hopkins, MEP for Hereford and Worcester, their ranks included distinguished captains of industry such as Basil de Ferranti, co-chair of his family electronics company, and Sir David Nicholson, a former chairman of British Airways, as well as some fairly exotic members of the House of Lords including the Marquess of Douro, later to inherit the title of Duke of Wellington.

The 17 Labour MEPs elected the redoubtable former cabinet minister Barbara Castle as their leader and joined the Socialist group, chaired by the Belgian MEP Ernest Glinne, as the third largest national delegation after West Germany and France.

While the British members were finding their feet and looking slightly lost as they searched for their new offices in the maze of corridors in the Council of Europe building, the political great and good from the rest of Europe converged on Strasbourg for this symbolic leap forward for post-war Europe of making the institutions more democratic. Indeed, such was the importance placed on this by the other 8 countries, that their newly elected MEPs included Willy Brandt, the former chancellor of West Germany, Jacques Chirac, the former French prime minister and future president, and Enrico Berlinguer, leader of the Italian Communist Party. Each of them had no intention to stay as an MEP for more than a few months, but had stood for election because they saw direct elections as a significant staging-post on the path to European integration. They knew that what had previously been a purely consultative Assembly would soon be transformed into a fully-fledged Parliament.

On an anecdotal level, as members were seated not by nationality but by alphabetical order in their political group, Roland Boyes, Labour MEP for Durham, was astonished to find himself seated in the chamber next to one of Europe's greatest living statesmen, Willy Brandt. On the first day, just before the official proceedings began, and although it was strictly against the rules, Boyes managed to persuade the Parliament's photographer to take a picture of the two of them together. Over the next five years, whenever visitor groups from his constituency came to his office in Strasbourg, Boyes would proudly show them the photo.

The solemn high point of symbolism in this first session was the election on Tuesday 17 July of Simone Veil as president of the Parliament. A former French minister of health, she was a survivor of Auschwitz and Bergen-Belsen and had lost both parents and a brother in the camps. In the eyes of her 409 fellow MEPs, she symbolised the reconciliation of Western Europe, and in particular France and Germany, thirty-four years after the horrors of the Second World War – the principal raison d'être for the creation of the European Community, a point not lost on the 81 British MEPs.

A different political culture: how the Parliament worked

When the British politicians arrived in Strasbourg for their first plenary session, and then in Brussels for their first committee meetings, they faced a wholly novel situation. Those coming from national or local politics had been used to sitting in the same chamber as the governing members (ministers or Council leaders), and to having clearly defined roles either as the opposition or the party supporting the administration. They understood their roles and the political hierarchies and levers.

Suddenly they were in a completely new setup, more akin to the United States or other presidential systems where major policy decisions were taken by the executive outside the legislature. In the

PART I: THE STORY 7

EP too, the Commission and the Council were not physically present "in the kirk", but sent draft legislation, or dossiers, across to Parliament to be considered by elected members who worked not vis-à-vis the relevant minister, but in a committee chaired by a fellow MEP and with a level of detailed scrutiny quite alien to national MPs.

Politically too, they found themselves in a new situation, where they sat within two political groupings: their own (national) political party – Conservative or Labour (initially, just the two) – but also within a European political family, each with their own elected whip to issue voting instructions. Indeed, the EP is the only multinational parliament or assembly in the world where members sit not by nationality but by political affiliation. Members tended to develop a strong loyalty to their political group as well as to their national delegation.

Over the years the Conservatives, as set out in the next chapter, moved between different political groupings, latterly sitting in the European Conservatives and Reformists group (ECR), set up with hard-right parties from Central and Eastern Europe after David Cameron took them out of the centre-right EPP group in 2009. Labour, on the other hand, always sat firmly in the Socialist group, which Pauline Green led from 1994 to 1999. It happened to change its name in 2009 (to accommodate Italian sensitivities) to the Socialists and Democrats (S & D), but throughout this book it is referred to as the Socialist group. (The equivalent party organisation, outside of Parliament, went through a name change earlier, from the Confederation of Socialist Parties to the Party of European Socialists, the nomenclature we also employ.)

For the national party delegations, internal elections were held for senior posts such as leader, secretary and whip, and then negotiations took place between all national delegations to elect the leader of the EP political group. By way of example, in 1994 it was the leader *pro tem* of the Labour Party, Margaret Beckett (following the tragic and untimely death of John Smith in May that year) who negotiated Pauline Green's designation and subsequent election as Socialist group leader, after Labour had won 62 seats in the 1994 election and become by far the largest national delegation in the group.

Within the Parliament, once the new political groups crystallised after each European election, negotiations took place for the position of committee chairs, on the strict basis of an allocation of points reflecting each group's number of MEPs (known as the D'Hondt system after the Belgian mathematician who invented it in 1878).

For most MEPs, the centre of their work was their committee, scrutinising proposals from the Commission and holding the relevant commissioner to account. Here an important role was that of rapporteur, with the job of preparing the draft report on proposed items of legislation to be voted on first in committee and then by the full Parliament in plenary session. Scope also existed for individual initiatives by members, for example on human rights worldwide or constituency-related issues, through procedures such as urgency resolutions, written declarations, and oral or written questions to the Council and the Commission.

The allocation of committee places, committee chairs and rapporteurs was decided in a carve-up between the political groups – and the president of Parliament was elected – every five years after each European election and again halfway through the parliamentary term. The president of the Commission was also nominated by the member state governments after taking account of the result of the European elections, and then formally elected by the EP for a five-year term.

As Parliament's legislative powers increased, the role of rapporteurs in committee became ever more influential in shaping the final item of legislation adopted by Parliament in plenary session. By the time of British withdrawal, some 80% of all EU legislation required the Parliament's approval, following a process of co-decision with the Council representing the member states. Parliament by this time had acquired a significant and often determinant role in the institutional partnership with the Commission and the Council.

This concentration on the detailed scrutiny of draft legislation (more akin to the role of the House of Lords) in committee produced a very different way of working, and culture, than the House of Commons. In addition to party political views, national positions also had to be accommodated, with the rapporteur and committee chair involved in building cross-national and cross-party consensus in order to secure agreement by a majority in plenary. For most MEPs, this soon came to be seen as a better way of doing politics, respecting different points of view and seeking to move forward rather than score points. In Caroline Lucas's contribution, she praises this more collaborative, less adversarial approach, which female politicians particularly appreciated. Even the fact of having a chamber in the shape of a hemicycle rather than with ranks of opposing benches reduces the hothouse atmosphere.

A word at this point on the use of languages. The European Parliament has one of the largest interpretation services in the world, making multilingualism a dominant feature of the institution. Every MEP has the right to listen and speak in his or her own official EU language in committee meetings and plenary sessions. As a result of this hugely ambitious policy, whereas in 1979 the EP had 6 official languages and 30 language combinations, by 2013 with 28 member states the number of official languages had grown to 24 with 552 language combinations. Amazingly, the system coped with this mammoth administrative challenge. One of the first impressions in entering the EP's buildings was the continuous surrounding buzz of foreign languages (mixed with a strange emerging quasi-dialect of lowest-common-denominator English).

Travel and the human side of an MEP's work

There was another reason for greater cross-party collaboration. Commuting from the UK to Brussels and Strasbourg (initially without the Eurostar so always by plane) led to unavoidable social contact with MEPs of other nationalities and political persuasions. Endless waiting for delayed flights, allocated seating – whether in cars to airports or on board – could mean forced conversations with normal political adversaries, perhaps even finding them human. Social contacts with MEPs from widely differing backgrounds were interesting and mind broadening. Many MEPs elected in the new member states after their countries' accession arrived with first-hand experience of the physical, psychological and political privations of life under totalitarian rule, be it fascism or communism. Many had gruesome but inspiring stories to tell. Sharing their experiences gave many British MEPs a new perspective on European unity and solidarity.

Other opportunities for cross-party relationship building occurred on missions undertaken by inter-parliamentary delegations, which visited legislatures around the world. MEPs frequently found that the further they travelled from Brussels, the more the EU was respected. Despite the risk of adverse press coverage about jaunts and freebies, these exchanges were greatly valued by MEPs, the delegation for relations with the US Congress being unsurprisingly a particular favourite among leading British MEPs. Its chairs over the 40 years included Geoff Hoon, Jonathan Evans (both subsequently to become MPs), Mel Read and Alan Donnelly. Likewise, the South Asia delegation was chaired by Neena Gill.

Even without these overseas trips, Strasbourg itself was a target of frequent attacks in the UK media as part of the "gravy train". Many MEPs, and almost all British members, were in favour of changing the system and abandoning the monthly trek for four days in Strasbourg (however quaint the city's old quarter La Petite France around the cathedral and agreeable the local cuisine). Edward McMillan-Scott led the "single seat campaign" to relocate all Parliament's activities in Brussels and eventually obtained widespread support. Ironically, however, the decision to formalise Strasbourg as the seat of the EP was taken under the UK Council presidency, with PM John Major in the chair, at the 1992 Edinburgh summit as part of a wider pattern of deals between member states. The EP itself had no legal power to challenge this decision, and no member state wished to trigger a major rumpus or conflict with France on the issue.

Especially before 1999, when the introduction of PR produced vast constituencies of millions of voters, MEPs had to tend to their constituencies much as MPs do, both in representing communities and businesses but also in reporting back to their 8 or 9 constituency associations or parties who had selected them as candidates and campaigned for their election.

These weekly trips to Brussels or Strasbourg (with MEPs returning to their homes and constituencies at weekends) took their toll on members and their families. While generous travel allowances partly compensated, these too attracted criticism, and certainly did not make up for missed school plays, birthdays and not seeing enough of their children as they grew up. In Part IV some MEPs' children give their perspectives on what this meant.

With a handful of notable exceptions (including Linda McAvan, a former interpreter; Veronica Hardstaff, a former French teacher; Joyce Quin, who had been a lecturer in French at the universities of Durham and Bath; Nicholas Bethell, a trained Russian interpreter who had also studied Arabic and Persian; Eluned Morgan, who spoke excellent Spanish in addition to Welsh; and John Hume and Daniel Hannan), few UK MEPs were able to converse in any language other than English. Initially, when French had been predominant, this lack of basic language skills was noticeable and occasionally a hindrance in negotiating behind-the-scenes deals with non-Brits. But as the years went by, and particularly after the arrival of 10 new member states in 2004, English gradually took over as the lingua franca.

Making and witnessing history

1979 to 2020 was a time of massive change across the continent, throwing up challenges and opportunities never envisaged by those first intrepid 81 UK MEPs. By the time Britain left, there were 28 members of the EU, with a combined population of 500 million. Its political geography had been transformed by a series of accessions that included not just established democracies like Austria, Finland and Sweden but also new democracies in the previously right-wing authoritarian states of Greece, Spain and Portugal and former communist states from Central and Eastern Europe. A single market had been created, a single currency common across 19 of the 28, and whilst in 2020 – as in 1979 – a Conservative government was back in Number 10, the domestic political landscape had radically changed, with Labour having become the pro-European party, and the Conservatives the Brexiteers.

The aim of this book is not to try to document everything that British MEPs did in those 41 years – that would be an impossible task – but to give a sense of their involvement in the major developments, and of their achievements and disappointments, and offer portraits of some of the more prominent of them as seen by their contemporaries.

The contributions therefore embrace many different perspectives – from political allies and opponents, government ministers, family members, party colleagues, the media and diplomats. Some are analytical and critical, others positive, even affectionate, yet others anecdotal or mildly technical. All show the human side of life as an MEP, as well as the politics. Different viewpoints are included, but with two important threads throughout: the reversal over the years of policies on Europe by the two main parties; and the paradox of the impressive influence exercised by British MEPs on EU decision making on a daily basis while receiving little attention from the UK media – a factor which may well have contributed to the once unthinkable act of withdrawal.

Britain's two referenda on EU membership, in 1975 and 2016, had very different results. Between these two dates was the gradual volte-face of Britain's two main parties as they each completely swapped positions on Britain's relations with the EU. Of the first 81 British MEPs elected in June 1979, on a turnout of 32.4% (the lowest in Europe where the average was 63%), the 60 Conservatives were all enthusiastic pro-Europeans ("a Heathite tribute act", as George Parker of the FT describes them in his chapter below), whereas the majority of the 17 Labour MEPs were staunch anti-marketeers, as they were then called. By the time Britain left forty-one years later, the situation was almost exactly the opposite, with the Conservative Party in thrall to Eurosceptics and UKIP, and Labour largely positive – albeit passively, especially under Jeremy Corbyn – about British membership.

The next two chapters describe this political "switch over", firstly by the Conservatives, and then by Labour. However, as Tom Fieldhouse points out in the chapter following, given that the Conservatives were in government for most of the 40 years, they exerted a predominant influence on the nature of Britain's relationship with

Europe; Labour were in opposition much of the time and it was under the Conservatives that the UK both joined and left the EU. Responsibility, credit or blame – depending on one's political standpoint – must therefore fall squarely on successive Conservative governments, from initially supporting entry and such major developments as the single market and successive enlargements, to finally bringing about the EU's only loss of a member state. It is for that reason that Fieldhouse contends that the Conservatives' evolving attitudes shaped both Britain's relationship with Europe, as well as the EU itself. He also attributes the 2016 referendum's 52:48 result as least partially to Conservative Euroscepticism (with not insignificant additional help from Nigel Farage and UKIP, some might say), which began to take form under Thatcher's confrontational tone and her battles which established an "us vs them" approach, where winning rather than cooperating defined the narrative.

The rest of Europe and the European Parliament looked on bemused and saddened at this latest resurgence of "British exceptionalism". No other mainstream centre-right party in the EU member states had ever contemplated withdrawal. Even our country's closest friends were forced to conclude that once again Britain, and in particular the Conservative Party, were still struggling "to reconcile the past they could not forget with the future they could not avoid"[1].

Other contributors also shed light on the principal factors behind British withdrawal, not least the introduction of proportional representation for European elections in 1999, which led to a fundamental change in the political landscape, and ultimately to Britain's departure (see especially Part I:5). Another reason was the flawed relationship between the UK's elected representatives in Westminster and in Brussels, which is noted by many of the contributors. While charged with representing Conservative Party positions in Europe, Conservative MEPs, as Fieldhouse underlines, had little role in determining the party's views on Europe; the same could

---

1 Hugo Young, *This Blessed Plot: Britain and Europe from Churchill to Blair*, Macmillan, 1998

also be said of the Labour Party, where domestic rather than European considerations dictated the party's stance.

Meanwhile, for most of those forty years, the British state – Downing Street, the Foreign Office and the UK Permanent Representation in Brussels (UKRep), Whitehall and, to a lesser extent, Westminster and the political parties – played an increasingly active part in the day-to-day running of the European Union, while simultaneously promoting British interests. The efficiency of our diplomatic machine was the envy of many other countries, so much so that for many years it was inconceivable in both the EU institutions and the upper reaches of the British political establishment that Britain would ever contemplate leaving the EU, especially as the UK had negotiated some very helpful opt-outs to protect its interests.

In maximising the UK's influence in the EU, our MEPs were a potentially important, even decisive, source of support – although it took Whitehall many years to wake up to this and understand the characteristics and mode of operation of this new species of politician. As the Parliament gained in power and influence via successive treaty changes, virtually no new legislation could be adopted at European level, nor commissioners appointed nor the EU budget approved, without its agreement. UKRep adapted accordingly and took on additional staff. Ivan Rogers, Britain's ambassador to the EU who resigned under Theresa May's premiership (see Part II:6), saw more clearly than most which way the wind was blowing, and the resulting need to lobby the European Parliament, including MEPs from countries other than Britain.

Paradoxically, almost at the very moment that UK influence on EU legislation reached its apogee, the country decided to leave.

The British contribution

Despite UK MEPs – with only a few exceptions – having little public recognition, for four decades they played a prominent role at all levels of the Parliament. Henry Plumb was president in 1987-89, and David Martin and Edward McMillan-Scott were both long-serving, successful vice-presidents. Pauline Green led the Socialist group, while numerous Conservative and Labour MEPs chaired major committees (notably Malcolm Harbour, Ken Collins and Claude Moraes), as did Liberal Democrats (Graham Watson and Sharon Bowles). Conservative leader Christopher Prout set in hand the Parliament's rules of procedure, subsequently updated by Richard Corbett, who also played a leading role in helping to secure, with others and through his active committee work, additional powers and competences for the EP.

Parliament's way of working was influenced by British MEPs, particularly with the introduction of question time, when commissioners and national ministers representing the Council of Ministers can be interrogated in plenary sessions. Almost unsung was the work of many rapporteurs on key issues, notably the then newly elected MEP Alan Donnelly on the reunification of Germany.

Within the Parliament's administration, albeit not as MEPs, senior British officials included above all Julian Priestley, as secretary-general of the Parliament for 10 years (1997-2007), a hugely influential figure who began work at the EP fresh from Oxford in 1973 and commanded universal respect for both his political skills and administrative competence. David Harley was EP deputy secretary-general, spokesman of the president and secretary-general of the Socialist group. Anthony Teasdale, former special adviser to Geoffrey Howe and Ken Clarke, held senior positions in the private office of two Parliament presidents and was subsequently appointed director-general of Parliamentary Research Services. Many other British officials, at all grades, made an important contribution to the day-to-day running of the institution, and were perfectly integrated into the prevailing multinational and multilingual work culture.

When the UK first joined, its MEPs were generally welcomed and British parliamentary traditions greatly respected (now, not so much – the decline of the UK's reputation and perceived trustworthiness in Europe generally is a subject for another day). UK MEPs played their full part in the activities of the EP at every level. They were appreciated for their pragmatic and generally non-ideological approach, although the minority federalist wing of the EP looked on askance at successive UK opt-outs and opposition to institutional progress. The effective role played by most UK MEPs was also helped by the fact that the UK was one of the four big member states and therefore had a sizeable number of MEPs.

However, over the last decade of UK membership, this generally positive image of our MEPs became somewhat tarnished by the increasingly Eurosceptic Tories leaving the EPP and above all by the large numbers of UKIP members and the antics of their leader. Although the great majority of MEPs of all political groups and nationalities joined hands in the chamber to sing Auld Lang Syne on the day of departure, there was a sizeable minority who heaved a sigh of relief and muttered under their breath "good riddance to the lot of you". While many shed tears, Farage and his troops whooped for joy.

2. The Conservative journey, from pro to anti

by Tom Fieldhouse

Tom Fieldhouse was senior aide to the Rt Hon Sir Oliver Letwin in 2014-19 and also served as deputy director of the cross-party Red Tape Initiative. He is currently a research fellow and networks coordinator at the UCL Constitution Unit.

Britain's relationship with Europe has pre-occupied the Conservative Party for over 70 years.

The party's attitude towards European integration evolved over time, responding to different tendencies within the party and to political events. Its thinking developed from initial lack of interest, through pragmatic engagement, then increasing Euroscepticism and ultimately to outright rejection. Because the party has been in government for most of this time, it heavily influenced the nature of Britain's relationship with Europe and with European integration.

It is, therefore, a paradox that despite representing Conservative views *in* Europe, Conservative MEPs, as a group, were relatively peripheral in determining the party's views *on* Europe. The hard work of Britain's MEPs was as valuable as it is unsung, and this book shines a welcome light on these individuals. However, the focus of this chapter is primarily on events at Westminster – from where the Conservative Party (and governments) are ultimately steered.

This chapter provides a broad outline of the Conservative Party's evolving attitudes towards European integration, which is essential to understanding Britain's complicated relationship with the European project. While I endeavour to be objective, it is important to note that when telling the story of the dramatic events of 2019, I do so from the perspective of having been an active participant.

Phases of Conservative thinking

Many pro and anti-European tendencies have co-existed within the Conservative Party, with thinking about European integration passing through five broad phases – evolving in response to domestic politics, international developments, differing stages of the European project, and the changing make-up of the party.

These are:

1) Uninterest to involvement (1945-75)
2) Pursuit of economic interests within the bloc (1975-87)
3) Bruges, conceptual divergence, and the rise of Euroscepticism (1988-97)
4) Euroscepticism becomes dominant (1997-2013)
5) Brexit and resolution (2013-20).

Care must be taken when applying labels like Eurosceptic or pro-European, as their meaning differs depending on the context. It is better to use distinct terms, such as anti-Europeans and Europhiles in the 1950s; anti-marketeers and pro-marketeers in advance of joining the European Economic Community (EEC); Eurosceptics, anti-federalists, and pro-Europeans in the 1980s/1990s/2000s; hard and soft-Eurosceptics in the 2010s; and latterly, Leavers and Remainers.

Uninterest to involvement (1945–75)

Between 1945 and 1975, Conservative thinking about European integration evolved from apathy to seeking membership of the EEC following a pragmatic reassessment of where Britain's interests lay.

Apathy

At the start, most Conservatives were uninterested in European political federation or economic integration, seeing no need to take part in such projects.

Britain was Europe's pre-eminent economy, its trade was with the Empire and Commonwealth[2], it was a global military power, and its most important partner was the United States. Many harboured doubts about whether novel integrationist ideas could ever overcome the historic enmities of war-torn Europe. Churchill represented a minority view when he called for the creation of a "United States of Europe". His lofty rhetoric helped create the Council of Europe in 1949, but his vision for European unity was vague. Some believe his motivation was peace and prosperity through federation, with Britain being part[3]. Others think he wanted to help the continent withstand the Soviet Union but with Britain remaining outside any supra-national structures. What is clear is that his government did little to advance European unity upon returning to office in 1951 – leading disappointed European politicians to pursue integration without Britain.

This began with the European Coal and Steel Community (ECSC), created in April 1951. While most Conservatives were ambivalent, they criticised the Labour government's refusal to participate in negotiations. However, some contrary tendencies began appearing when six anti-European Conservative MPs sided with Labour, concerned about moves towards political federation. This contrasted with a small number of new pro-European MPs, including Airey Neave and Edward Heath, who argued passionately for joining.

The next step came in March 1957 when the Treaty of Rome established the EEC. While there remained little interest in participating, earlier scepticism was giving way to concern that this new bloc would see Britain economically excluded and NATO undermined. The Conservative government, now led by Harold Macmillan, responded by establishing the rival European Free Trade Association (EFTA) together with six other non-EEC countries. This

---

[2] N. J. Crowson, *The Conservative Party and European Integration Since 1945*. Routledge, 2007

[3] Ben Patterson, *The Conservative Party and Europe,* John Harper, 2011

more limited undertaking with no sovereignty impingements still upset some Conservative MPs, who worried it might harm links with the Commonwealth.

Pragmatic re-assessment and seeking membership

This attitude was becoming outdated as Britain's economic and geopolitical position in the world was changing. Many colonies were seeking independence, the economy was stalling, the United States was leading the West, and Britain had been humiliated by Suez. Unlike other European countries, Britain's "unresolved identity"[4] vis-a-vis Europe meant relations were perceived as "a choice", rather than a common destiny. This made it easier for Conservatives to reassess where Britain's interests lay – gradually concluding that joining the EEC could remedy many problems.

This shift became manifest on 31 July 1961 when Macmillan announced his intention to seek membership. Entry was presented as a beneficial free trade exercise, with the challenges to accession being economic. Despite being advised that sovereignty would be impacted, Macmillan downplayed concerns to avoid a split[5], and eventually just 29 Conservative MPs abstained. However, during protracted accession negotiations the domestic political landscape became more challenging, with opposition amongst farmers and Labour's Hugh Gaitskell eloquently warning of the risk to national sovereignty. Ultimately, this first application foundered when it was vetoed in January 1963 by the French president, Charles de Gaulle.

Harold Wilson's Labour government launched a second application in May 1967. The Conservatives, under their new leader Edward Heath, had meanwhile continued their shift to a pro-accession mindset, so Labour's application put them in a difficult position. They responded by positioning themselves as pro-European while criticising Labour for ruining negotiations. This strategy depended on de Gaulle again vetoing, which he duly did later that year.

---

4 O. Daddow, "Margaret Thatcher, Tony Blair and the Eurosceptic Tradition in Britain", *The British Journal of Politics and International Relations,* Vol 15, 2013

5 C. Tugendhat, *The Worm in the Apple: A History of the Conservative Party and Europe from Churchill to Cameron,* Haus Publishing, 2022

The third attempt, shortly after Heath's election victory in 1970, finally succeeded. However, the Commons vote to approve accession was only decided by the size of the relative rebellions. Although by now most Conservatives seemed willing to support entry, their modest majority afforded great influence to 39 anti-marketeers who allied with Labour to oppose entry. Conversely, 69 Labour pro-marketeers voted with the Conservatives, allowing the motion to pass. Passage of the 1972 European Communities Act saw multiple rebellions but, on 1 January 1973, the Conservatives finally took Britain "in".

First delegation representatives

Britain was now entitled to send nominated representatives to the European Assembly. The 18 Conservative MPs and peers were dual-mandated, sitting in both the European and Westminster parliaments. This provided a direct link, although needing to be physically present for votes in both proved problematic. Most of the group, including their leader, Peter Kirk, had experience in either the Council of Europe or the Western European Union assemblies, and while most were former pro-marketeers, two (Derek Walker-Smith and Rafton Pounder) had been strong opponents. Whilst the delegation was energetic, they lacked collective influence, mainly because they sat outside the large and influential Christian Democrat grouping.

1975 referendum

An unexpected coda to this period was the challenge of keeping Britain "in" – precipitated by the minority Labour government that took office after the general election in February 1974 promising a renegotiation and referendum on membership. The Conservatives' campaign had been somewhat undermined when a small number of anti-marketeers advocated voting Labour to secure a referendum. Wilson went on to gain a slim majority in a further genral election in October, before putting the renegotiated terms to a referendum in June 1975. Meanwhile, Margaret Thatcher had beaten Heath for the leadership of the Conservative Party. While her views on Europe were still developing, she praised Heath for securing accession and, alongside the official Conservative Party machinery, actively supported the "Yes" campaign. Conservative anti-marketeers campaigned for "No". However, both passionate proponents and sceptics were minorities within the party; most were simply agnostic or would follow the party-line. The referendum result was 67% in favour of remaining – settling, for a while, the issue within the Conservative Party.

Pursuing economic interests within the bloc (1975-87)

With membership decided and anti-marketeers marginalised, pursuing Britain's economic interests within the bloc became the priority.

EEC budget

The first of many battles involving the EEC budget started shortly after Thatcher became prime minister in May 1979. Britain was in the uncomfortable position of being the second largest contributor whilst being the third poorest member on a per capita basis. Thatcher therefore decided to re-negotiate Britain's budgetary contribution – eventually securing a rebate of 66% at the 1984 Fontainebleau summit. Thatcher's combative approach masked the awkward reality that arriving late with a weak economy effectively made Britain a junior partner. Her nationalistic rhetoric distracted from her early domestic unpopularity. Some Conservatives, including most MEPs[6], worried that Thatcher's confrontational tone alienated Britain's European partners. More significantly, these battles started establishing an image of "us versus them" where winning, rather than cooperating, became the defining narrative.

---

6   https://www.telegraph.co.uk/news/obituaries/politics-obituaries/5828223/Lord-Kingsland.html

Direct elections and dissonance between parliaments

June 1979 saw the first direct elections to the European Parliament, when the Conservatives won 60 of 81 seats. Rather than join the European People's Party (EPP) which inclined towards federalism, they formed a new grouping, the European Democrats (ED) or European Democratic group (EDG). The MEPs were broadly pro-European. Some, like Madron Seligman and Bill Newton Dunn, strongly supported federalist projects like the single currency. Others, such as James Scott-Hopkins and Henry Plumb, were moderates, whereas Harmar Nicholls and Eric Forth were more sceptical about further integration. Ben Patterson suggests the selection process favoured pro-European candidates[7]. Some dual mandated MEPs returned, including Tom Normanton, Elaine Kellett-Bowman, Jim Spicer and Brandon Rhys-Williams, but fewer than before, weakening the link with Westminster.

The need to manage the relationship with MEPs was recognised but ideas such as assigning a Westminster whip or setting up a joint standing committee never materialised. Over time, this contributed to many MPs viewing the European Parliament with suspicion, sometimes accusing MEPs of "going native". Even early on, during Thatcher's budgetary battles, the relationship with the government has been described as "distant … and more Communautaire"[8]. MEPs of this period may reject such accusations, emphasising the European culture of trading co-operation for influence. Lord (Timothy) Kirkhope, who led the Conservative group of MEPs between 2004-07 and 2009-11, suggests that, by his era, this cognitive dissonance between Westminster and "over there" had worsened. He confirms that there were still no official structures integrating MEPs with the national party leadership[9].

The next European elections, in 1984, saw the Conservatives run another pro-European campaign where, unlike Labour (who advocated leaving), they championed further cooperation on foreign pol-

---

7 Patterson, *The Conservative Party and Europe*
8 https://conservativehome.com/2014/06/13/lewis-baston-the-national-election-that-saw-the-highest-conservative-vote-in-the-age-of-democracy/
9 Interview with Lord (Timothy) Kirkhope

icy, defence and the common market. But while remaining the largest party, they dropped to 45 seats. A few years later Conservative fortunes somewhat revived when former group leader Henry Plumb was elected president of the Parliament – the only Briton ever to hold the position.

Single market

The next significant moment was the creation of the European single market in July 1987, which many Conservatives saw as an opportunity to develop "Thatcherism on a European scale"[10]. The vehicle was the British-led Single European Act (SEA). Over the succeeding years, Eurosceptics and Thatcher herself came to regard the SEA as a double-edged sword that marked an undesirable "acceleration of the unification process and challenge to the nation-state"[11]. The Act expanded EEC competencies, establishing qualified majority voting in the Council of Ministers and granting greater powers to the European Parliament. At the time, however, the SEA was broadly accepted by the party. Indeed, at the 1987 general election the single market was presented as a key Conservative achievement. Where there were concerns about sovereignty, objections were muted in favour of emphasising the economic benefits – undermining later claims that the implications for national sovereignty were neither understood nor anticipated.

Bruges, conceptual divergence, and the rise of Euroscepticism (1988–97)

Thatcher believed the single market represented an end point, but this expectation was shattered when Commission president Jacques Delors heralded a new era of deepening integration. Consequently, Conservative attitudes to the European project over the next nine years would be defined by the rise of Euroscepticism, and the need to manage this conceptual divergence.

---

10 Crowson, *The Conservative Party and European Integration Since 1945*
11 Ibid

Bruges – the rise of Euroscepticism

On 20 September 1988, Thatcher made her famous Bruges speech, rejecting Europe's growing centralisation of power and the idea of a European state. Her cry was that "we have not successfully rolled back the frontiers of the state in Britain only to see them reimposed at a European level, with a European super-state exercising a new dominance from Brussels". The speech not only brought Euroscepticism into the mainstream, reinforced by the positive reception of much of the press[12], but it also saw ideology creep into the equation. The aftermath saw the founding of several Eurosceptic organisations, including the Bruges Group, rivalling the pro-European Conservative Group for Europe and exerting great influence during the following decades.

The Conservatives fought a disjointed campaign at the 1989 European elections, losing 13 seats and coming second behind Labour. Despite a manifesto lauding the achievements of Conservative MEPs and welcoming EEC activity in areas such as environmental protection, the rhetoric of senior spokespersons was "openly negative towards the Community".[13] This confused messaging, together with domestic unhappiness about the economy and the poll tax, contributed to defeat. Given the new parliamentary arithmetic, Christopher Prout, the MEPs' leader, applied on behalf of the ED to join the EPP, but was rebuffed over concerns about the compatibility of British Conservatism with the Christian Democratic tradition as well as Thatcher's perceived hostility. It was not until 1992 that a loose alliance was agreed – making the EPP the largest political group, and greatly increasing the Conservatives' influence.

The Rome summit in October 1990 was Thatcher's last. It followed the Madrid summit where she believed that movement towards a common currency had been paused in exchange for sterling's entry into the European Exchange Rate Mechanism (ERM). She was therefore aggrieved when the summit called for

---

12 A. Roe-Crines, "Margaret Thatcher and the Rhetorical Road to Brexit", in A. Mullen, S. Farrell and D. Jeffray (ed), *Thatcherism in the 21st Century: The Social and Cultural Legacy*, Palgrave, 2020

13 Patterson, *The Conservative Party and Europe*

an intergovernmental conference on monetary and political union. Her strident response of "No, No, No!" prompted the pro-European cabinet minister Geoffrey Howe to resign, sparking events leading to her own resignation. Because the party had evolved in Thatcher's likeness, the manner of her departure caused considerable resentment. Her deposition by, as she believed, pro-Europeans over a European issue, outraged many newer MPs who held views like hers and who would remain loyally receptive to her increasingly sceptical opinions after leaving office.

Maastricht

The new leader was John Major, whose tone was more collaborative. However, Euroscepticism was growing as Conservative MPs wanted a predominately economic relationship with the EU, whereas those on the continent envisaged more political integration. Major attempted to manage this conceptual divergence by carving out a special status for Britain within the Community.

The 1992 European Council in Maastricht is regarded as a key moment when the integrationist project accelerated. The EEC was re-named the European Union (EU), becoming an entity in international law and affording citizenship to its population. However, at the time, the concessions Major won were widely lauded. Instead of blocking further integration, he prioritised protecting British interests while not obstructing others from pursuing theirs. Rather than derailing the single currency, he secured Britain a permanent right to opt in or out. Instead of killing the social chapter, he encouraged its creation outside the EEC framework thereby absolving Britain of obligations. He also won agreement that law and order, foreign affairs and defence would be managed on an inter-state basis, and that "subsidiarity"' would be written into the treaty. For pro-Europeans, this allowed the benefits of membership without being part of a federalist entity. However, anti-federalists feared that Britain would eventually be dragged in that direction. Indeed, Thatcher (who was now mainly concerned about sovereignty) felt the extent of powers being ceded justified a referendum.

Ratification was delayed, firstly until after the 1992 general election which Major unexpectedly and narrowly won, and secondly when a Danish referendum rejected the treaty. This galvanised Conservative anti-federalists to ally with Labour, which objected to omission of the social chapter. This unlikely alliance, combined with Major's small majority and the decline in enthusiasm for the EU after Black Wednesday, made the bill's passage difficult. Conservative rebels fought a war of attrition tabling over 600 amendments. At one point the government only won by submitting itself to a confidence vote. The Conservative rebels were few but wielded great influence. Kirkhope offers a fascinating retrospective from the whips' office, suggesting the number of "real" anti-federalists was "small enough to count on one hand"[14] – and that most were using the issue to tether Major to the broader Thatcherite agenda. The bill finally passed in July 1993, but its divisive passage ensured Europe remained a toxic issue for the rest of Major's premiership.

European elections in June 1994 saw the Conservatives lose another 14 seats, to hold just 18, versus Labour's 62. The campaign made a positive case for the EU, but Major also tried to allay Eurosceptic concerns, promising to "fight for the kind of Europe we want: not a European superstate, but a Europe of nation states, working together". Nevertheless, he continued to endure rebellions on Europe, eventually forcing a confidence vote – which he won. The long running spectacle of Conservative infighting got worse during the 1997 general election, when one-third of candidates refused to support Major's policy of negotiating terms for joining the euro and putting these to a referendum[15]. The Conservatives lost the election in a landslide.

Euroscepticism becomes dominant (1997-2013)

Major's defeat began 13 years in opposition, during which Euroscepticism became embedded among Conservative MPs. A com-

---

14 Interview with Lord (Timothy) Kirkhope
15 T. Hepell, "The Ideological Composition of the Conservative Party from Thatcher to May", in A. Mullen, S. Farrell S and D. Jeffray (ed), *Thatcherism in the 21st Century: The Social and Cultural Legacy,* Palgrave, 2020

bination of defeats and retirements saw the number of pro-Europeans collapse to just 8.5% (from 29.6% in 1992) versus 84.8% Eurosceptic. This shift was reinforced by subsequent intakes and by political events continuing to push the party towards Euroscepticism.

Increasing Euroscepticism – the euro and European Constitution

The new leader, William Hague, opposed joining the euro for at least two parliaments, which seemed to align with public sentiment, as the Conservatives doubled their seats at the 1999 European elections (the first under proportional representation). Their campaign slogan of "In Europe, not run by Europe" articulated their evolving position: commitment to the single market, eastern expansion, environmental protection and, interestingly, free movement; but strong opposition to the euro, tax harmonisation, expansion of majority voting and a European army.

Around this time, the MEP group's leader, Edward McMillan-Scott, negotiated a loosening of the alliance with the EPP and a name change to EPP-ED. The party's increasing Euroscepticism prompted several MEPs, including James Moorhouse, John Stevens (via the short lived Pro-Euro Conservative Party) and Bill Newton Dunn (whose pro-European proclivities lost him the whip), to defect to the Liberal Democrats. Patterson suggests "these defections did not trouble the party unduly – most of the original Conservative MEPs had already been written off as having gone irredeemably 'native'"[16]. But they reduced the number of pro-Europeans. Kirkhope (who became an MEP in 1999) suggests that in 1999 the MEP group broke evenly between Europhiles, hostiles and moderates. Over his 16 years in the European Parliament, the Europhiles steadily declined but continued to be represented by people such as John Purvis and John Bowis (at least until 2009), whereas the hostile group – including Martin Callanan, Daniel Hannan, Chris Heaton-Harris, Roger Helmer, Nirj Deva and Den Dover – steadily grew, welcoming defections from UKIP, including David Campbell Bannerman (2011), Marta An-

---

16 Patterson, *The Conservative Party and Europe*

dreasen (2013) and Amjad Bashir (2015). The moderates included Kirkhope himself and others like Neil Parish, Giles Chichester and Sir Robert Atkins. Furthermore, in contrast to 1979, it appeared that taking an overtly pro-European position was now detrimental to a candidate's chances of selection.

Europe was central to the Conservatives' 2001 general election campaign, largely because Hague had made little headway against Blair on domestic issues. The undertaking to hold a referendum before transferring additional powers to the EU and the call to "Save the Pound!" demonstrated the Eurosceptic shift. However, European issues failed to resonate, and the Conservatives made only one net-gain. Hague was replaced by Iain Duncan Smith – a Maastricht rebel – who defeated the pro-European Ken Clarke. IDS was himself soon swapped for another committed Eurosceptic, Michael Howard.

European integration again took centre stage in July 2003, when the EU published a draft Constitution of Europe. This alarmed Conservatives, who opposed both the concept and its provisions. Although Blair agreed with Howard's demand that ratification be preceded by a referendum, the French and Dutch rejected the treaty in 2005; the process of ratification by the member states stalled and was then abandoned without the issue ever being put before the British people. This controversy overlapped with the 2004 European elections where the Conservatives opposed the new treaty. Although they remained the largest party, the Conservatives lost eight MEPs, whereas UKIP continued their advance, winning 12 seats, up by nine on 1999. Explaining UKIP's rise, Patterson recounts that: "For nearly 10 years the message had been that Britain was in danger of being submerged in a federal super-state ... many people not surprisingly concluded that we should get out while we could"[17].

Cameron, Lisbon and the ECR

Following Blair's third successive victory in 2005, the Conservatives again changed leader. Since 1997, three Eurosceptics had led the party, and opposing integrationist projects had become normal.

17 Ibid

While reform, rather than withdrawal, remained the majority sentiment, Euroscepticism was becoming embedded in the Conservative psyche and image[18]. The new leader, David Cameron, was elected as a moderniser, wanting to stop the party "banging on about Europe". But he was a self-proclaimed "Eurorealist", believing that while "membership of the EU was necessary for trade and cooperation ... Britain never would welcome the political aspects"[19].

During the leadership campaign, Cameron committed to taking Conservative MEPs out of the EPP and forming a new, Eurosceptic grouping. While this appealed to Eurosceptics, most of the MEPs were opposed, not wishing to partner with right-wing parties and anticipating a loss of influence[20]. Eurosceptics argued that because the EPP was federalist-inclined, the association was uncomfortable. As Hannan put it, "once we left, the EPP would lose a bad tenant and gain a good neighbour"[21]. Also, because all the political groups supported further integration, the Parliament lacked a de facto official opposition – which this would remedy. Kirkhope, who led the Conservative MEPs at the time, believes Cameron's need to win-over Eurosceptics was the main driver. He also asserts that while extensive due diligence allowed them eventually to find acceptable partners, leaving the EPP reduced their influence.

Despite Cameron's desire to avoid the issue, EU-related matters still required attention. In 2007, Gordon Brown had refused to hold a referendum on the Lisbon Treaty, which contained many of the provisions found in the abandoned EU Constitution. The Conservatives opposed the treaty and Cameron had committed to holding a referendum if he won power, and if the treaty had not yet become law. However, when he entered office in 2010, he instead promised a future "referendum lock" – on the grounds that a retrospective plebiscite about a treaty that had already been ratified made little sense. UKIP, the right-wing press and some Conservatives felt this was a betrayal.

---

18 T. Bale, *The Conservative Party: From Thatcher to Cameron*, 2nd ed. Polity Press, 2016
19 Tugendhat, *The Worm in the Apple*
20 Interview with Lord (Timothy) Kirkhope, June 2022
21 Patterson, *The Conservative Party and Europe*

The 2009 European elections saw Conservative seats remain relatively steady. However, UKIP increased to 13 seats, beating Labour to second place on vote share. These elections also saw the formation of the long delayed European Conservatives and Reformists group (ECR), marking a further embedding of the Eurosceptic mindset. At this point, the staunchly pro-European McMillan-Scott – a Conservative MEP since 1984 and group leader in 1997-2001 – protested against this new arrangement, defeating the ECR's official candidate for EP vice-president. He was ultimately ejected from the party.

Coalition government and pressure for a referendum

The 2010 general election delivered a Conservative-led coalition with the Liberal Democrats. Oliver Letwin, a senior minister in Cameron's cabinet, described his Conservative colleagues as ranging from "nascent Euro-outers through strong Eurosceptics to milder Eurosceptics"[22]. Pro-Europeans, other than Ken Clarke, had almost entirely disappeared. The party now undertook never to join the euro, indicating a further hardening of attitudes.

Events continued pushing the party towards Euroscepticism. In March 2012, the signing of the Treaty on Stability, Coordination and Governance in the Economic and Monetary Union outside the EU treaties – thereby circumventing Cameron's earlier veto of the EU Fiscal Compact – reinforced concerns that opt-outs and vetoes would not prevent absorption within a federal super-state. UKIP's rise on the Conservatives' right flank alarmed, and sometimes attracted, Conservative activists, MPs and MEPs – including Roger Helmer, who defected to UKIP in March 2012. Large-scale rebellions calling for a referendum applied additional pressure, such as in October 2011 when 81 MPs rebelled – including 49 from the 2010 intake[23] – further highlighting the Eurosceptic shift. Cameron also unwittingly contributed, as his own Eurorealist views, calls for re-

---

22 O. Letwin, *Hearts and Minds: The Battle for the Conservative Party from Thatcher to the Present*, Biteback Publishing, 2017

23 P. Cowley and M. Stuart, "The Cambusters: The Conservative European Union Referendum Rebellion of October 2011", *Political Quarterly*, 83 (2), 2012

form and regular arguments with EU leaders reinforced a negative narrative. The Conservative press was also influential as much of it was under the ownership of Eurosceptics like Rupert Murdoch and Conrad Black, resulting in unremittingly hostile headlines.

These pressures, combined with principle, electoral calculations and his own optimistic reformist instincts, led Cameron, in January 2013, to pledge that, if the Conservatives won a majority in 2015, he would renegotiate Britain's terms of EU membership and put these to an in/out referendum.

Brexit and resolution (2013-2020)

Cameron's referendum pledge marked the start of a dramatic period of "resolution", encompassing the 2016 referendum and internecine battles over the manner of departure.

Hard and soft Euroscepticism

While Euroscepticism was now fully embedded, there was an important distinction between soft Euroscepticism (seeking reform, opposing further integration) and hard Euroscepticism (which advocated leaving). Both had their roots in the same debates about sovereignty and globalism that had existed since the earliest days of the ECSC and EEC. Anti-Europeans, anti-marketeers and hard Eurosceptics regarded sovereignty as something "you either possessed, or did not, it could not be shared"[24]. They also increasingly embodied the hyper-globalist instincts of earlier anti-Europeans and anti-marketeers – believing that Britain's economic interests lay beyond Europe. Letwin observes that during the 2010-15 parliament "the mood amongst many of the Eurosceptics was subtly shifting from acceptance of the single market aspect of the EU to what was (in effect, if not explicit) a belief in exiting the EU altogether"[25]

---

24 T. Hepell, *The Ideological Composition of the Conservative Party from Thatcher to May*
25 O. Letwin, *Hearts and Minds*

Majority, renegotiation and 2016 referendum

UKIP's success continued as they became the largest party at the 2014 European elections (the Conservatives dropping to 19 seats and third place). However, at the 2015 general election, Cameron confounded expectations by winning a slim majority.

The renegotiation he secured in February 2016 is mainly remembered for the opprobrium it generated in the Conservative press, on the grounds that it did not go far enough on controlling immigration, which had become a key demand of both hard and soft Eurosceptics. However, it represented the largest potential restructuring of the EU since Maastricht. Cameron secured exemptions from "ever closer union", from contributing to Eurozone bailouts, and from joining the euro, with limits placed on the European Court of Justice's ability to expand EU law to Britain. Significantly, other EU countries could emulate these arrangements, allowing, as Letwin suggests, "the creation of a Europe of concentric circles with an emerging federal state at the centre and a free trade single market around it, so that Britain can remain in the single market without being drawn into the federal state"[26]. Others did not share this assessment, and several senior Conservatives declared for leaving – including Boris Johnson and Michael Gove.

The referendum forced Conservative MPs to choose between hard or soft Euroscepticism, with a sizeable 43.9% supporting Leave, but a majority backing Remain[27]. The MEP group also split, with Daniel Hannan, Amjad Bashir, Emma McClarkin[28], David Campbell Bannerman[29], Andrew Lewer[30], and Syed Kamall[31] backing Leave while the majority supported Remain[32].

---

26 Ibid
27 Hepell, *The Ideological Composition of the Conservative Party from Thatcher to May*
28 https://www.theparliamentmagazine.eu/news/article/conservative-meps-split-over-brexit
29 https://www.theguardian.com/politics/2016/mar/08/eu-referendum-11-of-20-tory-meps-back-staying-in-brexit
30 https://www.politico.eu/article/mays-new-wave-of-brexit-believers-euroskeptics-tories-uk-snap-election/
31 https://www.politico.eu/article/syed-kamall-senior-tory-mep-backs-brexit-eu-referendum-date-june-23/
32 https://web.archive.org/web/20160518101504/http://www.conservatives.in/meps

On 23 June 2016, Britain decided to leave the EU by 52:48. This result was influenced by many factors, but Conservative Euroscepticism certainly contributed: not only had successive Tory leaders embedded a negative narrative defined by battles and summit showdowns, but Euroscepticism within the party had been a powerful force driving the issue to this climax.

A party of Leavers

Cameron resigned and was replaced by Theresa May. Although she had supported Remain, May undertook to deliver the referendum result – her infamous "Brexit means Brexit". This demonstrated that, apart from a minority seeking a second referendum[33], Conservatives had now become Leavers.

Impasse, civil war, and a hard departure

Following the referendum there was no agreement about whether the future relationship with the EU should limit divergence so as to maintain access to the single market (soft Leavers) or whether Britain should cut free of the single market and customs union to strike new trade deals (hard Leavers). The final Withdrawal Agreement (and Political Declaration) May secured in late 2018 attempted to bridge these positions. However, the hard Leavers objected, triggering a confidence vote, albeit one which May won. They objected to the Northern Irish backstop and continuing close alignment. While May's deal delivered an orderly departure, ended free movement, and left the single market and customs union, for hard Leavers it threatened to delay or prevent signing trade deals as well as undermining sovereignty.

When the Withdrawal Agreement came before the Commons in January 2019, hard Leavers allied with opposition parties to vote it down by 230 votes – a new record. The Withdrawal Agreement was tabled twice more in March, but while the margins reduced, the defeats remained heavy.

---

[33] Shrinking further as many (including Conservative MEPs Richard Ashworth and Julie Girling) left.

Unless this impasse could be resolved by 31 March, Britain risked falling out of the EU on World Trade Organisation (WTO) terms. While hard Leavers accepted this, "no deal" represented much more than just a limited trading relationship. Because the government had not adequately prepared for "no deal", and because important details could only be resolved once Britain was a third party, there were few arrangements in place to mitigate the severe shock of an unmanaged exit. A small group of Conservative MPs and advisors (including myself) were so worried that their priority became preventing the country falling off this cliff edge: they therefore tried to break the impasse before an accidental "no deal" occurred. Undertaking some innovative and controversial parliamentary manoeuvres, they mobilised a latent cross-party majority against "no deal" by taking control of the order paper and holding a series of indicative votes, hoping to identify whether a majority for any solution existed; but no such majority appeared. Despite the choice fast becoming "no deal" or "no Brexit", many MPs stuck resolutely to their first preferences. This myopia went beyond the parliamentary party – a striking YouGov poll in June 2019 indicated grassroots Conservatives prioritised achieving Brexit over maintaining the unity of the United Kingdom. With time running out, the cross-party alliance (assisted by Dianne Hayter in the Lords) legislated, via the Cooper-Letwin Act, to force an extension.

Even this failed to produce a solution and May subsequently resigned. The extension meant Britain needed to participate in the May 2019 European elections. The Conservative campaign was low key, without even a manifesto, and saw only four MEPs elected: Daniel Hannan, Geoffrey Van Orden, Anthea McIntyre and Nosheena Mobarik, whereas the new Brexit Party won 29 seats. Hannan explained the results thus: "We voted to leave (the EU), and we haven't left – it's that simple"[34].

May was replaced by Boris Johnson who had resigned from the government over the Withdrawal Agreement. As the revised departure day of 31 October approached, Johnson's government tried to pressure the EU into offering a better deal. Unlike May, who

---

34 https://www.bbc.co.uk/news/uk-politics-48417228

might have accidentally caused "no deal", Johnson's entire strategy rested on threatening, and countenancing, a cliff edge exit. This alarmed those who had fought to avoid an unmanaged exit – prompting renewed cross-party efforts to legislate for another extension. To prevent this, Johnson dramatically prorogued Parliament (an action ruled illegal by the Supreme Court) but the same grouping managed to use the few days before prorogation to pass the Benn-Burt Act – mandating an extension to 31 January 2020. Johnson retaliated by expelling 21 Conservative rebels.

The de facto parliamentary lock on leaving without a deal incentivised Johnson to reach agreement with the EU. His new deal replaced the customs union backstop with a dual tariff front-stop, imposing a customs border in the Irish Sea. This allowed Britain to sign new trade deals but, if anything, undermined sovereignty more than May's deal – thereby losing the Democratic Unionist Party's support. Four UKIP MEPs (Lucy Harris, Lance Forman, Annunziata Rees-Mogg and John Longworth) defected to the Conservatives to support this deal. But before attempting to pass the deal through the Commons, Johnson persuaded opposition parties to have a general election. The Conservatives, campaigning on the new deal under the banner "Get Brexit Done", won an 80-seat majority and a mandate to deliver this hard – though, mercifully, managed – Brexit.

These ructions made British politics more polarised and ideological, and hugely affected the composition and attitudes of the Conservative Party. The ejection of rebel MPs in September removed the core of the liberal wing of the party. Hard Leavers, by contrast, had transitioned from a minority exploiting the tight parliamentary arithmetic to winning control of the government and the Brexit process. Additionally, every Conservative candidate at the 2019 general election had to sign up to Johnson's approach – completing the shift to becoming a party of hard Leavers.

So it was, that at 11pm London time on 31 January 2020, the Conservative Party, now fully committed to a hard departure, finally took Britain out of the EU. While Brexit-day was both loudly celebrated and regretted outside Parliament in London, at midnight in Brussels and Strasbourg the lights were quietly turned off after 47 years of British membership of the EU and 41 years in the elected European Parliament.

Bibliography:
Books

T. Bale, *The Conservative Party: From Thatcher to Cameron*, 2nd ed. Polity Press, 2016

N.J. Crowson, *The Conservative Party and European Integration Since 1945*, Routledge, 2007.

T. Hepell, "The Ideological Composition of the Conservative Party from Thatcher to May", in A. Mullen, S. Farrell and D. Jeffray (ed) *Thatcherism in the 21st Century: The Social and Cultural Legacy*, Palgrave, 2020

O. Letwin, *Hearts and Minds: The Battle for the Conservative Party from Thatcher to the Present*, Biteback Publishing, 2017

B. Patterson, *The Conservative Party and Europe*, John Harper, 2011

A. Roe-Crines, "Margaret Thatcher and the Rhetorical Road to Brexit", in A. Mullen, S. Farrell and D. Jeffray (ed) *Thatcherism in the 21st Century: The Social and Cultural Legacy*, Palgrave, 2020

C. Tugendhat, *The Worm in the Apple: A History of the Conservative Party and Europe from Churchill to Cameron*, Haus Publishing, 2022

Articles

P. Cowley and M. Stuart, "The Cambusters: The Conservative European Union Referendum Rebellion of October 2011", *Political Quarterly*, 83(2), 2012

O. Daddow, "Margaret Thatcher, Tony Blair and the Eurosceptic Tradition in Britain", *The British Journal of Politics and International Relations*, Vol 15, 2013

Webpages

https://conservativehome.com/2014/06/13/lewis-baston-the-national-election-that-saw-the-highest-conservative-vote-in-the-age-of-democracy/

https://www.telegraph.co.uk/news/obituaries/politics-obituaries/5828223/Lord-Kingsland.html

https://www.europarl.europa.eu/election-results-2019/en/turnout/

https://www.theguardian.com/world/2022/apr/26/lord-plumb-obituary

https://www.theparliamentmagazine.eu/news/article/conservative-meps-split-over-brexithttps://www.theguardian.com/politics/2016/mar/08/eu-referendum-11-of-20-tory-meps-back-staying-in-brexit

https://www.politico.eu/article/mays-new-wave-of-brexit-believers-euroskeptics-tories-uk-snap-election/

https://www.politico.eu/article/syed-kamall-senior-tory-mep-backs-brexit-eu-referendum-date-june-23/

https://web.archive.org/web/20160518101504/http://www.conservatives.in/meps

https://www.politicshome.com/news/article/brexit-full-timeline-history

https://www.bbc.co.uk/news/uk-politics-48417228

https://www.supremecourt.uk/cases/docs/uksc-2019-0192-judgment.pdf

Interview

Lord (Timothy) Kirkhope, House of Lords, 29 June 2022

3. Labour's journey: from anti to pro

by Richard Johnson

Richard Johnson is a senior lecturer in the School of Politics and International Relations at Queen Mary, University of London, researching US and UK politics. He is currently writing a book on the Labour Party's changing attitude towards European integration.

When Britain joined the European Economic Community in January 1973, Labour was entitled to send a delegation of 16 legislators, drawn from the Houses of Commons and Lords, to the European Assembly. Reflecting the party's Euroscepticism (to use a later term), however, party leader Harold Wilson refused to appoint any, a boycott which was not reversed until Britain voted in a referendum to remain in the EEC in June 1975.

Labour's initial refusal to send delegates to the Assembly was not an objection to the fact it was unelected. Proposals for an elected European Parliament were fiercely resisted within the party. In 1976, Labour conference voted in favour of a national executive committee (NEC) document opposing the direct election of MEPs. A survey in early 1979 found that 56% of Labour MPs were opposed to the European Parliament having more powers, compared to just 30% who were supportive. One opponent of the direct election of MEPs was Neil Kinnock. In a 1977 Commons debate, Kinnock warned that the European Parliament would attract people "with the most enormous resources at their command and power over nothing but their own egos". Labour's internal strife over the election of MEPs led to the first direct elections to the European Parliament being delayed by a year for the whole European Community.

The first elections to the Parliament eventually took place on 7 June 1979, and their timing could not have been more inopportune for Labour. Just a month earlier, the Callaghan government had lost power in a general election to Margaret Thatcher's Conservatives. Labour activists were traumatised, demoralised, and a little indignant at having been forced to take part in the European elections at all. One academic observed the "indifference shown by [Labour] party workers, the majority of whom despised the institution". Labour's campaign team was chiefly comprised of Eurosceptics, with Tony Benn and Eric Heffer at the helm. Their intention was to block the pro-EEC members of the party, who were a minority, from using the elections to imply that Labour had embraced the common market. Tens of thousands of party leaflets were "recalled, pulped, and reprinted at vast expense" because the slogan on the leaflets had said "Labour for Europe" rather than the non-committal "Labour and Europe".

The results bore out this mix of misery, apathy and, for some, antipathy. On a paltry 32% turnout, the lowest in the EEC, the Conservatives won 48% of the vote to Labour's 32%. The scale of the Conservative victory in terms of seats was even more pronounced, with the Tories winning three-quarters of all seats in Great Britain. Labour had been trounced, failing to win seats anywhere in the south outside London or even in its West Midlands stronghold. It captured only one seat in the northwest and just two constituencies to the Conservatives' five in Scotland.

Of the 17 Labour MEPs elected in 1979, just one had previous parliamentary experience. Recently retired as MP for Blackburn after 34 years, Barbara Castle was the group's only "star". Castle was a committed Eurosceptic, whose motivations for becoming an MEP were to stop the tide of further European integration. She wrote to Labour members in Bradford, explaining her decision to stand for a Parliament whose direct elections she had voted against, in these terms:

"I can assure you ... I have not changed my views about our membership of the Common Market ... [but] it would be madness for us to leave the field clear for the Eurofanatics ... to drag this country deeper ... to imprison us in a federal Europe ... I did so in order to go into Europe to resist any further undermining of the supremacy of the House of Commons, of British MPs and the British government ... otherwise representation ... would be monopolised by people who would seek ... to weaken the sovereignty of the British parliament"[35].

Castle had the celebrity status, experience and natural talents that made her the clear choice for leader of the newly formed British Labour group (BLG) of MEPs. She was described by one journalist as "the stormy petrel of the British Labour members ... and if some Brit has to give the EEC hell, then she is the one on whom we can rely"[36].

Yet Castle did not warm quickly to the European Parliament. "To the British MP, used to the benign authority of Mr Speaker and the strict control of the debating timetable, the conduct of European Parliamentary business has been incomprehensible", she complained. Castle summed up her first experience in the Parliament in characteristically vivid terms: "It is as though at a baby's delivery the midwife spoke a language the mother could not understand while the doctor, called in to perform the caesarean, turned out to be a faith healer". Castle even complained that the Parliament made her ill. "We Euro-candidates always knew it would be a headache to try to represent half a million British voters in a far-away meeting place. But we never realised the headache would be quite so literal. ...It has been like doing a complicated crossword in nine languages", she grumbled. "My seat for an aspirin [is] the heart cry of the new European MP after his or her first week in the European Parliament".

Castle was a product of the confrontational Westminster culture. Her combative style could sometimes cause upset, especially amongst non-British MEPs who prized conciliation and compromise.

---

35 Letter from Barbara Castle to John Doherty, Secretary, Bingley Labour Party, 24 August 1978/
36 Gordon Maxwell, 'Britain's Liveliest Crusader', Oldham Evening Chronicle, 17 January 1984.

This included fellow members of the Socialist group with whom she initially clashed. Castle also went to battle with Conservative MEPs, but from them she won a begrudging respect. Henry Plumb, their group leader, later recalled that "she was a fighter, but she was a sweetie"[37].

About 11 out of the first 17 Labour MEPs were Eurosceptic. In spite of their reservations, many made an effort to participate constructively. Castle reflected a year into the job, "The thing about my British Labour boys is that they are not cynical. They are not saying let's take our money and go home because this place stinks". She contrasted this with what she perceived to be the relative lack of vigour by many of the other nations' MEPs: "A lot of the Europeans don't carry their Europeanism too far. They don't miss their meals, for example. Our boys are puritans. They miss their meals and carry the vote".

An outwardly constructive pragmatism, grounded on a principled scepticism, summarised the Castle approach. Being an MEP did not cause her to abandon her scepticism. She said in 1982: "My belief in the correctness of ... criticism of the hotch-potch of free market economics and agricultural protectionism has been strongly reinforced by my first hand experience of how it works". In 1984, Gordon Maxwell, a Lancashire journalist, summarised Castle's views after a meal between the two over pizza and Beaujolais in an Italian restaurant in Strasbourg: "Basically, Barbara has no time for Europe as a community. She would have us out tomorrow because she sees no long-term satisfaction for this country in membership". Nonetheless, Castle recognised that leaving the EEC lacked public support back home and, therefore, "so long as we are in, she intends to fight to construct a community which has some point, purpose, and relevance".[38] After her 1984 re-election, she told a journalist, "We shall have to see how the Community develops, whether it gets over its crisis and whether it is capable of reforming itself. If it isn't, then the British people will want to sever their connections"[39].

---

37 Pollack, Anita, *Wreckers or Builders? A History of Labour MEPs, 1979-1999*, John Harper, 2009.
38 Gordon Maxwell, "Britain's Liveliest Crusader", Oldham Evening Chronicle, 17 January 1984.
39 "Why Victorious Barbara, 73, Just Cannot Slow Down", Bury Times, June 1984.

The Labour group had "strong anti-EEC credentials" but there were about half a dozen Labour MEPs who were true believers in the European project. Those who embraced the European Parliament wholeheartedly did so at their peril, with constituency Labour parties ready to deselect those seen to have "sold out" to Europe. Being called a pro-marketeer was "a highly abusive term indeed to apply to a Labour MEP". One of those deselected for his pro-EEC views was Michael Gallagher, MEP for Nottingham. After his deselection, Castle spent four hours pleading with Gallagher to choose a dignified retirement rather than switch parties, but it was to no avail and he became the first (and only) SDP MEP. He had accumulated a large sum of EEC funds for campaign purposes, reported to be about £100,000, which the Labour group demanded he hand over to them. Gallagher refused in dramatic fashion: "They might just as well have told the condemned man in the electric chair that he was expected to pay the electricity bill"[40].

The 1984 European elections, in which Labour nearly doubled its numbers from 17 to 32, also swelled the Eurosceptic ranks in the BLG. This time, Eurosceptic activists had made a more concerted effort to influence the selection process compared to five years earlier. Many of these new MEPs lacked a constructive attitude. Sheffield's Bob Cryer even refused to call himself an MEP, preferring the more antiquated "Labour Party Representative in the Common Market Assembly". Some of the Labour MEPs deliberately misbehaved during plenary sessions, racing toy woodpeckers down planks of wood on their desks. In one debate, the acting president of the Parliament switched off the microphone of Les Huckfield, Merseyside East MEP, nicknamed "Les Misérables". This not being the first time his mic had been cut off, a well-prepared Huckfield responded by producing a loudhailer. "In case you didn't hear what I said, I said get stuffed", he bellowed. The sitting was suspended. Merseyside West MEP Ken Stewart, who had served in the Parachute Regiment during the Second World War, told a group of German MEPs, "the last time I saw a German, it was at the point of a gun"[41]. Such comments tended not to win favour with non-British MEPs.

---

40 "Euro Swoop by the Left", Nottingham Evening Post, 17 December 1983
41 Interview with Richard Corbett, 18 March 2022

Castle's willingness to work constructively within Europe put her at odds with the harder line members of the BLG, who saw sabotage and intransigence as a more effective political strategy. In 1985, Castle was defeated in a leadership challenge by Alf Lomas, a more intransigent Eurosceptic and veteran left-winger. The Conservative foreign secretary, Geoffrey Howe described Lomas as someone "who can make the Militant Tendency look like rabid anti-Communists"[42].

Lomas dedicated his leadership to ensuring that Labour would not renege on its commitment to leave the EEC. In 1980 and 1981, party conference had overwhelmingly voted in favour of Leave. Withdrawal, as it was known at the time, was a central plank of the 1983 Labour manifesto. When Neil Kinnock replaced Michael Foot as leader later that year, he massaged the policy but could not abandon it entirely without a new vote of conference, which did not come until 1988. For the time being, Leave was now an option that Labour would exercise if the EEC refused to reform itself sufficiently. Leave was, as Kinnock put it, "a last resort instead of a first strike"[43].

In October 1986, the BLG sent a policy paper, written by Lomas, to the NEC which called for Labour to repeal Section 2 of the European Communities Act 1972, denying the automatic applicability of European law within the UK, and "for the return to the British Parliament of powers we had when we joined the EEC". It passed 18 to 13. The effect of this policy would have been for Britain to be ejected from the EEC, a position Barbara Castle had herself championed as BLG leader in a New Statesman piece, "Let them throw us out" in 1982. Castle had argued for a Labour government simply to ignore EEC law to which it objected and dare the Commission to eject Britain from the Community.

At a time when Kinnock was trying to push Labour in a more pro-European direction, these interventions were deeply unhelpful. The British Labour MEPs were seen by some as an embarrassment to the rest of the Labour Party. An internal report, written by the BLG, admitted, "Liaison with the PLP and the Party has not been effective". The party leadership chose broadly to ignore the BLG. Barry Seal, leader from 1988-89, recalls, "at that time, the party

---

42 "Howe tears into Labour euro-chief", Yorkshire Post, 22 June 1988.
43 Transcript of Chris Mullin interview with Neil Kinnock for Tribune, 11 July 1983

weren't bothered about us. It was as though we were elected and pushed to one side".

By the late 1980s, the BLG consisted of three factions: the hard-left Campaign group, the soft-left Tribune group, and the Labour right. Broadly speaking, the Campaign group was staunchly Eurosceptic, the right were (mostly) pro-EEC, and the Tribune group began as Eurosceptic but became more pro-EEC over time. Those who remained Eurosceptic were known by some members as "the Japanese", a reference to the Japanese soldiers who refused to surrender after the end of World War II. Alf Lomas rejected the comparison stating, "Well, the war the Japanese soldier was involved in was over, but unfortunately the class war that we are involved in, the war being waged by capitalism against the working class, is not"[44].

These divisions spilled over into bitter personal acrimony. Manchester West MEP Gary Titley, who became Labour group whip in 1989, described his experience as "hell on earth". Janey Buchan, a working-class Glaswegian who had previously been a member of the Communist Party, was particularly direct in her appraisals of other MEPs. At one Labour group meeting, Barbara Castle wished to make a contribution. A witness to this meeting recalled Castle waving her hands in the air, "Oi, I want to speak!". "Yeah, I can see you", replied Buchan, "You'll speak when you're called". "I want to speak now", pleaded Castle. "You shut up, you stupid fucking bitch" roared Buchan. Another MEP recalled that one of his Labour colleagues would shout down the corridor at my assistant, "You're still fucking working for that fucking bastard?". When the Birmingham West MEP John Tomlinson was in hospital, a motion was moved at a BLG meeting to send Tomlinson a "get well soon" card. An amendment was then raised that the word "soon" should be deleted.

Relations with the Socialist group were also poor. A decade earlier, Walter Kendall had argued that: "In outlook, organisation, and behaviour, the labour movement in Britain is closer to the labour movements of Australia and New Zealand half the globe away than it is to its nearest neighbours in France, Belgium, and the Netherlands

---

44 Alf Lomas, "Labour and the Common Market", 1 September 1986

across the narrow width of the English Channel". The Labour Party differed from the other parties in the Socialist group in its historical lineages (with little influence from Marxism and a strong influence of Christianity), organisation (with strong, formalised trade union links) and culture (combat rather than consensus). It is notable that the Labour Party is unique among all the socialist parties in Europe in having no post-war experience of coalition government.

Lomas had tried to withdraw the BLG from the Socialist group, in protest at their pro-Europeanism. He was blocked by the party leadership, however, receiving a personal summons to London to be dressed down by Neil Kinnock, who told Lomas that the BLG would not leave the Socialist group under any circumstances. Acquiescence did not mean total acceptance, however. At one Socialist group meeting, at least three Labour MEPs gave a Nazi salute to the Socialist group leader Rudi Arndt, a German SPD MEP, in protest at his leadership style. Arndt's father, a trade union leader, had been murdered by the Gestapo during World War II.

Labour won the 1989 European elections with 39% of the vote to the Conservatives' 34%, taking a majority of British seats in Brussels. Kinnock described it as the happiest night of his leadership. The party had stood on a pro-EEC platform. Nonetheless, the BLG was led at the time by Barry Seal, a Eurosceptic, and Labour still argued that it opposed further transfers of sovereignty to the EEC. After the 1989 European elections, the balance of power in the Labour group shifted decisively in the pro-EEC direction for the first time. Wayne David, who was elected in 1989, recalls that before this election, "the BLG was very much in the hands of the people who were antagonistic to the EU. And a number of us, inspired by Neil Kinnock, it has to be said, were keen to bring about a change".

This period saw a rapprochement between Labour MEPs and the national party. MEPs were allowed to serve as departmental liaison members with Westminster shadow departmental teams. The Labour MEPs' leader was made a full ex-officio member of the NEC; MEPs were given equal voting rights to MPs in Labour leadership elections; and MEPs were provided with representation on the national policy forum. It was also at this time (June 1990) that the BLG changed its name to the European Parliamentary Labour Party

(EPLP) and, with encouragement from the leader's office, Dianne Hayter was appointed chief executive by the new, pro-Kinnock officers. When asked whether the EPLP needed to make concessions to Kinnock in return for this increased power, Glyn Ford, who was EPLP leader from 1989-1993, replied: "Yeah. Be pro-European".

Ford, although not embracing the label "federalist", accepts that he was certainly of that tendency. This was a dramatic shift from the Eurosceptic Castle, Lomas and Seal leaderships. One of the curious developments during Ford's leadership is that the BLG leadership was now more strongly pro-European integration than the national party leadership. In March 1990, Neil Kinnock wrote a confidential letter to Ford, chastising the BLG for supporting a proposal to strengthen the European Parliament's powers. The letter is instructive because it demonstrates the delicate dance of authority between the Labour leader's office and Labour MEPs. Kinnock wrote:

> "I heard with considerable concern and surprise that the EP was due to discuss the above report at last week's session in Strasbourg and that the BLG had already agreed to support it without reference to the party. Whilst I accept that there has to be certain division of labour between members of the NEC, PLP and BLG, I do not expect it to be quite so rigid or distanced that it leads to unexpected policy initiatives."

Kinnock reminded Ford: "The party does not support the transformation of the EC into a union of federal type [sic]". He told Ford that Labour did not support the extension of qualified majority voting to all policy areas as a matter of course because it "would be too great a transfer of national sovereignty for any EC member state". Efforts to support co-decision between the Council of Ministers and the European Parliament were also, in Kinnock's view, a step too far: "to support co-decision goes well beyond party policy in ceding powers away from the electorate as represented by MPs at Westminster and ministers accountable to them there"[45].

In 1993, Ford was replaced by Pauline Green, a relative newcomer to the EPLP. Green, who had been partly brought up in West Germany in a British military family, was personally pro-European,

---

45 Letter from Neil Kinnock MP to Glyn Ford MEP, 19 March 1990

but she recognised that "people here were not completely sold on the European vision, and I thought you had to ... take people with you. So, you had to build slowly." While making a pro-EU argument, she "certainly fought against the federalists" because "they were going too fast and would lose the people".

Green had good personal relations with Labour leader John Smith. At the start of the 1994 European election campaign, Smith visited Green in Brussels and offered his backing for her to become leader of the Socialist group. She recalls with good humour, "to be honest with you – and people don't believe it because they think I'm a manipulative cow – I was absolutely stunned". On 11 May 1994, Green sat next to Smith at the top table of a Labour Party fundraiser for the European elections. Smith was late, and Green remembers feeling "a little cross". She then spotted him talking to Michel Rocard, former prime minister of France and first secretary of the Socialist Party. Smith gave Green a wink and a thumbs up. When he came over to give Green a kiss on the cheek, he whispered in her ear, "You've got the French." Hours later, John Smith was dead from a heart attack.

With Margaret Beckett as party leader, Labour achieved an exceptionally good result, winning 43% of the vote to the Conservatives' paltry 27% and securing 74% of the seats in Great Britain. After the elections, Green was elected leader of the Socialist group, demonstrating both Labour's increased numerical strength and its changed reputation as a pro-European party. Labour MEPs were now one-third of the entire strength of the Socialist MEPs in the EU (see figure 1).

To replace Green, the soft left, pro-European South Wales MEP Wayne David was elected EPLP leader. David saw his job as being a conciliator, arguing, "the very fractious relationships between Labour MEPs had to be brought to an end. Things were very difficult. Not just on a political basis, but on a personal basis ... I stood on a platform of being the person who would try to bring the group together".

In spite of David's efforts, some members of the EPLP and the national Labour Party continued to clash. The most dramatic of these incidents occurred in January 1995, on Tony Blair's first visit to Brussels as leader. Blair had recently proposed scrapping Labour's commitment to "common ownership of the means of production,

Figure 1. Relative size of the Labour group/EPLP within the Socialists group in successive elections

distribution and exchange" spelled out in Clause IV of the party's constitution. Secretly, the day before the visit, 32 Labour MEPs paid £10,000 for an advertisement, in the form of a petition, to appear on the front page of the Guardian, condemning Blair's Clause IV reforms.[46] The advert read: "more than half the European Parliamentary Labour Party have called for Clause IV part 4 to remain in Labour's constitution". The front page headline of the Guardian read "MEPs fight Blair reform". The advert was described as a damaging blow to Blair, who had recently called for party unity.

The advertisement only reinforced the longstanding view that the EPLP contained some highly troublesome, recalcitrant and unreconstructed members. "They are just not serious people", a Blair adviser assessed. Wayne David, who had been left unaware of this

---

46 The MEPs who signed were Richard Balfe, David Bowe, Roger Barton, Ken Coates, Peter Crampton, Alan Donnelly, Mike Elliott, Robert Evans, Alex Falconer, David Hallam, Mike Hindley, Stephen Hughes, Hugh Kerr, Alf Lomas, Mike McGowan, Hugh McMahon, Eryl McNally, Tom Megahy, David Morris, Clive Needle, Stan Newens, Christine Oddy, Barry Seal, Alex Smith, Shaun Spiers, Ken Stewart, David Thomas, Sue Waddington, Norman West, Ian White and Joe Wilson. "Labour MEPs Defend Clause IV", Guardian, 10 January 1995.

plot, bitterly regretted it: "A front page advertisement on the day that the Leader of the Labour Party was coming to Brussels was reprehensible". In David's view, the advert scuppered his efforts to repair relations between the EPLP and the national party:

> "That damaged the EPLP enormously in terms of our standing with the new leadership ... That was the EPLP shooting itself in the foot in the most crass way you can imagine".

Blair was furious, telling them to grow up. As Glyn Ford recalled, Labour MEPs were to be confined to the sixth circle of hell.

Downing Street exacted its revenge in 1998 when the Labour government rushed through a party-list proportional representation (PR) system to elect MEPs, abandoning first-past-the-post. Described as the "scorched earth policy", the leadership, under the direction of Peter Mandelson, used its new-found powers to set the order of the regional party lists by purging those MEPs who had opposed the Clause IV reforms, as well as the remaining Eurosceptics. Wayne David acknowledges that:

> "Certainly PR was a useful tool in ridding the EPLP of dissident, unhelpful voices. Absolutely. That was one advantage of the PR system undoubtedly... [it gave] ... the Labour Party centre powers to create an EPLP which reflected the politics of the leadership, which they did very successfully".

Another MEP who experienced this transition agreed: "it did change the dynamic. It allowed the national party to jettison some MEPs who were not part of the project. Some found themselves very low down on lists".

Just five (16%) of the 32 MEPs who signed the Clause IV petition were returned after the 1999 elections, compared to 17 (57%) of the 30 of those who did not sign (figure 2). In other words, 84% of those MEPs who opposed Blair's Clause IV changes either retired or were placed sufficiently low on the party list by the national leadership that they were not returned to the EP. As the Eurosceptic Labour MEP Barry Seal, who retired in 1999, recalled: "They systematically pushed everyone out who were in any way critical of the EU".

Figure 2. Incumbent Labour MEPs re-elected in 1999, sorted by signature of 1995 Clause IV petition

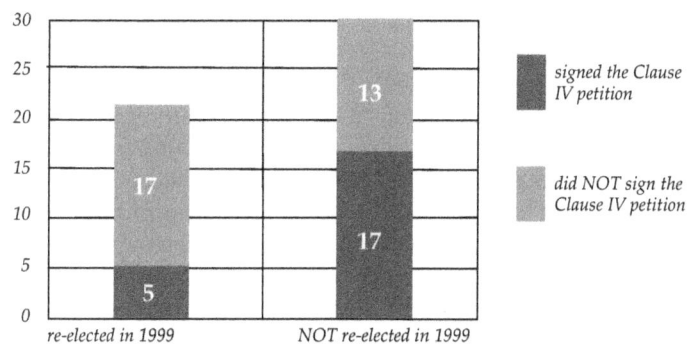

The 1999 election marked a decisive change for the EPLP. It was the end of Labour's Eurosceptic voice in Brussels. There were still about half a dozen Leavers in the EPLP as late the mid-1990s. Thereafter, all Labour MEPs were committed to Britain's EU membership. As a consequence, the EPLP became much more harmonious, both ideologically and personally. MEPs who served after 1999 describe an entirely different dynamic than the "ferrets in a sack" culture of the 1980s and early 1990s. Glyn Ford, who had served from the 1980s until the late 2000s, was almost wistful for the earlier years of tumult. Twenty-first century EPLP meetings were "very quiet. Towards the end, I almost never went to EPLP meetings because there was almost nothing of any interest. There was nothing happening ... We were all singing from the same hymn sheet, and it got boring".

There were some differences of opinion, however, over the extent of EU integration. It seems that a majority of Labour MEPs were on side with the New Labour government which, while pro-EU, expressed scepticism over some proposals for deeper integration. Simon Murphy, EPLP leader from 1999 to 2002, remembers: "For many within the European Parliamentary Labour Party, it was still an economic project ... We saw it more as a functional economic entity as opposed to this great United States of Europe". There were some Labour MEPs who believed in the dream of a federal Europe, but Murphy assesses that they "were never ultimately going to find complete favour with the national party because that wasn't where the national party was coming from on the future of Europe".

As leader, Murphy wanted to "keep the European Parliamentary Labour Party within the tent". It was important for the EPLP to be "seen as an organisation that could be relied upon" and for MEPs to be treated by the Labour government "as politicians who could be relied upon to support the national line". Murphy's successor as EPLP leader, Gary Titley (2002-09), adopted the same approach: "When I became Leader, I was determined to avoid any ructions with the party, which meant sometimes I'd sit on my hands and would keep my mouth shut where I would have liked to have got involved in the debate" – though he later reflected that he had perhaps done this too much.

Loyalty to the national line led to some (continued) friction with Socialist group MEPs. Murphy admits, "We were seen as, I think, part of the awkward squad". Tensions bubbled up at the time of the US-led invasion of Iraq in 2003, which was supported by the Labour government but opposed by nearly all the socialist parties in Europe. Gary Titley, EPLP leader at the time, remembers the period with great agony: "It was most difficult time of my political career because we got so much flack from the Socialist Group ... We were pariahs of the Socialist Group".

The following year, however, the tables had turned. In an effort to patch up relations within the European Parliament, Labour MEPs voted with the Socialist group in February 2004 to end national opt-outs for the working time directive. In so doing, the EPLP now found itself in opposition to the position of the Labour government, which supported the legal right to work for more than 48 hours per week. The EPLP faced a stern rebuke from the Labour government, and nearly two decades later Gary Titley professes "I still bear the scars of being savaged by Jack Straw" over the issue.

The size of the EPLP shrank dramatically over the course of the Labour government, due to the shift to proportional representation in 1999 and the rise of UKIP, whose first major breakthrough election occurred in 2004 when it won 12 seats. When Labour entered government in 1997, there were 62 Labour MEPs. When the Labour government ended thirteen years later, just 13 Labour MEPs remained. In the 2009 European elections, Labour fell to third place, behind the Conservatives and UKIP. It was the first election since universal suffrage in which Labour had lost Wales.

As the EPLP shrank, its membership became very cohesive, as Glenis Willmott, who became EPLP leader in 2009, observed. Willmott had become an MEP in 2006 after the death of Phillip Whitehead and greatly valued the consensual political culture of the Parliament. She reflected that on arrival:

> "I was very impressed with the way that the Parliament worked. It seemed much more modern than our [UK] Parliament. It wasn't the same sort of atmosphere – screaming and shouting at each other ... Everybody had to reach a consensus to get anything through [the EU] Parliament. So, it was a much more comfortable way to work because it was less confrontational".

The previous cultural frictions between a combative British left and consensual European socialists had seemingly dissipated. The standing of the EPLP within the Socialist group had also changed quite markedly. Willmott believes that under her leadership the EPLP was held in high regard within the Socialist group: "Other European Socialists were always keen to liaise with us".

Relations with the national party also warmed, especially after Labour went into opposition after the 2010 general election. When Ed Miliband became leader, he gave the EPLP leader a place in the shadow cabinet. Willmott saw this as a significant development which ensured that the collective view of the EPLP was expressed at the heart of the policy-making process. For example, she was able to make the case against Labour supporting a referendum on EU membership in advance of the 2015 general election, given that Labour MEPs tended to believe that if a referendum was held, the public would vote to leave.

The Conservatives won a majority in the 2015 general election with a manifesto pledge to implement a referendum on the EU, which Prime Minister David Cameron then held in June 2016. The referendum campaign was a difficult time for Labour MEPs, who felt that the national party had returned to its habit of sidelining them, in part out of the sense of the awkwardness of MEPs campaigning to keep their own jobs. Willmott looks back gloomily at the campaign, reflecting: "It was a horrendous time".

In 2017, Willmott retired from the European Parliament. In what was to be the swansong of the EPLP, its most pro-EU leader ever was elected. Richard Corbett had been active in the pro-European movement since a student at Oxford during the 1975 referendum, when he served as organising secretary of the Labour club. Corbett had spent his entire career working in the European Parliament, beginning as an intern in 1976 and rising as a European civil servant and member of the political staff of the Socialist group. He was a very well-respected bureaucrat. When Corbett first became an MEP shortly before the election of the Labour government in 1997, he found his pro-Europeanism out of step with the party leadership. Simon Murphy remembered, "what he wanted to see happen was definitely not what the national government wanted to see ... It was too federalist, too integrationist". Corbett served as an MEP from 1996 until his defeat in 2009. In the interlude that followed, he was an adviser to the European Council president, Herman Van Rompuy. In 2014, Corbett was returned at the European election in which Labour made its first gains in the Parliament for 20 years with 20 seats, one more than the Conservatives but 4 less than UKIP.

As EPLP leader, Richard Corbett was determined to stop the implementation of the 2016 referendum vote, even though the Labour Party had stated in its 2017 general election manifesto that it would accept the result. Corbett used his position in Labour's shadow cabinet repeatedly to make the case for blocking the 2016 referendum. Despite some initial hesitations, the EPLP collectively decided to work to stop the UK's withdrawal from the EU. As Corbett recalls, "I think everybody [in the EPLP] came to the view that if there is an opportunity to reconsider Brexit, to stop it happening, then we should do it because it's a national error".

Labour leader Jeremy Corbyn, however, was personally highly sceptical of the idea of stopping Brexit. Corbyn himself had emerged from the Campaign group, which had traditionally been much more sceptical about the EU. In the 2008 and 2009 Irish referendums over the Lisbon Treaty, Corbyn visited Ireland to urge a No vote, whereas Corbett advised the Yes campaign. As Britain faced its final European elections in 2019, Labour's position reflected some of Corbyn's remaining ambivalence about efforts to block leaving the EU, while also containing a second referendum pledge that implied support for staying in. The results were Labour's worst, with the size of the EPLP cut in half, winning just 14% of the vote.

One of the final, consequential acts of the EPLP was to vote for the centre-right German politician Ursula von der Leyen to become European Commission president in 2019. The Socialist group had huge misgivings about von der Leyen, and the group split almost in half. German, Dutch, French, Austrian, Bulgarian, Belgian and Slovenian social democratic MEPs all pledged to oppose her. Deputy EPLP leader Seb Dance met with von der Leyen to find out if she would be prepared to extend the Article 50 exit deadline for the United Kingdom if the UK Parliament requested it. As Corbett recalls, "We got that commitment from her. So we decided to vote for her". Von der Leyen's Commission was approved by just 9 votes on 16 July 2019. There were 10 Labour MEPs who supported her, thus making the crucial difference.

There is a certain irony that in the years when Labour MEPs were led by a broadly Eurosceptic leadership, the public appetite in Britain for leaving the EEC was at an historic low. Yet, as the leadership and the EPLP itself became increasingly pro-EU, the mood in the country grew more sceptical. It was at this point -- when the EPLP had finally become a cohesive political force in Europe, respected within the Socialist group and in the Parliament, as well as influential in shaping Labour Party policy on Europe – that the UK left the EU. The 2020 withdrawal fulfilled the vision of those early Eurosceptic Labour MEPs, and some, like Barry Seal, even lived long enough to vote Leave in the referendum. But, as a sign of how the parties had flipped on the issue, withdrawal was now being implemented, not by a socialist Labour government, but by the Conservatives.

Author's note:

I thank the following leaders of the EPLP for agreeing to be interviewed: Barry Seal (1988-89), Glyn Ford (1989-93), Pauline Green (1993-94), Wayne David (1994-98), Alan Donnelly (1998-99), Simon Murphy (1999-2002), Gary Titley (2002-2009), Glenis Willmott (2009-2017), and Richard Corbett (2017-20). I am grateful to the EPLP insider who agreed to be interviewed on the condition of anonymity. Glyn Ford and Richard Corbett kindly shared unpublished reflections, and Wayne David provided additional archival material.

Bibliography

Baker, David, Andrew Gamble, Steve Ludlam, David Seawright, "Labour and Europe: A Survey of MPs and MEPs", *Political Quarterly* 67:4 (Oct), 1996.

Baker, David, Andrew Gamble, Nick Randall, David Seawright, "Cast from the Same Pro-European Mould?". *Politique europeéne* 6 (hiver), 2002.

Broad, Roger. *Labour's European Dilemmas: From Bevin to Blair*, Palgrave, 2001.

Geddes, Andrew. "Labour and the European Community, 1973-93: Pro-Europeanism, Europeanisation, and their Implications". *Contemporary Record* 8:2 (Autumn), 1994.

Grahl, John & Paul Teague. "The British Labour Party and the European Community", *Political Quarterly* 59:1, 1988.

Johnson, Richard. "Neil Kinnock and Labour's European Policy" in K Hickson (ed) *Neil Kinnock: Saving the Labour Party?*, Routledge, 2022.

Jones, Eileen, *Neil Kinnock*, Hale, 1994.

Kendall, Walter, *The Labour Movement in Europe*, Allen Lane, 1975.

Pollack, Anita. *Wreckers or Builders? A History of Labour MEPs, 1979-1999*, John Harper Publishing, 2009.

4. The Liberal Democrats' arrival

by Graham Watson

Sir Graham Watson was an MEP from 1994 to 2014. From 1999 to 2002 he chaired the Citizens' Rights, Justice and Home Affairs Committee and from 2002 to 2009 he led Parliament's Liberals in the group of the European Liberal, Democrat and Reform Party (in 2004 renamed as the Alliance of Liberals and Democrats for Europe, ALDE). He is the author of ten books including "Building a Liberal Europe" (John Harper Publishing, 2010).

Alone among the EU's member states, the UK initially decided not to apply a system of proportional representation for its elections to the European Parliament. Instead, it held first-past-the-post elections in single member constituencies. This had the effect of denying the Liberal Party and its Social Democratic partners any representation in the first, second and third legislatures (1979-94), though the party received up to 18.5% of the votes cast.

Absence of representation did not mean absence of influence, however. The Liberal Party was represented in the unelected European Assembly prior to the first direct elections in 1979 by Lord Gladwyn and Russell Johnston MP. Both had become well known and liked by their continental colleagues. Incensed at being denied UK members by an electoral system which had an impact not just on UK representation but ipso facto on the balance of forces in the European Parliament as a whole, EP Liberal group leader Martin Bangemann invited Russell Johnston, who had come close to being elected to represent the Highlands and Islands of Scotland, to attend and enjoy voting rights at all meetings of Parliament's Liberal group during the first directly elected mandate of 1979-84. Moreover, Bangemann appointed the British Richard Moore, a former aide to the leader of the Liberal Party, to the staff of the Liberal group. Johnston represented UK Liberal opinion in political discussions within the Liberal group. Moore contributed decisively to Parliament's resolutions on global affairs through the application of his considerable knowledge and negotiating skills in inter-party discussions.

It was not until 1994, however, that the Liberal Democrats won the Somerset & North Devon and the Cornwall & West Plymouth constituencies. The party contends it should also have won the Devon & East Plymouth European constituency: a candidate called Richard Huggett stood for election as a Literal Democrat. Appearing on the ballot paper above Liberal Democrat candidate Adrian Sanders, he polled over 10,000 votes, some 4.3% of the total. Had the returning officer used his power to disqualify Huggett, whose candidature was clearly a ruse to assist the Conservative candidate, the "victor", Giles Chichester would not have clinched the seat with his 31.7% of the vote against the Liberal Democrats' 31.4%. Indeed, the Liberal Democrats came within a hair's breadth of winning all four seats on the southwest peninsula that night, failing by less than 1% to win East Devon & Dorset.

As the two MEPs representing the Liberal Democrats in the 1994-99 legislature, Robin Teverson and I shared the spoils. I served as whip of the Liberal group for the first half of the mandate, he for the second. He joined the committees for Regional Affairs and Fisheries, I the committees for Economic & Monetary Affairs and Budgets. Robin Teverson played a key role in Cornwall being granted "Objective 1" status, giving the county the right to higher levels of EU funding support than previously, and he sought reform of the common fisheries policy. I concentrated on parliamentary oversight of the functioning of the EU's internal market and preparations for the introduction of the euro. We welcomed James Moorhouse to our ranks in October 1998, a Conservative who switched party to the Liberal group in protest against the Conservative Party's opposition to UK membership of the euro. He was the first of three Conservatives who switched to the Liberal Democrats: Bill Newton Dunn and former UK Conservative group leader Edward McMillan-Scott followed, in 2000 and 2010 respectively.

The belated introduction of a proportional voting system for European elections under Tony Blair allowed the Liberal Democrats ten MEPs in the 1999-2004 mandate. It thus brought to the Parliament's Liberal group a fair share of the UK's representatives; and it also spared the European People's Party and Socialist groups the "adverse pendulum" effect of the UK's hitherto disruptive electoral law. The Liberal Democrats decided that their lists of candidates should be zipped (female-male-female-male and so forth in half the constituencies, with the other half male-female and so forth) to ensure gender balance.

The 1999 election thus saw Elspeth Attwooll (Scotland), Nick Clegg (East Midlands), Chris Davies (North West), Andrew Duff (Eastern region), Chris Huhne and Emma Nicholson (South East), Sarah Ludford (London), Liz Lynne (West Midlands), and Diana Wallis (Yorkshire & The Humber) elected alongside me as Liberal Democrats. I led the team for the first half of the Parliament, while serving as chairman of the Committee on Citizens Rights & Freedoms, Justice & Home Affairs, while the new MEPs found their feet. Elected subsequently in 2002 as leader of the European Parliament's Liberal group, I left the internal arrangements of the UK Liberal Democrat delegation to Diana Wallis, my successor as UK delegation leader.

The Liberal Democrats, the UK and the European Union were well served by the talented MEPs elected in 1999. Liberal Democrat MEPs in the fifth term were able to boast considerable individual achievements, including the European Arrest Warrant, the obligation of openness and transparency forced by Parliament on the European Central Bank, monopoly-breaking telecoms legislation and key pillars of the EU's private international law.

Three members of that intake – Chris Davies, Liz Lynne and Emma Nicholson – had previously been MPs. Another two, Nick Clegg and Chris Huhne, were to leave the European Parliament (in 2009 and 2010 respectively), gain election to the Commons and serve as cabinet ministers.

Elspeth Attwooll and Emma Nicholson each sat for ten years in the EP, Liz Lynne and Diana Wallis for twelve-and-a-half. The latter served with distinction for five years (2007-12) as one of Parliament's vice-presidents. Three members of the "class of 99" were to serve for three legislatures, with one of them, Chris Davies, returning for the final six months of UK representation in 2019-20.

The Liberal Democrats never elected an MEP in Wales, but the sixth legislature (2004-09) saw a Liberal Democrat MEP elected in North East England. Fiona Hall was re-elected in 2009 and served for two mandates.

As Liberal Democrat MEPs moved on, they were succeeded by other candidates. Thus Sharon Bowles (South East) joined the EP in 2005, with Catherine Bearder (South East) and George Lyon (Scotland) in 2009, and Phil Bennion (West Midlands) and Rebecca Taylor (Yorkshire and The Humber) in 2012. Upon her re-election in 2009, Bowles chaired the Committee on Economic and Monetary Affairs and was made a life peer in 2015.

Unsurprisingly, the members who served for longest made the greatest impact. Sarah Ludford made an important contribution in justice and home affairs and has continued such work in the UK's House of Lords since 2014. Diana Wallis has more parliamentary reports to her name than any other Liberal Democrat MEP and can take credit for much of the Rome l and Brussels ll packages of law. Liz Lynne was active in drawing attention to the needs of people with disabilities and fighting their corner in policy formation. Chris Davies can claim credit for introducing the financial mechanism that is the basis for the EU's €20 billion Innovation Fund to support low-carbon technologies. Andrew Duff worked on the EU's Charter of Fundamental Rights and on the EU's draft constitution which saw the light of day in the 2009 Lisbon Treaty. Catherine Bearder worked to ensure action against trafficking in wildlife, particularly of endangered species.

Our actions were not always popular in the UK. I was widely pilloried by UK Conservative and UKIP MEPs for having proposed the European Arrest Warrant mechanism and for subsequently piloting the legislation through the House. Their arguments that it constituted an attack on the principle of habeas corpus clearly did not hold water, however, since it soon became the most widely used legislative tool available to governments in the fight against cross-border crime.

Converts from the Conservative Party Bill Newton Dunn and Edward McMillan-Scott had each served in the EP for many years before joining the Liberal Democrats. At the start of the ninth legislature, in 2019, the former was the only MEP who had been elected to serve in the first direct elections in 1979, forty years earlier. The latter served for ten years (under different party labels) as a vice-president of Parliament and was active in establishing the EU's Instrument for Democracy and Human Rights.

The party's vote in the nine European elections between 1979 and 2019 oscillated between ten and twelve per cent, with three exceptions. In 1989 it fell below 10% as the Liberal-SDP Alliance was pushed into fourth place, behind the Green Party. In 2014 the party paid the price for an unpopular coalition with the Conservatives: its vote fell to 8% and it secured only one MEP, Catherine Bearder (South East England). In 2019, by contrast – in the wake of the Brexit referendum – the Liberal Democrats beat the Labour, Conservative and Green parties, taking almost 20% of the vote, though the Brexit Party topped the poll.

Of the 16 Liberal Democrat MEPs elected in 2019 (seven men and nine women), four had served in previous legislatures, including Martin Horwood, who had been an MP. They were joined by Naomi Long, leader of the Alliance Party of Northern Ireland (the Liberal Democrats' sister party in the Province), and comprised a major component of the renamed Renew Europe group. Lucy Nethsingha, as chair of the Legal Affairs Committee, and Chris Davies, as chair of the Fisheries Committee, were the last two UK representatives to chair committees in the European Parliament.

The Brexit saga playing out at Westminster made the position of the 2019 intake very difficult; the very limited duration of their mandate deprived them of the opportunity for significant achievements. Nonetheless Catherine Bearder, Anthony Hook and Judith Bunting (South East), Phil Bennion (West Midlands), Chris Davies and Jane Brophy (North West), Barbara Gibson and Lucy Nethsingha (Eastern Region), Shaffaq Mohammed (Yorkshire & The Humber), Bill Newton Dunn (East Midlands), Sheila Ritchie (Scotland), Caroline Voaden and Martin Horwood (South West) and Irina von Wiese, Dinesh Dhamija and Luisa Porritt (London) all took their seats in Strasbourg for the UK's unexpected "grand finale" in the EP. All were active in campaigning to stop Brexit.

The parliaments to which the Liberal Democrat MPs were elected in 1994 and 1999 were quite different from those which had preceded them. To some extent, the early parliaments had been composed either of former members of national parliaments who had been "put out to grass" or younger politicians seeking the first rung on the ladder towards a national parliamentary career. That was beginning to change: the EP began to attract convinced European federalists who sought to build European political careers.

While the European Community was not yet a federation, it was already more than a confederation. Politics at Westminster and in other member state parliaments appeared to be often stagnant and, at worst, in decline. The Commons had lost much of its power to oppose legislation during the 1980s; with the advent of the 1990s it appeared also to lose many of its powers to control the executive, powers increasingly exercised through external statutory agencies.

While the powers of the European Parliament at that time were more restricted than those of national parliaments, the expansion of the EP's powers through the Maastricht and Amsterdam treaties was already redressing the balance. This dynamic made Brussels and Strasbourg attractive places to be. Combined with the development of political parties at European level and the early stirrings of a European demos, some found a political excitement in Brussels and Strasbourg which national politics could not match. While national parliaments were often hidebound by tradition, the European Parliament was a crucible of a fascinating and world-changing European experiment.

One frustration in representing the UK in the European Parliament was that, like Russia, the UK perceived itself as only partially European. Some of its leaders appeared to believe the Atlantic Ocean was narrower than the English Channel. Moreover, its political establishment often reacted to the development of powers at European level by seeking to downplay and even to disparage the work of MEPs. Indeed, it was not until the turn of the century that MEPs were allowed passes to the Palace of Westminster; and these were subsequently withdrawn when the British National Party succeeded in electing MEPs.

Any frustration was balanced, however, by the opportunities offered. Since the proportional representation election system normally gives no party an absolute majority, opportunities to pilot legislation through the house are shared out among the different political parties. To become a rapporteur, or pilot, can give even a back bench member decision-making power over legislation akin to that of a government minister in a national parliament; the chairs of committees with legislative powers enjoy this privilege frequently. However arduous the task of making laws in a parliament whose members speak many different languages, and however long the voting sessions, MEPs could make legislation; and it seemed a far preferable way of settling our differences than firing machine guns at each other from the trenches of a European war.

Liberal Democrats did not see in the development of the EU any loss of sovereignty for the UK. In contrast, by pooling our sovereignty with others we were able to offer greater protection and enhanced opportunity to UK citizens. The European Parliament thus became increasingly attractive to those who welcomed what Churchill had called "a wider sovereignty and a common citizenship for the distraught peoples of this powerful and turbulent continent". Though dismissed by Prime Minister Theresa May in 2017 as "citizens of nowhere", our support for the European Constitution agreed in 2006 lay not least in the desire for rules which set down clearly which competences were to be exercised by the EU institutions, which powers were rightly the province of national governments, and how decisions should be made in the areas where power is shared. The proposed European Constitution also enshrined in law the rights of the citizen against arbitrary abuse of power and was the first EU treaty to give member states a formal right to secede from the EU and to limit effectively the powers exercised at the centre. As such, one might have expected the UK to welcome it. Instead, it became a pawn in the ill-informed UK debate about Europe which even the BBC, mandated by its charter "to educate and to inform", did little to enlighten.

Developments in communications technology had a considerable impact on the work of MEPs. Those elected in 1994 started their mandate with correspondence from constituents of which over 90% was received via the Royal Mail and finished it with mailbags which were almost entirely electronic. Email became a powerful tool for mass communication with constituents or party members. The following decade saw the growth of social media, with the launch of Facebook in 2004 and Twitter in 2006. Liberal Democrat MEP Martin Horwood was the first representative of the party to receive (in 2019) over one million "likes" in response to a post on Twitter.

My newsletters to constituents between 2004 and 2014 show that I detected an acceleration in the UK's disengagement from the EU. This was reflected in our language. While schoolchildren of the 1960s and 1970s were increasingly taught to consider "Europe" as consisting of the British Isles and the continent, by the turn of the century it had once again become commonplace to consider Europe as something other than our islands, and to speak of "going to" or "coming from" Europe.

Although the Liberal Democrats were the only consistently pro-EU party at Westminster, national party leaders nonetheless approached the European Parliament in different ways. While David Steel was a passionate European who regularly attended European Liberal conferences and even stood as a candidate in the 1989 European election in the Central Italy constituency (in protest against the UK's first-past-the-post voting system), some of his successors paid the party's MEPs less attention than they would have liked. Notable exceptions were Charles Kennedy and former European Commission official and MEP Nick Clegg; both engaged – the former in opposition and the latter in government – frequently and fervently in Europe's democratic processes. As deputy prime minister, Clegg hosted a summit of the leaders of EU liberal parties at Admiralty House.

Other MPs – and the party's representatives in the Lords – took an active interest in EU affairs, struck up good relationships with the MEPs and secured meetings with European commissioners and other officials. Some of their colleagues in the lower house showed little interest, being concerned essentially with the pavement politics in which the party took pride. To the regret of the MEPs, a few MPs fell for the British myth of superiority, regarded their chamber as the "mother of parliaments" and looked down snootily on those representing the party in Brussels and Strasbourg.

In the first parliament in which we were represented, the MEPs were welcomed at meetings of the Westminster parliamentary party, offered speaking slots at the party's annual conference and were otherwise involved in Liberal Democrat activity at UK level, although this did not extend to being promoted by the party's press office to UK broadcasters. In the 1999-2004 legislature, with ten MEPs, the leader of the party in Brussels was invited to parliamentary party meetings and given an ex-officio place on the party's national executive. But below the surface, tensions simmered: the party's campaigns department too often appeared to view MEPs primarily as cash cows and sought to use funding intended to promote their European activities to promote MPs instead.

To counter this tendency, Robin Teverson and I employed jointly a member of staff in London to fight our corner. The practice was continued by later Liberal Democrat MEPs; and around the turn of the century, with the move of its headquarters from Queen Anne's Gate to Smith Square, the European Parliament's office in London agreed to make office space available to the political groups to maintain such a presence. Head of office Martyn Bond showed acute sensitivity to the needs of MEPs and was widely respected across party lines.

The UK Liberal Democrat delegation in the EP formed a part of the group of the European Liberal, Democrat and Reform Party, later renamed the Alliance of Liberal Democrats for Europe and – in 2019 – the Renew Europe group. The group was led during the first forty years of the directly elected Parliament by Martin Bangemann, Simone Veil, Giscard d'Estaing, Yves Galland, Gijs de Vries, Pat Cox, Graham Watson, Guy Verhofstadt and Dacian Ciolos. The UK delegation was led successively by Graham Watson, Diana Wallis, Chris Davies, Andrew Duff, Fiona Hall, Catherine Bearder and Caroline Voaden. The history of the Parliament's Liberal group from 1979 to 2009 is related in the book *Building a Liberal Europe*, published by John Harper in 2010.

Twice during the period 1979-2019 the Liberal Democrats hosted the annual congress of the European Liberal Democrats. Thus in 2002 in Bath and in 2013 in London, Europe's Liberal Democrat parties came together for their annual policy making and representational bash. European politics played an important role too at the annual Liberal Democrat party conferences, where representatives of our European sister parties were frequently present and occasionally offered a speaking slot on the conference floor. Such links were particularly valued by the party since, although the UK's first-past-the-post voting system normally denied it representation in UK government, continental Liberal parties were frequently in government, either on their own or in coalition. Thus access could be gained to the details of discussion at meetings of the EU's heads of state and government in the European Council. There were invariably European commissioners from continental Liberal parties, though never one from the UK (unless Roy Jenkins, a Labour appointee, be thus counted in regard to his later position).

Some continental right-wing politicians felt a greater affinity for the UK's Liberal Democrats than for its Conservative Party. Though his party was affiliated to the EPP rather than the Liberal family, and thus a sister party to the UK's Conservatives, José Manuel Barroso became the only European Commission president to address a conference of a UK political party – the Liberal Democrat conference in Brighton in 2007. (His predecessor Jacques Delors had addressed the TUC in Bournemouth.)

When David Sainsbury moved (in 2014) to set up a Referendum Council to prepare the Yes/Remain Camp for the likely forthcoming referendum campaign, the Liberal Democrats were represented by Danny Alexander MP, Baroness Suttie and this author. Together with Lord (John) Kerr and latterly Peter Wilding, we opposed the strategy proposed by Craig Oliver (Conservative) and Peter Mandelson (Labour) because they sought to say nothing positive about UK membership of the EU, preferring to argue simply that leaving would cause damage to the country's economy. Our contention was that this would leave the pro-EU campaign constantly on the back foot and would not motivate people to vote to remain.

Our avowedly pro-European argument in the 2014 European election campaign cut little ice with the electorate, however; and the unpopularity of the policies of the Conservative/Liberal Democrat coalition saw the party's representation cut from twelve MEPs to just one. In the general election the following year the Liberal Democrats suffered a severe electoral defeat. Reduced at Westminster from over fifty MPs to just eight, the one remaining MEP was soon recruited as the party's official spokesperson on EU affairs. Although the party was represented in the Remain campaign for the 2016 referendum, it was never happy with the campaign's implicit defensiveness.

It seems ironic that the moment of greatest public enthusiasm for the European project since the 1975 referendum coincided with the moment at which the Brexit Party topped the polls, in the 2019 European election. The fissiparous nature of the 2016 referendum and its aftermath had pushed voters more decisively into one camp or the other. Prime Minister Theresa May's term as Conservative Party leader – already foreshortened by four parliamentary defeats of her Brexit proposals – was ended decisively by her party's losses in that election. Opposition leader Jeremy Corbyn's refusal to oppose Brexit added to the Liberal Democrats' triumph; never before had the party elected so many MEPs. The unreal nature of the UK's participation in the 2019 European election, however, curtailed our celebration.

5. The move to proportional representation and the rise of UKIP

by Lorin Bell-Cross

Lorin Bell-Cross is a journalist and former parliamentary aide to John Spellar MP. His specialist interests include the Labour Party, antisemitism and opposition to proportional representation.

"UKIP has supported a representative electoral system for many years now. The result of the referendum merely goes to highlight the disconnect between the political parties and the public." Nigel Farage[47]

The use of Britain's traditional first-past-the-post system (FPTP) had long been queried in the case of European elections, partly because it resulted in having British MEPs sitting alongside MEPs from every other country who had been elected on a different, more proportional basis. But another objection was that the large European constituencies evidenced more clearly the impact of this system on smaller parties. Thus, for example, in 1989, the Greens won 14.5% of the vote (almost three times the Liberal Democrats' share – the "tra-

---

47 Independent, 1 July 2016

ditional" third party) and thus might have taken a dozen seats under a proportional system, but they won none at all.

By contrast, the 1994 European election saw Labour reap the benefits of FPTP with 62 seats, taking 71% of the GB seats on 42% of the vote (in similar fashion the Conservatives had won 60 seats in the 1979 election). The SNP and Liberal Democrats only won two seats between them, despite getting 16% (2.5 million) and 3.1% (under 0.5 million) of the votes respectively.

Despite the clear advantages FPTP had for Labour, its 1997 manifesto pledged: "An independent commission on voting systems will be appointed early to recommend a proportional alternative to the first-past-the-post system" – part of a deal between Tony Blair and the Liberal Democrats. Whilst this was not delivered for Westminster, the elections to the Welsh Assembly, Scottish Parliament, London Assembly and European Parliament all adopted some form of proportional representation in time.

The resulting 1999 shift to proportional representation (PR) for the five-yearly European elections, supposedly brought about to move the UK closer to a "common" EU system, had enormous consequences for the Labour Party but ultimately even more for the Conservative Party, and ultimately the UK.

The 1997 Amsterdam Treaty committed members states to "greater uniformity" in their EP electoral systems but did not define any particular system. The one chosen by Home Secretary Jack Straw (despite dire warnings from some, including one of this book's editors) – a system of multi-member, enormous regions comprising electorates of millions – was particularly damaging, partly because voters could only opt for a party and not for named candidates, and partly because it effectively ended any meaningful MEP constituency link. The proposal was voted down six times in the Lords (because of the closed list which gave so much power to the party hierarchy) and necessitated use of the Parliament Act to overcome this resistance.

When it became clear that the new Labour government would introduce PR for European elections, the Referendum Party, which Sir James Goldsmith had launched in 1994, contemplated contesting seats, realising the potential of the new system for a party like his with a geographical spread of support sufficient to elect MEPs. He realised that, for example, in an 8-seat constituency the threshold to take a seat would be about 12.5%. Goldsmith had been elected to the European Parliament in France in 1994, on the list of the French Majorité pour l'Autre Europe. His death in July 1997 left the field open in the UK to the then rather demoralised and divided UKIP whose incoming chair, Nigel Farage, quickly recognised the potential[48] of PR. He himself chose an 11-seat region needing only 8% to take one of the seats. Thus the pro-EU Tony Blair, via this change to the voting system, gave UKIP the tools to make electoral headway, with profound consequences over the following two decades.

However, the immediate impact was on political parties' method of selecting candidates and on their campaign machinery, which had to be reconfigured to fight elections in a different manner. Previous Euro constituencies contained between 8 and 10 Westminster seats. Henceforth each would have about 70 Westminster seats and elect 9 or 10 MEPs in a proportional manner.

The selection of candidates across these large constituencies was drastically affected for both main parties, with MEPs less accountable to local party members and with a transfer of power from local parties to party leaders. Inevitably, the centralisation of candidate selection from an area of around 10 constituencies to around 70 impacted the ability of potential candidates to campaign for selection and greatly empowered the central authority. This soured relations in both the Labour and Conservative parties.

In the case of Labour, candidates at variance with the party leadership were placed low down on the list, usually in unwinnable positions, with the more favoured placed towards the top, regardless of local support or their record in the European Parliament. Less immediately, a similar pattern emerged with the Conservatives, with ructions between its delegation in Brussels and Conservative Central Office. The 1999 elections also saw the first appearance of Conservative Eurosceptic MEPs with Roger Helmer, Chris Heaton-Harris and Daniel Hannan elected.

There was another impact felt in both parties – the widening gulf between MEPs and the national party. In this book, both Christopher

---

[48] Michael Crick, *One Party After Another: The Disruptive Life of Nigel Farage,* Simon & Schuster. 2022 pp 79-82

Tugendhat (former Conservative EU commissioner) and George Robertson (former Labour shadow Europe minister) comment on the distance which had earlier developed between directly elected MEPs and their party (in comparison with the former Assembly comprising members of the UK Parliament). But while the need to keep close to the national party hierarchy in order to retain an advantageous list position for the subsequent election might have been expected to persuade MEPs to follow their party line, in practice, on a day-to-day basis, there was far less involvement with anyone in the national party. Euro-constituencies had disappeared. And in contrast to having a close relationship with their MPs and council leaders when representing 8 to 10 Westminster constituencies and thus only a couple of local authority areas, this was effectively impossible over 70 seats. Socialist group leader Pauline Green (as noted by Dianne Hayter in Part III:8) regretted the real loss of contact with her community as well as with the initially one, later 7, Labour MPs who kept her in touch with the UK party.

While the 1999 election was a lot more proportional (Labour won 33% of the seats with 26% of the vote), its real impact was on new or smaller parties which suddenly had a better chance of success under the new system. Unlike under FPTP, they were able to present voters with a convincing message that their vote would no longer be "wasted" as it would add to the regional vote share.

As Rob Ford and Matthew Goodwin note in their study of UKIP, the change to the electoral system was exactly the opportunity smaller parties needed to make gains:

> "The new system, commonly used in Europe, makes it much easier for smaller parties, and those with evenly distributed support, to win representation. If each region elects six MEPs, then a party winning 18% of the vote in any region will elect an MEP, whereas under first-past-the-post they would win nothing. The British electorate recognised and responded to the changed incentives offered by the new system, backing smaller parties in far larger numbers now they were freed from the 'wasted vote syndrome'."[49]

---

49 Ford, R & Matthew, G, *Revolt on the Right: Explaining Support for the Radical Right in Britain*. Routledge, 2014.

It didn't take long for the impact to be seen. In 1999 UKIP elected for the first time three MEPs, including the then unknown Nigel Farage (alongside Michael Holmes and Jeffrey Titford) – making these the first of 66 people over the next 20 years to become UKIP (or its successor, the Brexit Party) MEPs. Farage himself would remain an MEP until the UK left the EU in 2020. Although Euroscepticism in the UK wasn't new, the proportional system fuelled UKIP's ability to win seats. It similarly allowed the Greens, Liberal Democrats and the Scottish National Party (SNP) to make gains, particularly at Labour's expense.

The low bar required to pass the electoral threshold even enabled the British National Party (BNP) to gain elected office. Whilst ultimately of much less consequence than UKIP, the avowed extreme right-wing and racist BNP not only gained seats under PR, but thereby gained financial and publicity resources which were of national significance. It took two seats in the North West in the 2009 European elections, whereas it is extremely unlikely it would have won anything under FPTP because its vote was so widely but thinly distributed. This was not the first time PR had aided the extreme right; even in the supposedly liberal capital, the BNP took a seat on the London Assembly in 2008, forcing the then London Assembly member, James Cleverly (later a Conservative cabinet minister), to sit next to someone with openly racist views.

Supporters of PR champion the opportunities granted to smaller parties under PR, even as some regret how it paved the way for UKIP to force its agenda into the mainstream and ultimately led to Brexit. By its own admission, UKIP would have found achieving its goal more challenging – if not impossible – under FPTP, whereas PR altered how it was perceived by the public. Whereas in the 1997 general election UKIP attracted barely 100,000 voters, under PR in the 1999 European election (with a much lower total turnout) it won nearly 700,000. Indeed, as Michael Crick has noted, "thanks to PR, a new party had emerged into the political stage that questioned the whole existence of the EU and Britain's involvement with it".[50]

---

50 Crick, op cit, p.110

It would not be an exaggeration to describe Nigel Farage as the most influential figure in 21st century British politics never elected to national office. It is hard to imagine Britain voting to leave the EU without his impact on the Conservatives and his presence in national politics, given how he was able to generate a laser-like focus on the question of British membership of the EU.

Over time, the proportional system for European elections saw the share of the vote move away from Labour and the Conservatives, with smaller parties thriving at their expense. In 1999 Labour and the Conservatives held 75% of the Euro seats between them; by 2014, just 53%. From 1999, MEPs from smaller parties could set up a physical presence in the areas they represented with funding from the European taxpayer. This enabled then to bed themselves into the relevant media and gather greater attention and profile.

With hindsight, the 2009 European elections should have been a major warning sign for Labour, when it was relegated to third place in vote share, behind the Conservatives and UKIP. This represented a significant breakthrough for Farage and UKIP, achieving a record 16% of the vote and equalling the number of Labour MEPs (13 each) – something unimaginable in 1994. Although UKIP failed to translate this share of the vote into seats in the 2010 general election, its increased presence meant it had more EU resources at its disposal and more opportunities to campaign across the UK, especially with Farage's use of online platforms such as YouTube: his speech mocking incoming European Council president Herman Van Rompuy as having "all the charisma of a damp rag and the appearance of a low-grade bank clerk" produced millions of views online.

One advantage for UKIP was that a motivated Eurosceptic electorate would vote for them in European elections, unlike in general elections where withdrawal – UKIP's flagship policy – was not of central importance.

While PR saw Labour lose seats to other parties, its impact on the Conservatives – and the future of Britain in Europe – was even larger.

The result of the 2010 general election – a Tory-Lib Dem coalition – was the perfect result for UKIP. For the first time in 13 years, the Conservatives were in government but in partnership with a Europhile party, providing opportunities for Farage to create discomfort for the new government. Europe had already played a key role in amplifying the divisions within the Conservative Party before 1997, so it was not an issue Cameron could ignore. Early in the coalition, he saw his largest rebellion when 81 Tory MPs defied the whip to vote for a referendum on Britain's membership of the EU.[51] This wouldn't be the only such rebellion. The Euroscepticism in the Tory party, exacerbated by UKIP's presence in British politics, meant Farage was able to fuel divisions within the Conservative ranks and ensure Europe was never off the agenda.

The tensions over Europe set the agenda for the subsequent, historic 2014 European election – the first since 1910 when neither the Labour Party nor the Conservatives won a national election. UKIP topped the poll on 27%, Labour came second on 25% and the Conservatives third on 23%.

The momentum generated – and the political headache for David Cameron – wouldn't go away, as the campaign to get Britain out of the EU took off. To ramp up the pressure on the Conservative Party, two Tory MPs – Douglas Carswell and Mark Reckless – defected to UKIP. Not only did they cross the floor, but UKIP's insistence on holding a parliamentary by-election meant that UKIP won its first ever national parliamentary seats. Sensing vulnerability – and worried about the potential splintering of the Conservative vote (and indeed, further defections to UKIP) – David Cameron pledged to hold an in-out referendum on EU membership.

UKIP and Nigel Farage had thus successfully exploited the advantages PR afforded them. Their political success was not guaranteed solely by PR – that would not be giving enough credit both to UKIP's abilities organisationally and to Farage's skills as a politician. However, such abilities would have been more limited without an electoral system that gave UKIP seats at the expense of established parties. Through this platform they used their publicity, influence and the threat of splitting the Conservative Party over Europe to win the promise of a referendum. Without UKIP's electoral success under PR and its influence on the Conservative Party,

---

51 Guardian, 25 October 2011

the in-out referendum on Britain's membership might never have happened.

UKIP's vote had been turbo-charged in 2004 when TV star (and ex Labour MP) Robert Kilroy-Silk was catapulted onto a prime list position by Farage, making him one of the best-known British names ever to contest a Euro election. He brought untold publicity to UKIP, which then came third with 16.1% of the vote, relegating the Liberal Democrats to fourth position and electing 12 UKIP MEPs across every region except the North East. In Kilroy-Silk's East Midlands region UKIP won 26%, ahead of Labour. The increase from 3 to 12 MEPs produced a four-fold increase in EP resources.

UKIP's effect on the Conservatives was to produce both Cameron's withdrawal from the EPP (see also Part III:13 on Daniel Hannan) and the referendum promise, as he sought to retain Eurosceptic support within his party and prevent defections to UKIP either by MPs or by voters.

However UKIP, supercharged by PR, wasn't an exclusively Tory problem, though that is how it was foolishly treated by many in the Labour Party. This was perhaps because, as Tim Montgomerie outlined at the time:

> "At the next UK general election [2015], fought under the first-past-the-post system, most experts think [UKIP] will struggle to win many – if any – seats, but that does not mean it won't influence the result. Although it is siphoning off votes from all parties, it is winning the lion's share of its support from the Conservative Party".[52]

So, whilst UKIP was squeezing the Conservative Party to get a policy change on Europe, senior figures in the Labour Party failed to see UKIP as posing any significant threat to Labour.

Others did notice. Though then just a university student, the present author wrote in his student paper:

---

52 Tim Montgomerie, "Britain's Tea Party" The National Interest, September/October 2014, No. 133, KASSINGER'S VISION: How to Restore World Order, September/October 2014, Center for the National Interest Stable URL: www.jstor.org/stable/44151198

"Labour should by alarmed by UKIP's success ... they can ill afford to treat UKIP as an exclusively Tory threat. Despite Labour gaining 291 seats and retaining South Shields, UKIP's popularity is growing in safe Labour seats, coming second in the Rotherham by-election last year. More worrying was Labour's failure to break through in the South of England ... UKIP, rather than Labour were able to make larger gains."[53]

Labour's inability to appeal to potential UKIP voters was to cost it greatly. Proportional representation, introduced (your author thinks unnecessarily) into the UK by the Europhile Tony Blair and the more sceptical Jack Straw for Euro-elections, not only led to UKIP's electoral success but also to the referendum and to the weakening of the old two-party duopoly.

Labour remains fully supportive of PR wherever it is already in use. The Conservatives, however, now seek to remove it from some local elections, perhaps recognising the gift Labour gave to UKIP via PR, despite Boris Johnson having successfully exploited the referendum to gain the keys to Number 10.

---

53 Nouse, 5 May 2013, https://nouse.co.uk/2013/05/05/the-fruitcake-rises-what-the-future-holds-for-ukip

Nicholas Bethell, seen here in 1978 when he was a nominated Conservative member from the House of Lords. He won a seat in the first direct elections in 1979.

Barbara Castle was the biggest name in British politics ever to make the move to Strasbourg. Here she is with her political assistant Anita Pollack, who herself went on to become an MEP.

All photos © European Communities/European Union except where indicated

Three of the first contingent of elected Conservative MEPs: (l-to-r) Stanley Johnson (father of Boris), Ben Patterson and Edward Kellett-Bowman, 26 January 1980.

Derek Enright (left) fell out with hard-line anti-marketeers in the Labour Party in the 1980s and was deselected, while Roy Perry (right) fell into disfavour with Eurosceptics in the Conservative Party two decades later and was dropped down the list of candidates to make him unelectable. See Part IV "As their children saw them" for portraits of both.

A 1980s gathering of British MEPs and others: those seen, from left to right, include at position 2 Geoff Hoon, 3 Jack Stewart-Clark, 6 Madron Seligman, 7 Barbara Castle, 9 Winifred Ewing, and 11 Ben Patterson.

Basil de Ferranti (right) in good humour at a November 1985 meeting of the influential pro-single market Kangaroo group. He and German MEP Karl von Wogau were the main founders of the group.

Christopher Prout, the leader of the Conservative MEPs, speaking in February 1987.

Ian Paisley's protest against the visit of "the Antichrist" Pope John Paul II on 12 October 1988 led to his expulsion from the chamber. But he discreetly worked with fellow MEP, Catholic nationalist leader John Hume, in pursuit of peace in Northern Ireland.

John Hume in Strasbourg on 1 October 1998 after receiving the Nobel peace prize. With him is Pauline Green, leader of the Socialist group.

David Martin was the longest-serving of all British MEPs, sitting continuously from 1984 to 2019. The photo is from 13 February 2019.

Bill Newton Dunn: uniquely, he was an MEP at both the start and finish of British membership of the elected Parliament (though he did not serve all parliamentary terms). Here he is seen with his family – including the 10-year-old Tom Newton Dunn who writes about his father in Part IV – in Strasbourg, 1 April 1984.

Glenys Kinnock: worked for development at the global level and for the South Wales valleys.

Sharon Bowles: Liberal Democrat who played a key role as chair of the Committee on Economic and Monetary Affairs at the height of the eurozone crisis.

Syed Kamall: Conservative co-leader of the European Conservatives and Reformists group who backed Leave in the 2016 referendum.

Dianne Hayter, chief executive of the European Parliamentary Labour Party, with party leader John Smith shortly before his sudden death in May 1994.

Dianne Hayter with George Robertson (centre): he reflects on Labour's relations with its MEPs in Part II.

II: AS OTHERS SAW THEM

1. The view from the coalition government

by David Lidington

Sir David Lidington KCB CBE is chair of the Royal United Services Institute. A Conservative MP from 1992-2019, he was for 20 years on the front bench in opposition, and then in the governments of David Cameron and Theresa May, when he was successively minister for Europe, leader of the House of Commons, secretary of state for justice, and minister for the Cabinet Office, in which capacity he acted as deputy to Prime Minister May.

It was lunch with José Manuel Barroso that rammed the message home. Or, to be strictly accurate, it was the placement at the president of the Commission's table.

We were back in the early part of the coalition government. David Cameron had told his party to "stop banging on about Europe" and I had been tasked with promoting a positive British agenda for the EU, centred on completing the single market. (In those days, Conservative ministers still talked about the single market as one of Margaret Thatcher's greatest achievements!)

I'd struck up a cordial working relationship with Barroso's chef de cabinet, Johannes Laitenberger, and had hosted an enjoyable dinner for the Commission president in London, bringing MPs, special advisers and think tank leaders together for a lively and constructive debate. This was the return trip, when I led a similar UK team to Brussels to lunch with President Barroso.

I was seated opposite the president. Around me and Barroso were clustered a small group of Conservative and Liberal Democrat MEPs. Not only were they given seats close to the president, but he treated them with particular respect. Barroso understood that these men and women had been key to his re-election as president in 2009, would have a large say in whether or not the Commission's policies would be enacted, and had the ultimate power to remove him from office.

This is not just a theoretical power. Every five years, when a new Commission is nominated, the Parliament holds confirmation hearings for the men and women nominated by member states, and it has become almost expected that the Parliament will flex its muscles by blocking the appointment of one or two nominees. In 2014, we feared that this might happen to Jonathan Hill, whom the Cameron government had nominated as commissioner for financial services. By that stage, the referendum debate had generated a bit of anti-British feeling at Strasbourg and in the aftermath of the 2008 financial crash a number of MEPs, especially but not only on the centre-left, felt that the UK, seen as the home of freewheeling "Anglo-Saxon capitalism", should not get this portfolio.

We pulled out every stop to get Jonathan confirmed by the Economic and Monetary Affairs (ECON) committee. Kay Swinburne and Ashley Fox lobbied their fellow-MEPs and fed back to me and to our permanent representative in Brussels. We analysed the position of each member of ECON and tried to identify who, in Strasbourg or their national capital, might be best placed to influence them. I remember calling ministers in a number of countries to ask them to help with their MEPs. From both Brussels and London, we talked to the EPP to check and double-check that their promised support for Jonathan was real. It was an exercise, a successful one, in which the UK government and Conservative MEPs worked hand-in-glove.

That tableau on the 13th floor of the Berlaymont had encapsulated the truth that my officials in the Foreign Office and my own experience in the Council had taught me: that the European Parliament, love or loathe it, had growing institutional weight within the EU and any member state government (or any other organisation) that wished to protect and advance its interests needed to find a way to work with the Parliament's members.

Every minister in the coalition government (2010-2015) had to grapple with the novel experience of working with colleagues from a different political party. My own coalition of Conservative and Liberal Democrat MEPs presented a particular challenge, stretching as it did from ardent federalists like Andrew Duff to UK nationalists like Roger Helmer, and I tried, with varying degrees of success over the years, to remain sensitive to the beliefs and priorities of both party groups and to seek their help in lobbying for the coalition government's EU policy objectives.

On anything to do with the single market, Malcolm Harbour and Vicky Ford were both staunch allies and an invaluable source of intelligence as to how opinion was shifting within the Parliament. More unexpectedly, I found myself also working closely with Sharon Bowles, especially after she became chair of the ECON committee with responsibility for financial services legislation. Sharon had been the Liberal Democrat candidate in my constituency at two general elections, but we were able to work well, as indeed she did with Treasury ministers.

The way that the European Parliament does business, no single group having a majority and compromises and trade-offs being struck between the different political factions, meant that I also dealt with Labour MEPs, sometimes attending part of their group meeting and at others speaking to a key Labour MEP one to one.

I tried to see the Conservative group collectively every time I went to Strasbourg. Often, I'd get there in the evening and meet my MEP party colleagues in whichever restaurant they were dining. Those were pleasant occasions. For the most part, different opinions about Britain's membership of the EU were kept under wraps, and we would run through a mixture of policy updates and gossip about the internal politics of the Parliament and its various political groups.

The following day I would usually have a more formal meeting with the Conservative delegation, where we would discuss what

EU business the government wanted to see achieved or blocked and they would ask me about the mood in Whitehall and Westminster. Our MEPs (and I think this was true of those from all UK parties) felt undervalued by London. I thought they were right. To do their job of scrutinising and amending legislation demanded hard work (especially from committee chairs and rapporteurs) and dedication, and the power that MEPs collectively had over EU law making was real.

Those meetings were always cordial, but after David Cameron's Bloomberg speech in January 2013, when he committed the Conservative Party to a referendum on EU membership, and as we approached the 2016 referendum, the dividing lines within the Conservative delegation gradually showed more above the surface. Different members of the group passionately backed both Leave and Remain, and while I saw my job as trying to maintain a focus on the crunchy reality of the legislation before the Parliament, the sense of a common enterprise among Conservative MEPs became harder to sustain.

Having said that, Syed Kamall showed, when leader of the ECR, that it was possible still to work effectively within the institution. Senior MEPs from other political groups, particularly the European People's Party, spoke to me about the respect that they had for Syed, despite a pretty fundamental policy disagreement about the UK's place in the European Union. And by allying the ECR with the larger EPP group on particular votes, Syed and the Conservative delegation were key to securing greater clout for the centre-right as a whole within the Parliament.

Of course, it was not just me or the Foreign Office that maintained contact with British MEPs. Ministers and officials from other departments also enlisted their support as essential allies to get the outcome that we as a government wanted on financial services, on agriculture and on fisheries. UK MEPs, with Conservatives to the fore, pursued a campaign over several years to end the practice of discarding, whereby fishermen would dump perfectly good fish (though by now dead) back into the sea out of fear that common fisheries policy rules would penalise them if those fish were landed. Treasury ministers briefed our MEPs on the relevant committees about the amendments that they wanted to financial services regulations and directives. DEFRA supported Julie Girling in her campaign to ensure proportionate rules on the labelling of honey.

Most of Whitehall understood that what MEPs thought and how they voted was important to our country's interests. A new legislative measure might leave the Council in a form with which we were content, but then face amendments in parliamentary debate and in trilogue (the negotiations held jointly between Parliament, Commission and Council) that stood to cause real problems for British industry.

What I sometimes found frustrating was the reluctance of some (though by no means all) of my ministerial colleagues to take the Parliament as an institution seriously and show it the respect that MEPs felt they deserved. Few ministers regarded visiting the Parliament as a priority, and I was unsuccessful in trying to persuade my government colleagues that we should encourage the House of Commons to allow UK MEPs more access to the dining and social facilities of the House. Occasional formal dialogue is important, but not a substitute for the kind of trusted working relationship that is built up through frequent contact and conversation.

Despite the UK being now outside the EU, the decisions that the European Parliament makes, the details of the legislation it considers, will still affect our national interests. Any British company that trades with the European Union, invests in the EU, transfers data to or from the Union, has operations inside the Union, or relies in any way on EU patent law to protect its intellectual property has and will continue to have an interest in the requirements of European law. The European Parliament is thought to be the second most lobbied institution anywhere in the world, second only to the United States Congress. Other third countries that have important trade ties to the EU – the US, Norway and Switzerland, for example – have large teams of diplomats and other government officials assigned to monitor and seek to influence the decisions of EU institutions, including the Parliament. Our own experience of the role that MEPs (and the Parliament institutionally) play should persuade any UK government that this should be a priority for us too.

2. The view from Tony Blair's No. 10

by Roger Liddle

Roger Liddle is a Labour member of the House of Lords. A lifelong pro-European, he was political adviser on Europe in 10 Downing Street from 1997-2004, served in the cabinet of Peter Mandelson when he was EU trade commissioner, advised the president of the European Commission on a new approach to social Europe and chaired a panel of experts on industrial policy in the Business Department in 2008-10.

Little did I realise on my appointment to the No 10 Policy Unit in May 1997, with election of the new Labour government under Tony Blair, that I would end up in love with the European Parliament.

By background and temperament, I was a British pro-European, but not what I would describe as a "Europeanist". My languages were deplorable; my detailed knowledge of the workings of the European institutions at best sketchy; my personal networks across the EU as yet limited. Yet I had been a staunch Labour pro-European since the late 1960s; was an enthusiastic campaigner for "Yes to Europe" in the 1975 referendum; and the then contemporary Labour figures I most admired were on the beleaguered pro-European wing of the party. Europe therefore played a significant (though not decisive) part in my decision to join the SDP. It was to be Neil Kinnock's brave leadership, and in particular his strong reaffirmation of Labour as a pro-European party that started me on the road back to Labour. That pro-European commitment was also crucial to the creation and success of New Labour. It underpinned the Blairite political credo of a dynamic social market economy, open to the world, combined with moderate redistribution, strong public services, and a "high standards" road to competitiveness.

Labour came to office in 1997 as a united pro-European party but without a detailed European agenda. Labour was "pro Europe, pro-reform in Europe" as the catchline went. We recognised that not everything in Europe was perfect. Since the end of the "*trente glorieuses*" (the thirty years of economic growth after 1945) economic performance had been halting, growth weak and unemployment far too high. Many European welfare states were clearly under strain due to unaffordable entitlements in face of growing demographic pressure. Poor performance undermined the public legitimacy on which European integration depended. In academic language, New Labour put the rise of Euroscepticism down to a lack of "output" legitimacy.

In the 1997 campaign, Tony Blair skilfully used the European question to demonstrate that Labour was a united party fit for government, whereas the Conservatives were bitterly divided. Yet apart from a commitment to sign the social chapter, from which John Major had opted out at Maastricht in 1992 (under extreme pressure from Conservative anti-Europeans led by Michael Howard), Labour had been careful not to offer policy hostages to fortune, or more correctly commitments that presented the Daily Mail and Sun with easy target practice. Blair insisted that it was being "pro" or "anti" that mattered. Indeed, throughout his premiership he always successfully cornered the anti-Europeans as antediluvian opponents of European cooperation with outdated ideas of national sovereignty – an argument that, sadly, pro-Europeans failed to land in the 2016 referendum. Blair was serious: Britain under his premiership would play a leading role in Europe. But it was left to our time in government to work out what the precise nature of that role would be.

His first port of call for ideas was *not* the European Parliament or EPLP. First and foremost, the Tony Blair of that period saw himself as a social democratic moderniser. He had grave doubts as to where the EPLP stood on what for him was the central question of politics. His relations with the EPLP had got off to a bad start when a group of Labour MEPs had, in the autumn of 1994, put their names to an advertisement opposing his plan to scrap the existing Clause Four of the party constitution. So instead of seeking counsel in Brussels and Strasbourg, he got on a plane to Malmö to tell a congress of European socialists that the centre-left in Europe had to "modernise or die". Tony had an unerring gift for making an impact.

He then dispatched me as his adviser to the capitals of Europe to preach the gospel of social democratic modernisation and work out how to give this project European substance. The diplomatic service was wheeled into action to support this mission, overall successfully. Across the EU I breakfasted, lunched and dined for New Labour Britain, as well as attending and addressing conferences and seminars beyond number on the future of Europe. The New Labour message was generally received with surprising positivity. The Nordics had introduced wide-ranging welfare state reforms in the 1990s, with innovative active labour market policies to tackle unemployment and social exclusion, and a determination to raise employment participation levels with radical policies for childcare and maternity and paternity rights. Their economies had substantially deindustrialised; investment in research and innovation as well as wider educational opportunity were seen as the high road to a successful "knowledge and service" economy. Dutch Labour under Wim Kok, in coalition with the Liberals, was seeking to follow the same path. The new leadership of the SDP under Gerhard Schröder pitched themselves as reformers determined to restore German competitiveness and ultimately delivered on it with Agenda 2010 in a spectacular way. In Southern Europe, the Greek and Portuguese Socialists, and the Olive Tree coalition in Italy, had similar aspirations for reform but found it difficult to overcome deep-seated institutional resistance in their societies. The Spanish Socialists were still smarting from their loss of power following sixteen years of Felipe González governments, but under Joaquín Almunia remained New Labour in orientation. As a broad generalisation, in politics, New Labour had much to teach; but in policy we had much to learn. If there was a problem, it was in France. The Socialists held the premiership under Lionel Jospin. An impressively deep thinker, but leading a sharply divided French left, he resented New Labour lectures on modernisation, while quietly pursuing reformist policies. The French Socialist view resonated strongly in the Socialist group in the EP.

Gradually, however, Downing Street came to realise that Europe faced an institutional as well as a policy problem of legitimacy, which enlargement from 15 to 25 then 27 would make much more difficult. The public in many member states increasingly saw "Brussels" as an unaccountable bureaucracy making decisions on their behalf that reached into the "nooks and crannies" of everyday life, as Douglas Hurd memorably put it. Here, Blair became eager for new ideas. He did not oppose strengthening the EP's powers – as evidenced in the treaty changes he willingly signed up for – but he was very sceptical whether the public would view the "parliamentarisation" of the EU as a great advance in accountability and democratic control. He toyed with proposing a directly elected EU president but came to the view that it was too radical an idea for his generation. But he did agree that the vacuum of leadership needed to be addressed. That led him to argue, along with French president Jacques Chirac, for the need to strengthen and constitutionalise the role of the European Council and create the position of its own full time president. In addition, he wanted a slimmed down Commission to become an effective executive concentrating on Europe's big priorities, and accountable to both the European Council and EP. Much of this thinking eventually made its way into the Lisbon Treaty. The tragedy for Blair, and in my view for the EU as well as the future of British membership, was that because of Iraq he did not become the first European Council president in 2009.

To drive support for these reforms, officials pressed us to engage more deeply with Brussels and the European Parliament. In London, Colin Budd recommended more active involvement in the Party of European Socialists as a means of overcoming what, prior to 1997, had been increasing UK isolation in the European Council. Tony was always ambivalent about this, fearing it might damage his relationships with centre-right leaders. However, Robin Cook as foreign secretary became president of the Party of European Socialists. He drew up the manifesto for the 1999 European elections which committed the PES to a European Charter of Fundamental Rights. This charter came to be seen by the British as very problematic, but it had very distinguished British lineage.

In Brussels, Stephen Wall, then our brilliant permanent representative, argued strongly that the government had to pay more attention to the European Parliament, as its influence over policy making was bound to increase because of forthcoming treaty change. He reasoned that it was inconceivable that this process would not result in an extension of the EP's powers of legislative co-decision, its ability more generally to hold the Commission to account and its strengthening role as a counterweight to the previous dominance of the Commission and the Council of Ministers in European decision-making. The Foreign Office had previously taken the view that it was Britain's engagement in the Council of Ministers and the work carried out by British officials in the myriads of Council working parties that mattered in influencing legislation. It now became essential to get on top of what was being decided in the European Parliament.

So began my love affair with the EP. Reporting back to Blair, I worked at multiple levels. There was an element of the EP that operated as a kind of European House of Lords. Two prominent examples stick particularly in my memory: Giorgio Napolitano, the ex-Communist, then chair of the EP's constitutional affairs committee who went on to be president of Italy, and Michel Rocard, former prime minister of France under Mitterrand with a justified claim to be one of the greatest social democrat revisionists of the late twentieth century. They were both keen to talk, fascinated by what Blair stood for, emphatic in their to-be-forlorn hope that Blair would lead Britain into the euro. They reasoned, in my view accurately, that this would end once and for all Britain's semi-detached relationship with the European Union. The 2016 referendum result was a direct result of this advice not being taken.

Then there were the key committee chairs and vice-chairs, and the lead spokespeople of the main political groups. I dealt mainly with the committees in the social and economic field. I was invariably impressed by the grasp these members had of both the key long-term issues and their current dossiers, but even more by the culture of how they operated. There were of course occasional "point scorers" but their main efforts were directed at reaching constructive compromises within the committee that leant towards their individual and party view. There could be no bigger difference with the confrontational, and unproductive, style of Westminster politics.

There was also a group of younger members who saw themselves as a cross-party ginger group for the reform of the Parliament itself. They were sparky and full of new ideas on the future of the European Union. They showed a much-needed capacity to think outside the often conventional thinking of the Brussels bubble.

Finally, there were the Brits themselves. I dealt with individual members from all the groups, but never UKIP. Initially the most positive were those Conservative MEPs who were alarmed and disgusted by their party's drift to Euroscepticism. Some were at heart passionate supporters of British membership of the euro and deeply frustrated by what they saw as the Labour government's unnecessary prevarication. I did my best to provide assurance of Blair's commitment, over dinners in Strasbourg restaurants, with leaked and exaggerated versions of my remarks occasionally reaching the Daily Telegraph and causing mini-explosions between No 10 and No 11 back home.

A significant group of Liberal Democrats came on the scene with the introduction of the regional list system for the 1999 elections. As a longstanding supporter of electoral reform, I believe a version of the Scottish and Welsh system that retains individual constituencies, but with a top up list to make the representation more proportional, would have been better. However, PR brought some great talent to the Parliament in the shape of future cabinet ministers such as Nick Clegg and Chris Huhne. One Lib Dem MEP became a good friend in the shape of Andrew Duff, who along with Labour's Richard Corbett, are two of the great intellectual authorities on the workings of the European institutions and how they should be reformed. This was especially useful in the work of the 2002-03 Convention of the Future of Europe in which I became closely involved and which laid the foundations for the Lisbon Treaty.

The EPLP itself made a great contribution to the work of the Parliament. I'm not going to name names, because the list would be too long. They were ambitious for the Labour government to play a leading role in Europe with most in favour of our adopting the euro. There were, however, some tensions. The more "Stalinist" of London-based Labour disciplinarians thought Labour MEPs in Brussels and Strasbourg should blindly follow the dictates of London government policy. I never took that view myself. Labour MEPs could only be effective for Britain if they were seen by their Socialist colleagues to be serious players in the Parliament and that meant sometimes being seen not to follow the London line. There were also points of real difference over the economic reform agenda. The Blair government offered only cautious and much delayed support for some social and employment legislation because Downing Street was understandably anxious to keep business on side, especially given that Labour had a significant domestic employment rights agenda of its own, most obviously the national minimum wage. MEPs with trade union loyalties were very disappointed by this. In retrospect the information and consultation directive could have played a much bigger role in building industrial partnership at home.

As time went on, Tony Blair himself began to take the EP more seriously. This reached a notable climax in the second British presidency of the Council under his premiership in the second half of 2005. It was a difficult moment for Europe. The French and Dutch had just voted down the Constitutional Treaty: it was the first populist backlash of the losers from globalisation which carried a grave warning for the future. Also, the failure to settle the European budget had dominated discussion in the June European Council under the presidency of Luxembourg. In his report to the Parliament, Luxembourg prime minister Jean-Claude Juncker castigated the British for their obstructionism. The following day Blair came along to open the British presidency. He was received coolly at first. But after ten minutes of his speech, a critical audience had been totally won round. It was a remarkable speech drawing attention to how the social situation in Europe was feeding intense Euroscepticism. As Blair put it, the trumpets were sounding outside the walls of Jericho. How right he was. And on that day, I felt most of the assembled MEPs from across the member states were ready to listen and to follow. Tony could have led Europe: what a historic opportunity that we missed.

3. The view from Labour in the Thatcher and Major era

by George Robertson

Lord George Robertson was a Labour MP from 1978 to 1999. He was shadow secretary of state for Scotland from October 1993, then becoming UK secretary of defence with the election of the Blair government in May 1997. He left that position in October 1999 to become secretary general of NATO.

I took over the European portfolio on the Labour front bench after the severe defeat in the 1983 general election. Promotion? Some saw it as a poisoned chalice. So much in the 1983 election manifesto (dubbed by Gerald Kaufman MP "the longest suicide note in history") helped to defeat us; Europe was just one nail in the coffin. The Labour policy to "leave the European Community without a referendum" was exploited mercilessly by the Tories and added to our incredibility.

Following the general election defeat, Neil Kinnock was elected party leader and he charged me with changing the policy on Europe. But there was a condition: "do it without anybody noticing". Change it, I helped to do, and in the process made myself invisible as well. It took a decade, and Maastricht, before I surfaced again.

One of my roles was to watch, listen to and advise Labour MEPs. I was also to see that they did not embarrass the party back home.

I got to know the MEPs – which the bulk of Labour MPs refused to do. I visited them, encouraged them, and used them to good effect. Mostly however they were ignored, a traditional Labour Party mistake.

Since 1979 they had been directly elected, rather than the old system where national MPs were seconded to the Parliament. It was, though I supported it at the time, not a good idea. Instead of European issues being an integral part of the business of national parliaments, the big multi-national issues were hived off to Brussels. National ministers were involved, but national MPs were not. We had solved one democratic deficit by creating another.

I got to know the MEPs. I knew the good ones, the productive ones and the starring ones. I could see those who were making an impression in the Parliament and who were doing a brilliant job for Britain and the party. I was also aware of the less-than-useful ones – but luckily, they were in the minority. It was indeed a remarkable collection of people. They worked hard on subjects close to people in their daily lives. After all, laws were written there which took precedence over national laws. But the industrious MEPs were usually out of sight back at home – except of course when frivolous reporters like a mop-haired Daily Telegraph hack called Boris Johnson invented a regular straight banana story to feed nascent Brexiteers.

That process of taking the party from "leave without consulting the people"' to being fully Europhile was never going to be easy. Margaret Thatcher's Euro-enthusiasm, for example for the single market, had produced in Labour an opposite and equal reaction. If she was for it (and bizarrely at that time she was), we were against it. Politically understandable – but wrong-headed.

When the Single European Act – which implemented Mrs Thatcher's adviser Lord Cockfield's dream of a single market in 1987 – came to the House of Commons, George Foulkes, Donald Anderson and I spent long, lonely hours monitoring its progress – and pretending to oppose it. We were unseen by most, except the Brexiteers – rebels as yet without a name.

The turning point came in the drizzle of Bournemouth in September 1988. A Frenchman came to town and changed the

Labour outlook on Europe with one single speech. Jacques Delors' speech to the TUC opened trade union eyes to the potential of the EU's social dimension, circumventing the Thatcher revolution. The unions – then strongly entrenched within Labour – were bowled over.

We were on our way. But we were heading for Maastricht and the biggest European jump forward. Mrs Thatcher flipped sides, attacking Delors, and was removed by her own MPs in November 1990.

In the same month the remarkable "Assizes" took place in Rome. This one and only conference of 250 national MPs and MEPs was convened by the Italians in 1990 to consult parliamentarians before the next big treaty. Given that it was national MPs who ratify treaty changes, it is a matter of regret that such a conference never happened again. As the leader of the British delegation to Rome, I was persuaded to vote for a tough final statement by a silver-tongued Italian Communist, Georgio Napolitano (who was later to become a fine Italian president), who then promptly abstained himself. Tories tried to make mischief from the rhetoric but domestic interest was negligible.

Then came the Maastricht Treaty itself – with the opt-out from the social chapter, the fig-leaf produced by John Major to keep his fractious tribe together. What followed was a debilitating year of parliamentary guerrilla warfare with over 204 hours of debate with 26 Tory MPs aligned with my Labour team, making John Major's life a nightmare. I was ably assisted in the procedural tactics by newcomers (and subsequent cabinet ministers) Steve Byers and the former MEP Geoff Hoon.

It has to be said that this war made the Europhile folk in both the British and European parliaments very nervous. At Labour's Europe conference in Brighton on 8 November 1992, Jean-Pierre Cot, the leader of the European Parliament's Socialist group, demanded "Don't play Russian roulette with Maastricht".

But I had proclaimed at the start of the process that "we are out to wreck the government, not the treaty". Indeed. The PM had eventually to call an amazing vote of confidence to get the social chapter opt-out through. But the Tories were holed below the water line and Tony Blair's first act after the 1997 victory was to implement the social chapter.

Labour was firmly anchored in support for the sensible integration of European countries in the European Community. I was rewarded for the Maastricht war with a place in the shadow cabinet – and the Scottish portfolio. Promotion? Some said it was a poisoned chalice.

4. As seen by a German MEP

by David McAllister

David McAllister, a former minister-president of Lower Saxony, has been a German Christian Democratic Union (European People's Party group) member of the European Parliament since 2014. He is chair of the Committee on Foreign Affairs and co-chair of the UK Contact Group.

In 2012, the president of the European Commission, José Barroso, said in an interview for the New Statesman that he believed that Europe without Britain at the heart would be less reform driven, less open and less international. A few decades before, German chancellor Ludwig Erhard had even gone so far as to say: "Without Britain, Europe would only remain a torso".

Whether one or both of them were correct in their assessment is, after slightly more than two years since Brexit, still uncertain. But I firmly believe that the British departure from the European Union offers no additional opportunities and has many drawbacks.

One of those drawbacks is the different working atmosphere in the European Parliament and the loss of valuable insight and expertise into different policy areas. I had the pleasure of working alongside many dedicated British colleagues from 2014, when I first was elected as an MEP in Germany, until 31 January 2020, when the 73 UK members finally left the European Parliament.

Over these six years, the contributions of colleagues from the

Conservatives, Labour, the Liberal Democrats and the SNP were invaluable in sculpting a balanced European future. Since the 1970s, Europeans had designed an integration process that balanced the French tendency to centralise with the British proclivity for individualism. Through Brexit, this careful balance has lost its focal point, and it now lies with the remaining 27 EU member states to define a new way forward.

The departure of British MEPs has left some tangible gaps at the European Parliament that either cannot be filled at all or only with great difficulty.

There are, first and foremost, the good professional and sometimes personal relationships with many UK colleagues that cannot be replaced. I have fond memories of Vicky Ford, Timothy Kirkhope and Charles Tannock (Conservative) and of Neena Gill and Wajid Khan (Labour), as well as of Alyn Smith (SNP) and Irina von Wiese (Liberal Democrats), to name just a few. Among others, I would like particularly to mention Geoffrey Van Orden (Conservative), who represented the East of England between 1999 and 2020. Geoffrey and I were members of the Foreign Affairs Committee and I greatly valued his input as an accomplished expert on foreign and security policy. He also remembers my late father with whom he was stationed in West Berlin in the 1970s. When he left the European Parliament on 31 January 2020, I lost a great colleague and a good friend.

Another notable manifestation of the gaps that the British exit created lies in the change to the culture of debate and the loss of a certain type of humour and wit that I can only describe as quintessentially British.

While English remains the Parliament's lingua franca, it is now far more seldomly used as an instrument of debate in its own right. Most of our political discussions in working groups, committees or in the plenary are still conducted in English, but few colleagues are able to contribute to those debates as native speakers. Consequently, certain elements of political speech, like the use of humour or irony, are now simply less common.

During their 47-year tenure, British MEPs' command of the English language could occasionally lead to some confusion among non-native speaking colleagues. My former British colleague, Richard Corbett, once recalled that another German MEP was left wondering why British member Michael Cashman had called him a "waterproof coat". All Mr Cashman really had said was that this member's knowledge of obscure European treaty articles made him sound like an anorak. This anecdote is as much proof of the effortlessly poignant British contributions to the Parliament's debate culture, as it reemphasises the value English native speakers added to the EU's political environment.

Over the years, the UK's contribution to the European project was of course a hundred times greater than a strong command of political rhetoric and occasional humour. Whether it was Winston Churchill's 1946 speech in Zurich, where he first proposed "a kind of United States of Europe"; or the development of the European Monetary System (EMS) under the leadership of British Commission president Roy Jenkins in 1979 that would form the foundation for the euro; or Margaret Thatcher's campaign for the UK to remain in the European Economic Community (EEC) in 1975 wearing a pro-Europe jumper; or whether it was Britain's first woman prime minister leading the way in adopting the Single European Act (SEA), which resulted in the creation of the European single market, thus making her a critical architect of European integration – for nearly fifty years, the UK was one of the main forces for European stability, prosperity, innovation and even integration.

In later years, British critics of the EU, especially on the far right of the political spectrum, often became the centre of media attention. But as an MEP who worked alongside many UK colleagues, I can testify to the commitment and hard work of British MEPs who contributed more to the European Parliament than those who placed Union Jacks on their tables in the plenary. Although the nature of politics caused me to disagree with my Labour colleagues on issues like social or finance policy, and even though, as a German Christian Democrat, I have a different approach to European integration than most of my former Conservative colleagues, I never had any doubt that their contributions understood, in their core, the significance of British involvement in Europe.

Colleagues from the Conservative Party were often an especially important voice when it came to vital EU reform. By this, I do not necessarily mean the details of their proposals, but the general impetus they gave to cooperate more closely where useful, and less intensely where a subsidiary institution might be more effective.

This principle certainly still holds true today — for example in the European Union's common foreign, security and defence policy. Here, Britain's exit means that EU members can and should cooperate more closely in future. Before, the UK was most certainly one of the main opponents of deeper security and defence integration. I remember that by just uttering the words "European army" you could send literal shivers down the spines of some British colleagues.

After all is said and done, I miss our colleagues from England, Scotland, Wales and Northern Ireland, their commitment to the European cause as well as their contributions to European parliamentary life greatly.

Or, as we sang together with our British colleagues on 29 January 2020 in the plenary in Brussels:

> And there's a hand, my trusty feire,
> And gie's a hand o' thine;
> And we'll tak a right gude-willie waught,
> For auld lang syne.

5. The view from the Commission

by Christopher Tugendhat

Lord Christopher Tugendhat was a Conservative MP from 1970 to 1977, then becoming European commissioner for budget control and financial institutions until 1985. Among his subsequent roles, he was chairman of the Royal Institute of International Affairs (Chatham House) from 1986 to 1995. He is a member of the House of Lords European Affairs Committee and author of "The Worm in the Apple, A History of the Conservative Party and Europe from Churchill to Cameron", Haus Publishing 2022.

"The Forgotten Tribe" is an apt title for a book about the British members of the European Parliament. When they were at work at its three locations in Brussels, Strasbourg and Luxembourg during the years that Britain was a member of the European Union, their efforts were too often ignored and denigrated by politicians and the media in this country. Now that Britain is no longer a member, it is as if the waves have closed over them, a sad ending to the high hopes and expectations that were expressed at the time of the first direct elections in 1979. I welcome this opportunity to contribute to a volume dedicated to keeping their memory alive.

When the first direct elections were held in 1979, I was a member of the European Commission and Roy Jenkins was its president.

We both hoped that a new democratic era was about to open in the EEC, as it then was, and that British MEPs would play an important role. When the initial plenary session opened in Strasbourg, the Parliament's French president, the concentration camp survivor, Simone Veil, told Roy that she regarded the British Conservatives as the best of its various groups, a judgement with which he broadly concurred.

It was indeed a remarkable group. Among its members were Sir David Nicholson, a former chairman of British Airways; Sir Peter Vanneck, a former lord mayor of London; Sir Henry Plumb, who had led the National Farmers' Union and would go on to become president of the Parliament; and Sir Fred Warner, a former ambassador to Japan, along with others drawn from politics and other fields. Its range of experience and expertise was formidable. The much smaller Labour group had no big names from outside politics, but its leader, the former cabinet minister and campaigner for withdrawal in the 1975 referendum, Barbara Castle, was a major figure in British politics. In Westminster terms, she far outranked her Conservative opposite number, Sir James Scott-Hopkins, a one-time parliamentary secretary at the Ministry of Agriculture.

Before 1979, Assembly members had been drawn from the national parliaments of the member states. The direct elections were supposed to create a direct link between the citizens of Europe and the European institutions to complement those that existed within the member states. In countries in which membership of the EEC was not an issue, this was all very well. MPs and MEPs saw themselves as colleagues pursuing their parties' aims at the national and the European level. In their minds the two spheres of activity were complementary and equally valid. In Britain attitudes were different. The hostility of some MPs to British membership of the EEC, and of many others to any transfer of powers from the national to the European level, meant that over time those who sat at Westminster came to regard MEPs as upstarts and rivals.

In her masterly study, *The First British MEPs* about those MPs who also sat in the European Assembly from 1973 to 1979, the former MEP, Caroline Jackson argues that they should have established a procedure whereby members of the European Parliament could report back to and liaise with their Westminster colleagues. They didn't see the need to do so because they were members of both institutions. Among the newly elected MEPs in 1979 were a small number of MPs and several peers and the personal link between Westminster and Strasbourg was thereby maintained. But this was the last election at which the so-called dual mandate was allowed. Thereafter the failure to create such a procedure, in Jackson's words, "helped to create in Westminster the atmosphere of suspicion of Europe as a threatening territory of the unknown and the misunderstood".

Over the years several ideas were put forward to create a constructive link between politics at Westminster and in the European Parliament. One was that for the duration of their mandate a number of MEPs should become temporary members of the House of Lords, as are the bishops. Another was for the creation of a joint committee, or committees, made up of members from both parliaments. Either scheme might have done much to bring about effective co-operation between MPs and MEPs in pursuit of the British national interest. The knowledge and insights that MEPs had of the progress of draft directives and other EU initiatives and how to influence them, and of issues coming down the track, could have been of inestimable value to MPs. The support of MPs could likewise have strengthened the hands of British MEPs in dealings with the Commission and with their colleagues in other parliamentary groups. In the end, however, nothing was done.

As time passed, several former MEPs of all parties became MPs or members of the House of Lords. Some became ministers and Nick Clegg became deputy prime minister. In other countries a small number did even better by becoming prime minister, like Helle Thorning-Schmidt in Denmark. The most spectacular rise, however, was that of Jacques Delors, who, in 1981, went straight from being a French MEP to minister of finance in Paris. Thereafter, in 1985, he became president of the Commission. Those British former MEPs who went on to make careers in the Lords or Commons brought useful experience with them from which both Houses and governments have benefitted, but the underlying problem of the relationship between the British members of the two parliaments was never resolved.

Nor did direct elections to the European Parliament ever become significant events in their own right in the British political calendar. The balance of parties in the European Parliament and the effect that balance might have on the Commission and the Council of Ministers never engaged the interest of the British people. The elections were seen, throughout the time Britain was a member of the EU, as being second order events; like local elections, primarily of interest as tests of public opinion that showed where the parties stood in the public's estimation.

Paradoxically, the only British political party to have derived real benefit from the direct elections was UKIP. The change, with effect from the 1999 elections, from first-past-the-post in territorial constituencies to proportional representation and a regional list system had two consequences. One was to make it easier for Eurosceptic Conservative candidates to get elected by securing high positions on the Conservative lists. The other, and far more important, was to open the way for UKIP to win seats and to raise its profile to an extent that it had never previously been able to manage. Between then and 2016, under the charismatic leadership for most of the time of Nigel Farage, it used the European elections to become a highly influential player in British domestic politics.

And this was not the only paradox. By winning seats at Strasbourg, UKIP's MEPs gained access to the Parliament's generous arrangements for pay and allowances. As a result, the most federalist of the European institutions found itself in the anomalous position of simultaneously providing members of a party dedicated to getting Britain out of the EU with financial backing and a platform from which to promulgate their views. For UKIP this support was of inestimable value. Rarely before in politics can the law of unintended consequences have worked to such perverse effect.

6. The view from the UK Permanent Representation

(i) by John Kerr

John Kerr was the UK permanent representative from 1990-1995. Prior to that he had experience of the Council of Finance Ministers, ECOFIN (as private secretary to chancellors Howe and Lawson) and the European Council (as FCO under-secretary for Margaret Thatcher). Subsequent roles included those of UK ambassador in Washington (1995-97), permanent under-secretary at the FCO (1997-2002), and secretary-general of the Convention on the Future of Europe (2002-03) chaired by Giscard d'Estaing. He has been a crossbench member of the House of Lords since 2004.

It was all going so well ...

With Queen Elizabeth II's visit to the European Parliament in Strasbourg, early 1992 probably saw the apogee of British influence in the Parliament. The Maastricht agreements had been widely seen as a success for John Major; his drive, with Jacques Delors, for completion of the single market was generally supported in the European Parliament; and our stress on the need to respond to the green shoots of new democracies in Central Europe – the theme of the queen's address to the plenary – had broad cross-party endorsement. We were in the mainstream, rowing with the current. Ian

Paisley apart, there were few mavericks in our team; Black Wednesday and the rise of Euroscepticism still lay in the future; and UK MEPs still believed their jobs well worth doing.

And they were as powerful as they were professional. Labour fielded the largest national group in the Parliament's largest political group. Henry Plumb's successful term as president was over, but the Kohl/Major understanding, brokered by Chris Patten, made Christopher Prout's Conservatives the largest national component in the EPP group. Committee chairs and rapporteur appointments naturally followed. And links to the Commission, where Bruce Millan and Leon Brittan held the key regional and competition portfolios, were good, partly thanks to the skills of Commission secretary-general David Williamson (later Lord Williamson of Horton).

But a cynic might say that in those days it didn't always greatly matter. Parliament then still had relatively few powers other than on budgetary issues. Full legislative parity with the Council came later, with the 1997 Amsterdam and 2001 Nice treaties. Influence, and a veto, on external international agreements came even later, when the 2009 Lisbon Treaty finally delivered on the 2003 Convention commitments. The Parliament with which I worked still had to discover the institutional muscle it used to bring down the Santer Commission in 1999. In political terms it was still the junior partner of the Council, in some ways still a debating society, passing resolutions with more ambition than traction, cajoling rather than compelling, influential but not decisive.

So, while I hope my UKRep was helpful to our MEPs, they weren't as front and central in our work as they became for my successors, co-operating with a more powerful Parliament, as well as facing some MEPs who would rather have had it that we all packed our bags and went home. In my time we tended to be all on the same side. So my memories are more of briefings than of battles: the big challenges I faced were from other member states, in Councils, COREPER, and inter-governmental conferences.

Of course, it wasn't all plain sailing with our MEPs. I remember mixed feelings about the 1992 Edinburgh European Council agreement that Strasbourg would continue to host most plenary sessions, and about our 1994 effort, in the context of EU enlargement, to align

Council weighted votes more closely with national populations. But I also recall near total support for our drive to bring the Uruguay Round of trade negotiations to a satisfactory conclusion; to help Austria, Finland and Sweden to join; and to get accession negotiations started with countries further east.

I remember also how widely respected in Brussels were Christopher Prout's drafting skills, the political acumen of David Martin and Pauline Green, the passionate intensity of John Hume, the ferocity of John Tomlinson's strictures, as vice-chair of the Budgetary Control Committee, on waste and lax accounting, Fred Catherwood's real world market expertise, Henry Plumb's avuncular charm chairing the EU/ACP Assembly, and Madron Seligman's concert standard piano-playing.

I also recall how useful a non-binding resolution, slipped through the Parliament by an astute MEP, could be in a midnight Council battle. In 1994 the Scottish Highlands and Islands should have ceased to be eligible for Regional Fund support: Aberdeen's surging oil wealth had driven per capita GNP far too high. Cue a private conspiracy with the redoubtable Winnie Ewing, and a bad-tempered horse-trade with Delors ended happily for the Highlands when I was able to push across the table her EP-approved text relegating Aberdeen to the Lowlands. Some only move mountains: she could move a whole city.

"These were the days, my friend. We thought they'd never end". I wish they hadn't.

(ii) by Ivan Rogers

Sir Ivan Rogers was the UK permanent representative from 2013-2017. His career has included roles in both the private and public sectors. His time at the Treasury included secondment to Brussels as chief of staff to European commissioner Leon Brittan and in 2003-2006 he was principal private secretary to the prime minister, Tony Blair. In 2012 he became adviser on Europe and global issues to Prime Minister David Cameron.

A rather fine recent Charlemagne column in the Economist began:

> "Aside from war, illness and retirement planning, nothing can possibly be less funny than a 'Trilogue'. This arcane facet of law making in the EU involves shutting elected MEPs, officials representing the bloc's 27 Member States and boffins from the European Commission in a room until a deal is thrashed out, often late at night ... *Parlement*, a multilingual satirical show whose second season is out this month, takes a crack at turning Brussels into a punchline. For the fans of the EU, it is a serious moment."

Ah, trilogues!

I must confess that I rarely found them too comic myself, but I was never in any doubt about their importance in delivering or thwarting our national objectives, nor of the importance of those MEPs, British and otherwise, who were central to them.

I once asked my French opposite number, a glutton for Brussels and Strasbourg punishment and back for a second term in post, what had changed most in the years since his marathon stint early in the century in the permanent representative role. "The rise of the European Parliament, and the rise of the Germans", he replied. He forbore from adding "the progressive disappearance of the Brits", but he meant it. And he regretted that, as actually most senior French mandarins do, publicly or not – at least in regard to classically sceptically tempered Brits, not Europhobic ones.

To a fair degree, the rise of German influence, which had not been that enormous in the Brussels of the 1990s that I, like John Kerr, experienced (in my case from a seat as chief of staff to a British vice-president of the Commission), was also a story of the rise of the European Parliament, in which German weight was considerable on both centre-right and centre-left, and whose rise was, to an extent, at the expense of the Council.

By the time I returned to Brussels, the EU was decidedly less "intergovernmental" than it had been in the world John Kerr so ably describes. It was never that "my" commissioner, Leon Brittan, completely ignored the Parliament as he set the direction of EU trade policy back in the nineties. He paid the EP due attention and listened to parliamentarians' perspectives. But ultimately, they could not do anything much if he ignored them. The Council called the shots, and the Commission did not live in fear of being reined in or undermined by the EP.

Three things changed that.

First, the demise of the Santer Commission at the hands of the EP, which demonstrated that it, unlike the Council, had the power to turf out the Commission in its entirety. The Commission inevitably is most wary of – some would say in hock to – those who can sack it: this imbalance is a mistake. Second, the Nice Treaty, which shifted the institutional balance significantly in the EP's direction. Third, the Lisbon Treaty, which took that process a whole lot further, and introduced a world in which the vast bulk of legislation was subject to the co-decision process – renamed, accurately enough, the "ordinary legislative procedure" – which put the EP on an equal footing with the Council in well over 80 defined areas of EU policy making, covering the vast bulk of the EU's areas of competence.

In practical terms, what did this mean for those of us inside the government machine? It meant that there were, for every bit of legislation at the EU level, parallel detailed processes of discussion, scrutiny and amendment inside the Council and inside the Parliament, and that legislation was only finalised when the two processes had been reconciled in the final bunfight that was the trilogue.

And while the trilogue formally put all the institutions on an equal footing, from my seat one often felt that the EP had rather an advantage over the Council: continuity and depth of expertise often felt greater on the EP side of the table (and on the Commission's) than on the Council's – where, despite some reforms to strengthen continuity between presidencies, the Council interest was primarily represented by a rotating presidency which had its six months in the sun once every 14 years, and whose interests could sometimes seem dominated by the need to chalk up some visible achievements for its term of office, rather than worrying excessively about the content of the legislation.

The result for us? As I put it to many ministers, football-literate or not, what you agree in the Council (and, I didn't add, frequently want to proclaim as a great personal negotiating triumph) is only the half time score. But the match has a second half too, and it might well go to penalties. As we know, the Germans win at those, after all. So you need not to concede, and ideally to score more goals, in the EP.

Thus in my years as a sherpa and at UKRep, the Parliament really – really – mattered. It could decisively change, even overturn, things we thought we had delivered inside the Council. And it increasingly flexed its muscles to influence how the original draft legislation first emerged from the Commission.

I almost certainly devoted more time and effort than any of my predecessors to the EP. Because I had to. One simply could not achieve results unless one did, and one had to know and have good working relations with all the key people in the main functions on individual key pieces of legislation, as well as the big players in the main parties in the EP. I was, I should add, helped immensely in trying to navigate our way through this by experienced UK MEPs in all three major parties. And I had an entire – excellent – section of UKRep devoted to professionalising our effort with the Parliament alongside the subject experts who needed to be as capable in the ways of the EP as in advising ministers visiting for Councils.

However, some ministers and departments acted more effectively on the message than others. Some deeply resented the power of the EP, but in practice consistently underestimated it; others recognised that they would not ultimately get what they wanted unless they navigated the EP's side of the legislative machine as well as they did the Council's.

Did large tracts of Whitehall, notably at the top level, ever much understand the EU even when we were in it? Not really. And they understand it no better now they are on the outside. But UK MEPs across all parties played an often noble role in educating officialdom and ministers on the complex realities of a world largely beyond their ken.

As bureaucrats, though, we faced three further issues in my time.

First, the political reality of the EP pre-2014 was the dominance of the agenda – both policy and institutional – by a "grand coalition" of the three big "mainstream" political groups, the EPP, the Socialists and ALDE. The Conservative Party, while the larger party – and the party of the prime minister, chancellor and foreign secretary – in the UK coalition government in office from 2010 to 2015 was therefore, by dint of being in the ECR group, not represented in the inner counsels which dictated the Parliament's collective stance on key issues. This was a deliberate choice by a prime minister, David Cameron, who had won the leadership of his party promising to take the Conservatives out of the EPP, because of its essentially Christian Democrat commitment to ever closer union, and to found a separate genuinely conservative Eurosceptic reformist bloc on the right.

In practical terms, for me – and this became particularly true after the 2015 general election as we embarked on the Cameron attempt at renegotiation of the UK's terms of membership – I faced the reality that the EP's position on Cameron's negotiating objectives was completely central to whether we could deliver them, but none of the key EP decision makers, who had the power to block or neuter texts we needed, was actually British. Several of the key players in deciding the EP's final stance on Cameron's demands remarked to me with some surprise that every one of them had been seen and briefed by me individually before they met to agree their position. This was not by chance; no senior British political figure would ever put the requisite shoe leather in. But it meant that I devoted vastly more time to non-UK MEPs than British ones over those crucial months, for the simple reason that they had much greater scope to mess us up or help us to deliver. I saw more of the German EPP delegation than of the Conservatives over those months: they told me they saw comfortably more of me than they saw of my German opposite number. I did the same with other key players.

The second issue was that because one of the UK coalition partners (the Liberal Democrats) was passionately opposed to an in-out referendum, while the other (the Conservatives) was committed to holding one should it win the impending 2015 election, there was a severe limit on what one could appropriately say or do to roll the pitch for the challenge that lay ahead. Civil servants work solely for the government in office and can't freelance in the interests of potential future ones. This was a clear impediment to preparing the ground for what lay ahead. And that in turn contributed to there being a rather limited understanding in Brussels of UK political realities and needs when the renegotiation began.

The third issue was that as a result of the 2014 European Parliament elections, in which UKIP came first, about one-third of the UK's MEPs were UKIP and hence committed to working for the UK's withdrawal from the EU. The "system" of course was used to sharing HMG material with every one of the country's MEPs, fondly believing it maximised the chances of our phalanx of MEPs advancing HMG negotiating positions. But in a world where that degree of multi-partisan commitment to certain core national aims had completely disintegrated, ministers, understandably, were reticent about sharing too much, believing that, however carefully drafted it might be, it would just get used against them.

Even as regards the Tory ECR group, it was completely clear to UKRep officials that some members would campaign for exit regardless of what Cameron achieved; others were equivocal at best, and still others would campaign to remain regardless of the outcome of the negotiation. The acute tensions – sometimes, frankly, obviously bitter and personal – within the governing party's own delegation were palpable at every stage. And for those who wanted "out", the imperative, after all, was not to help deliver British legislative successes, but to demonstrate British helplessness and to brandish evidence of British "defeats". With MEPs, as indeed with many ministers, some wished the UK to lose qualified majority votes precisely because it would help to advance the cause by enabling them to claim we had been outvoted on essential national interests.

This was therefore no longer remotely like the world of 1990s UKRep, and the issue of European parliamentary power, and growing Conservative Party and thence HMG aversion to it, is under-examined by comparison with other factors contributing to Brexit. And it is not solely, even if it is primarily, a Conservative story.

Inevitably, this macro story therefore dominates reflection, certainly from the perspective of someone who only ever sat inside the executive, on the final years of the UK's EU membership.

But it would be quite wrong to diminish the formidable achievements of many MEPs – across all the major parties – even during those years. We consistently had dedicated and high calibre people who, regardless of their views on the end state of European integration, were pretty tireless in their efforts to deliver better legislation.

Amongst the Liberal Democrats, Sharon Bowles made a quite remarkable personal contribution as chair of the ECON committee on key financial and regulatory issues at the very height of the Eurozone crisis; and Catherine Bearder, soldiering on as the lone Liberal Democrat MEP post-2014, was equally formidable on environmental issues. Andrew Duff had departed by 2014 but remained a fount of creativity on institutional thinking – a committed federalist utterly pragmatic about what arrangements might need to be fashioned for the exiting UK.

From UKRep, we constantly looked for policy wisdom and delivery to figures as diverse as Malcolm Harbour, Vicky Ford and Kay Swinburne on single market and financial services issues; to Timothy Kirkhope on a welter of difficult interior ministry and judicial issues; and to Charles Tannock and Geoffrey Van Orden on security, defence and foreign policy questions.

On the Labour side, David Martin, remarkably, was still going strong, still formidable and invaluable on trade. Richard Corbett, fresh from his "sabbatical" from the Parliament in the cabinet of the European Council president, Herman Van Rompuy, brought a welter of institutional expertise and wisdom, having played an important personal role over many years in moving the Parliament beyond the "talking shop" stage. Neena Gill was highly active on key financial sector and tax questions. Glenis Willmott was a much-admired delegation leader who also did some remarkable work on medical devices. Claude Moraes did a formidable job chairing the Civil Liberties, Justice and Home Affairs Committee right at the heart of what were frequently neuralgic issues between the Home Office of Theresa May and the EP. I could go on and on.

The point is this. The EU as a whole benefitted hugely from the expertise, the wisdom, the breadth, the temperament, the professionalism, the humour and even the constructive healthy scepticism of so many good British MEPs over the decades. Those contributions won't be forgotten, and the imprint on what the EU has now become is indelible. The UK has been a force for democratic values, freedom, stability, competition, liberalism in its widest sense. The European project benefitted from all of it and is frankly the poorer without it.

But British involvement on all these fronts does not end with Brexit, and the task for future political generations will first to be part of repairing the deep distrust which now bedevils the cross-channel relationship, and then to create the means by which the UK can play its proper role on the European continent and remember the values for which it stands.

7. A journalist's view from Brussels

by George Parker

George Parker has been the political editor of the Financial Times since 2007, having previously been the FT's bureau chief in Brussels. He is a regular presenter of Radio 4's Week in Westminster.

In the days before Brexit, most British journalists who spent their adult lives watching events in the EU through the prism of Fleet Street and Westminster politics arrived on assignments in Brussels with certain preconceptions. The overriding one was that Britain was permanently on the backfoot and that Europe was something that "happened" to the UK. The best that could be achieved, even by pro-Europeans like Tony Blair, was to try to put the brakes on the federalist juggernaut.

Arriving in Brussels in 2002 as the Financial Times' bureau chief after a decade covering British politics, I was inevitably carrying a fair bit of baggage. However, that was quickly discarded as the impressive nature of the UK's engagement with the EU became apparent. The first thing, largely invisible back home, was the way in which UK soft power was deployed across the city. The people shaping EU decisions – the lobbyists, the accountants, the law firms – were dominated by British firms and Brits.

By the time I arrived, English was firmly established as the bloc's working language: the days when British journalists had to ask British nationals questions in French in the European Commission press room (as Jacques Delors insisted) were over. Even the media consumed by senior EU officials included bastions of British liberal influence including the BBC, the FT and the Economist. UKRep, the British diplomatic mission in Brussels, was regarded as one of the most effective – if not the most effective – of its kind.

Europe looked enviously at the financial capitalism roaring away in Blair's Britain. The financial crash was not even a cloud on the horizon. When Charlie McCreevy arrived from Dublin as the EU's internal market commissioner in 2004, he told me that if he left Brussels having regulated almost nothing in the financial services sector, he would have succeeded.

Indeed, the caricature of Britain as some kind of "victim" of the EU seemed farcical at that time, particularly as viewed from Paris. Free market liberalism was the order of the day and EU enlargement to the former communist east – Margaret Thatcher's dream of a wider, not deeper Europe – was about to be realised in 2004.

Back in 2002, the main action in the European Parliament revolved around the European Convention – the Convention on the Future of Europe – set up under the auspices of the venerable Valéry Giscard d'Estaing, with grand ambitions about capping the EU project with its own constitution and giving it greater powers and heft in the world. Blair was understandably nervous. Giscard told the conventioneers that his constitution would last for 50 years and that its drafters might one day have statues erected in their honour in their home villages. I spent many hours at the European Parliament building in Rue Wiertz getting to know some of these visionaries and trying to unpick what was going on.

The first thing I realised was that Britain was taking this Convention more seriously than some other countries, notably France and Germany. The view in Paris and Berlin seemed to be that Giscard could do his thing and that they would stitch things up later, in time-honoured fashion. Blair decided to try to shape it from the beginning. Peter Hain, the Europe minister, was despatched to try to ensure that any new powers were wielded through the inter-governmental route – notably via a new European Council president and EU foreign affairs chief – rather than via the federal/European Commission model.

Sitting at Giscard's side was the wily diplomat Sir John Kerr, a veteran of Maastricht negotiations, who had a hotline back to London. Gisela Stuart MP, who later became a staunch Brexiteer, was Labour's representative on the "praesidium". By engaging, the Brits started to shape the end result in their favour.

Delors, in a foreword to a 2004 Notre Europe report – *Leading from Behind, Britain and the Constitutional Treaty* by Anand Menon – noted "the pro-active, imaginative and positive attitude of the British delegation during the first phase of the Convention". He also said the British "internal coordination machine" was "widely held to be the best in Europe". Menon reckoned that "the final draft of the constitutional treaty chimed remarkably well with the stated preferences and priorities of its negotiators" and "that this was so was due in no small part to the effectiveness of the British representatives within the Convention". France, perhaps in part because of all this, rejected the text in a referendum in 2005.

All of this was going on in the European Parliament building, but the main business of MEPs in the chamber and on their committees also revealed an influence of British legislators which – again – was rarely noticed back home.

It was unusual for the UK to be out-manoeuvred on issues of financial services legislation – although whether that was a good thing was hotly debated a few years later when the whole edifice of Anglo-Saxon financial capitalism came tumbling down.

Of course, by the 2000s the main interest in British MEPs fell on Nigel Farage, first elected in 1999, and his UKIP comrades, with their Union Jack-waving and occasional confrontations with Blair. It is a remarkable fact that Farage, never elected to Westminster, sat in the European Parliament from 1999 until the bitter end of Brexit in 2020. Farage was always a convivial figure on the EP scene – and a regular in the Old Hack pub. But in retrospect the Euroscepticism he represented should have been taken much more seriously at the time, and not just in Britain. Although Brexit was a distinctly British phenomenon, anti-Brussels nationalism clearly is not.

But even while Farage was hogging the headlines, a cast of highly capable British MEPs was shaping decisions and doing the donkey work of shaping legislation that would impact on the lives of people back home. The REACH chemicals legislation, for example, was decried as too burdensome by industry at the time, but now UK companies are desperate to stick to the existing EU rules rather than comply with some new British version of the same thing.

Nick Clegg, a bright young Liberal Democrat MEP, and I would occasionally catch up for lunch at Poivre et Sel, off Place Luxembourg. He was credited with helping to shape "local loop unbundling" – driving the broadband revolution. The last time we met in Brussels was in 2004; six years later he was Britain's deputy prime minister.

The Conservative group of MEPs were in transition from a Heathite tribute band to a harder nosed group, anxiously looking over their shoulders at Farage, but they continued to hold influential roles. Edward McMillan-Scott was a vice-president of the EP, while Neil Parish chaired the Agriculture Committee, a job he subsequently performed while an MP at Westminster.

Others were highly respected in their field. Arlene McCarthy chaired the Internal Market and Consumer Protection Committee, while the redoubtable Glenys Kinnock acquired a strong reputation as a campaigner on international development. Michael Cashman, the former East Enders actor, took up human rights issues, while Claude Moraes campaigned on civil liberties.

During the 2000s the pro-EU Liberal Democrats also took up civil liberties issues while Caroline Lucas, one of two British Green MEPs in that era, went on to become Westminster's first Green MP. Theresa Villiers and Vicky Ford were among Tory MEPs who went on to represent seats in the House of Commons.

Collectively they formed a "forgotten tribe" of Brits in Brussels: legislators, lobbyists, journalists, lawyers, diplomats. They may not get much thanks for the work they did during that time (indeed some may feel that Brexit has rendered it largely worthless) but their legacy is an impressive one all the same.

III: THE MAIN PLAYERS

1. Barbara Castle

by Anita Pollack

Anita Pollack was Barbara Castle's research assistant from 1980-89 and then MEP for London South West from 1989-99. She was European officer for English Heritage from 1999-2006, and until 2012 a consultant on European heritage. Anita is the author of two books on Labour MEPs: "Wreckers or Builders?, a history of Labour MEPs 1979-1999" and "New Labour in Europe: leadership and lost opportunities" (both John Harper Publishing).

Barbara Castle was a star. She had a distinguished career of nearly 35 years in the House of Commons, holding cabinet posts in Harold Wilson's governments in the 1960s and 1970s. She was then sacked as secretary of state for health and social security in 1976 when James Callaghan became prime minister and chose not to stand for Parliament in the May 1979 general election that would result in Labour's shattering loss to Margaret Thatcher's Conservatives.

At getting on for 69 she might have taken retirement, but politics was her life blood. Despite her record as an opponent of Britain's membership of the European Economic Community – and indeed of direct elections to the European Parliament – she stood in the European elections a month later and was elected for Greater Manchester North. In taking the road to Strasbourg she was likely influenced by her husband, Ted Castle, who had been made a life peer in 1974 and was a member of the British delegation to the European Assembly from 1975 until direct elections. (He died in December 1979.) She was still of the view, shared by many in her party, that the EEC was a rich man's club. But during the hustings for selection in February she argued that "we anti-marketeers have to face the realities. We should be inside it fighting creeping federalism"; and she felt "the battleground was shifting inevitably to Brussels".

Plenty has been written about Barbara Castle in numerous books and articles over the decades, and in the diaries she published covering her years in Wilson's cabinet, but for the most part her ten year stint in the European Parliament, during which she was leader of the British Labour group (BLG) for close on six years, has been ignored. The British political commentariat has largely tended to ignore our politicians' presence in Europe.

The 17 Labour MEPs elected in 1979 were largely unknown outside their local areas and only six were in favour of EEC membership. Only four, including Barbara, were women. Because of her high national profile it was obvious that Barbara would be elected BLG leader, a post she held until 1985.

Given that the prevailing mood in local Labour parties was still against membership of the "common market", many parties had made little or no effort in the first European elections. Some European socialist colleagues grumbled that had the Labour Party taken the elections more seriously, the size of their political group would have been even larger and given them more influence in the new Parliament. However, the British Labour group, despite being small in relation to the total UK delegation of 81, was the third largest national delegation in the Socialist group. Already a French speaker, Castle endeared herself to members by taking German lessons. As leader of a national delegation, she served as one of the vice-chairs of the Socialist group where, despite her anti-common market stance, she was highly respected as a senior left-wing British politician and a long-standing elected member of Labour's national executive committee (NEC). After becoming leader of the British

Labour group, she persuaded the Labour Party to include her on the NEC, though the position came without voting rights.

Castle's personal mission was to reform the Common Agriculture Policy (CAP), which took the lion's share of the budget in those days of butter mountains and wine lakes. One of her key concerns about the CAP was its effect on food prices and she made much of this in her campaigning not only during the 1975 referendum campaign, but also as an MEP, being particularly opposed to any possibility of VAT being levied on food. Eschewing the Foreign Affairs Committee ("home of former prime ministers and other self-important types, hot air and travel", she muttered) she chose to work on the Agriculture Committee, stuffed full of farmers. Undeterred by her minority position there, she tabled amendments to reports at every opportunity, particularly attempting to reduce subsidies in the budget. She was especially enraged at surplus milk powder being fed to cows and made much of that in the press. She found an ally in the agriculture commissioner, Finn Gundelach who was a charismatic CAP reformer but who sadly died of a heart attack before long in post. Castle quickly enlisted the help of one of the senior officials at the European Commission and would hold regular meetings with him, trying to devise ways of reducing the power of the farmers. Her efforts often did not find favour with the Socialist group agriculture spokespersons but, undeterred, she would table her own amendments in committee and in plenary, time and again seeing her efforts defeated despite her passionate speeches. In later years she commissioned a Scottish academic to produce a substantial agricultural reform paper.

With her charismatic reputation from her time in Westminster, Barbara was a favourite of the British journalists and would take herself off to the press bar in Strasbourg to toss juicy soundbites to "the boys", as they largely then were. She avoided writing press releases, not needing to, as journalists would frequently stop by her office to see whether she had anything to say on the issues of the day. Being primarily a political animal, she never slacked in attacking Tory MEPs and was particularly critical of what she perceived as their Cold War mentality.

Castle had many points of issue with the Parliament and continental ways of operating politically. She hated coalitions and the way governments were elected by proportional representation, felt there were too many languages and complained about the lack of cut and thrust in debate. She said the Parliament had no powers and wanted to stop it getting any. The ponderous way the Parliament proceeded meant there was "no flexible response to events as they unfold". Publicity was awkward because votes were held the next day and not after the wind-up of debate.

When the next five-year term was looming there was a reorganisation of Euro-constituency boundaries and Castle had to engage in local campaigning to win the new seat of Greater Manchester West. She was in no doubt that it was important for local Labour parties to campaign in the 1984 European election and berated those who stood on principle against doing so, saying that what was happening in Europe was affecting all our lives.

As a frequent contributor to the New Statesman, in September 1982 she chose to use that platform for a pragmatic article reversing her stance on membership of the EEC, arguing to stay inside and fight for reforms – "let them chuck us out" she wrote. She was not the only "anti" to come to this conclusion, but she faced opposition from a number of her fellow Labour MEPs who were determined to remove her as leader, which they did in 1985.

Taking her role as a vice-chair of the Socialist group seriously, one of her successes was being part of a mission to Athens in advance of Greece joining the EEC, to persuade the Greek left-wing party, PASOK, to join the Socialist group rather than the Communists. She was also part of a Socialist delegation to Moscow to see Gorbachev. This senior position did not stop her left-wing activities, however. When Ronald Reagan visited the Parliament in 1985 it was Barbara who led a left-wing walk out.

In addition to her work on agriculture and attempting to reduce the UK contribution to the budget, Castle was a vocal advocate of animal welfare, particularly opposing battery farming and imports of baby seal skins. Her other main campaign was against the Spinelli report on the Treaty on European Union. Besides passion, Castle had courage too. When in 1986 French wine growers were besieging the Parliament in Strasbourg, she went out to the street in the cold, all five foot of her, and talked to the leaders of the demonstration. As with many other Labour MEPs she was an enthusiastic participant at question time but remained bemused that the Commission tended not to take it seriously, making only dull responses.

Throughout her ten years in the European Parliament Castle remained an important Labour figure at home and was always in demand as a speaker. When she decided to retire at the 1989 election, she was given a life peerage (in 1990) and continued her campaigning work from the Lords – by this time concentrating on campaigns for a fair deal for pensioners.

2. Ken Collins

by Anita Pollack

Ken Collins was a visionary who led the way in developing European environment policy – and who sought to go a step further to improve the functioning of the EU institutions, through making them more democratic and participatory. He maintained that environment policy is only really effective if citizens participate in its formulation and that it must cross frontiers, with pollution knowing no boundaries and fauna and flora always failing to respect Europe's frontiers. The combination of these factors meant that Collins put his mind to pushing not only stringent environment policy through "his" committee but also relished it being in the vanguard for EU institutional change and reform – a process of democratisation constantly on the EU political agenda during the 1980s and 1990s.

One of only six pro-European Labour MEPs elected in the very first European Parliament elections, Collins was a moderate local and county councillor, European Movement member and town planner. He became the longest serving chair of the Environment Committee, taking that role from 1979 to 1984 and 1989 to 1999, when he retired from Parliament. He was a vice-chair from 1984-87 and Socialist group spokesperson on environment from 1984 to 89. He was also deputy leader of the British Labour group from 1979 to 1984.

Collins was always a passionate believer in the European Community, often against the prevailing current of opinion in the Labour Party. In 1982, when Labour's national executive committee produced a paper promoting the case for UK withdrawal from the EEC, he wrote a substantial commentary on it and a further paper on environment, public health and consumer protection. He and the other pro-European Labour MEPs formed the Red Rose group in 1980 and began holding discussion dinners, also open to staff, on the Monday evening of the Strasbourg sessions. When some pro-Europeans split from the Labour Party and formed the SDP, Collins remained loyal to Labour and did not defect.

In his role as chair of the Environment, Public Health and Consumer Protection Committee, Collins was actively and persistently on the look-out for ways to increase the Parliament's powers and was fond of using arguments about the costs of not protecting the environment. As early as 1980 he chaired Parliament's first public hearing on a consumer action plan, a high profile event held in Dublin Castle.

At the same time, he was working on proposals to protect workers from lead in petrol and to ban the toxic herbicide 245-T. Following the 1980 Isoglucose judgment, when the European Court of Justice struck down some legislation because the Council of Ministers had adopted it before Parliament had given its opinion, Collins used this judgment as a delaying tactic to force policy concessions on numerous dossiers in the years before the Parliament had formal environment powers. His first such use was threatening to refer back to committee a proposal about meat inspection in the face of the commissioner's refusal to negotiate. Soon he had representatives of both Commission and Council in his office concerned about disruption of the meat industry and prepared to make concessions. He delighted in saying the Parliament at that time "had no teeth but made effective use of its gums".

His was the first committee to instigate systematic questioning of presidency ministers in the early stages of their presidency, requiring ministers to reply to each question individually. Commissioners, too, were questioned at committee meetings and Collins promoted jointly sponsored conferences or hearings with the Commission and international experts with the aim of prompting the development of progressive environmental legislation. He was an outspoken critic of the lack of democracy and transparency on the part of the European Commission, specialising in bone-crunching tackles on hapless Commission officials who had the misfortune to be responsible for a dossier before his committee.

After the Seveso disaster (a toxic chemical leak in Italy in 1976 affecting thousands of people and animals), Collins was instrumental in getting a committee of inquiry established in 1983 on the treatment of toxic and dangerous substances. By 1984 the Environment Committee was working on a framework directive on reducing emissions from industrial plants. There were subsequent battles over BSE, nitrates and lead in drinking water and many others, including consumer protection and public health, such as the food hygiene directive.

In what is now seen as one of the EU's core initiatives in farming and consumer policy, and as years ahead of its time, Collins as rapporteur on hormones in farming started to demonstrate a passion for resolving some of the biggest issues involved in the interconnection between science, technology, politics, law and food policy. The EU has become over the years a main battleground between proponents and opponents of the use of science and technology in farming and its regulation; many of these arguments became focused on Collins' committee.

On the hormone ban – foreshadowing the later arguments about bovine growth hormone (BST) in milk production, antibiotics in animal feed, cloned animals in the food-chain and ultimately the use of GMOs in farming – Collins set out the need for a new regulatory framework which he christened the need for a "fourth hurdle". In addition to the three traditional licensing hurdles of safety, quality and efficacy used for licensing drugs and other technologies, new and emerging agricultural technologies should be subjected to an additional "socio-economic and environmental assessment", alongside sweeping transparency for consumers and society generally. This approach incensed industrial players who simply wanted the market to decide – and preceded later battles over the application of the precautionary principle.

The potential impacts of some of the new agricultural technologies coming to fruition in the 1980s and 1990s were too important for consumers and the environment to be left to the whims of the market. Collins' socialist values, with scepticism about the ability of the marketplace always to satisfy human needs, were the perfect frame from which a new model of regulation along the lines of the fourth hurdle concept could be designed.

Collins was a good match for the multinational agricultural pharma company lobbyists sent to get their products to farmers with next to no assessment of what those products might mean for society beyond their immediate and short-term safety. In the words of two leading pro-technology spokespeople of the era who wrote of Collins' work on what became the hormone ban:

> "Ken Collins is the Socialist Member of the European Parliament for the Scottish constituency of Strathclyde East. A tough, able and earthy self-made man, Collins is proficient at the art of alternating scathing and soothing rhetoric. He looks, and behaves, like a football team manager. He hates losing".

It was not only the proponents of new agricultural technologies – usually giant US corporates – who were unhappy with Collins' regulatory zeal and entrepreneurship. Paradoxically, the Greens (entering Parliament in numbers mainly after the 1989 elections) were as adamantly opposed to Collins' new approach with the fourth hurdle as were the industrial players. This was because Collins' fourth hurdle might conceivably on occasion be jumped – whereas the Greens' absolutism looked forward only to outright bans.

Collins never lost sight of the fight for declining industrial regions such as Strathclyde East. Typical of his work was his participation in the campaign to save Ravenscraig steel mill and the Glasgow Caterpillar plant. He sought to be creative with EU competition law, meeting with the then competition commissioner, Sir Leon Brittan to establish whether there was a way to force British Steel to find a buyer for Ravenscraig rather than seeing it close with the loss of thousands of jobs. On the fight to save Caterpillar, he and fellow MEP Joyce Quin brought workers from Glasgow and

Newcastle to Brussels and organised joint campaigning with workers from the Gosselies plant (near Charleroi) in Belgium.

With the 1987 Single European Act came Article 100A, covering legislation concerning the single market and permitting majority voting in the Council of Ministers. Environmental considerations were now written into the treaty for the first time. Here began long years of battle where the committee sought to change the legal base in legislation so that instead of being purely environmentally based, needing unanimous voting, it could come under Article 100A, with majority voting which removed a blocking veto from individual countries. The treaty also gave a second reading for Parliament under the co-operation procedure, giving Parliament power to ensure that more of its amendments were accepted by the Council of Ministers. After a second reading the amendments carried by qualified majority of Parliament could only be rejected by ministers acting unanimously. This gave Collins and his committee opportunities to ensure progressive environment, public health and consumer legislation. An early battle was over exhaust emissions and with it the shift to lead-free petrol, which required cars to be fitted with catalytic converters. The new geometry of Council voting by QMV allowed Parliament and Commission to force more stringent standards through a somewhat reluctant Council.

Another successful campaign came following a temporary committee of inquiry in 1988-89 which would eventually lead to the setting up of the Medicines Agency and Food Safety Agency.

The Maastricht Treaty, which came into force in 1993, brought a further environmental clause, and powers of co-decision for policies brought forward under Articles 100A and 130s (environment) and a third reading process – conciliation. Collins loved this and likened it to a game of poker. Here he institutionally innovated again, creating what has become today's norm in EU law-making, namely use of the trilogue, bringing together a small group of representatives of the EP, Council and Commission to plot a way forward towards an agreement which the institutions can then ratify.

During the 1990s, Collins' committee became one of the largest, most powerful and heavily lobbied in the European Parliament. Its meetings were open to the public and became hugely popular, necessitating the use of Parliament's largest committee room. Its decisions had an enormous effect on the health of our environment and Europe's citizens. Collins also pushed for the creation of the European Environment Agency and was impatient at how slow the Council was to bring it into being. He consolidated his position by becoming chair of the Conference of Committee Chairs which had power over setting the Parliamentary agenda. In this role he was also able to attend the Conference of Presidents (involving the political group leaders). Such was the workload and power of his committee during the 1990s that there were moves to split off its remits for public health and consumer protection. These Collins successfully defeated on more than one occasion, believing a big committee with wide-ranging competences would always be more influential than several smaller committees composed of policy enthusiasts focusing only on their area of interest.

The Amsterdam Treaty, which came into force in 1999, contained for the first time sustainable development as a cornerstone of EU policy. This was something which Collins had advocated for years, alongside demanding that the Commission must prepare an environmental impact study for proposals with a significant environmental implication.

During his time as chair, the main subjects covered included air and water quality, urban environment, waste disposal, chemical substances and industrial risks, and there was many a battle to ensure better implementation of European directives.

Collins worked closely with the Labour Party in the UK in developing its environment policy. He collaborated with Chris Smith MP, then shadow environment minister, drawing up the backbone of environment policy for the Labour government elected in 1997.

There was an enormous amount of sheer hard work involved in all this, but the social side of life was not ignored. Collins initiated cross-party Christmas parties for all members of his committee and staff, which became very popular, with much singing – including from Collins, who had a fine voice and was fond of Scottish folk songs. This convivial event was abandoned after he left.

In 1999, after leaving the European Parliament, Collins became chair of the Scottish Environment Protection Agency (SEPA), serving until 2007, during which time he liaised closely with European institutions. He was appointed to a Commission-run high level group on Europe's energy intensive industries and the environment. Again years ahead of its time, here Collins contributed to a group which set out decades before the concept entered everyday debate, the need for Europe to consider establishing a carbon border adjustment mechanism to ensure an industrial level-playing field with industries elsewhere – and to counter environmental free-riding by other nations.

He was knighted for his services to environmental protection in 2003. In 2004 the University of Paisley (now University of West of Scotland) awarded him an honorary doctorate and later his old University of Glasgow awarded him a doctorate of science.

3. Basil de Ferranti

by Alistair Lexden

Lord Alistair Lexden OBE is a Conservative peer and historian, whose main academic publications are on late nineteenth century party politics. After teaching at Queen's University, Belfast, he was deputy director of the Conservative Research Department, working on national and European elections, between 1979 and 1997.

Basil de Ferranti (1930-88), known affectionately as Boz, personified the Conservative Party's determination during the early years of Mrs Thatcher's leadership to work wholeheartedly for progress in the European Community. "We are the European Party", she declared in 1977. The 1979 Conservative election manifesto sternly rebuked the Callaghan government, under which "our country has been prevented from taking advantage of the opportunities which membership offers". Britain, it continued, should "play a leading and constructive role in the Community's efforts to tackle the many problems which it faces".

This objective was enthusiastically supported by the 60 Conservative MEPs elected in 1979, the party's largest ever contingent in the European Parliament. From the first, de Ferranti occupied a prominent position among them, recognised in his appointment as a vice-president of the Parliament immediately after his arrival in 1979. Indeed, he had seemed almost destined to make a significant contribution to European affairs from the moment that Britain joined the Community in 1973 under Ted Heath, for whom he had a high regard (the feeling was mutual).

Europe was the natural sphere for his blend of political and entrepreneurial talents, which had been fostered within a family famous for its technological brilliance and who had always given fervent support to the Conservative Party since the beginnings of Ferranti International, founded by his grandfather, Sebastian Pieto Ziani de Ferranti, in 1905. The family's origins can be traced back to eleventh century Florence, with twelfth century Doges of Venice also reputed to be among their forebears. Few could claim more impressive European credentials.

A charming old Etonian with a Cambridge degree in engineering (a rare combination), Basil de Ferranti established early in his career a reputation as a man who looked constantly to the future, exemplified most conspicuously by his boundless enthusiasm for developing and marketing computers. His obituary in The Times noted that "in the 1960s he foresaw the time when the computer terminal would be as commonplace in the home as the telephone".

His passion for innovation, pursued both in Ferranti itself and in pioneering computer firms, most notably ICL of which he became managing director in 1964, helped convince him that Britain would only reap the full benefits of the technological revolution which was gathering pace, if it was at the forefront of the European Community.

He brought to the European Parliament political experience gained at Westminster early in his career. Elected for Morecambe and Lonsdale (a seat in which Ferranti was a major employer) at a by-election in 1958 when he was 28 (making him the "baby of the House"), he joined the ministerial ranks in July 1962 as parliamentary secretary at the Ministry of Aviation, a post for which he was obviously well-fitted. But the appointment lasted less than five months. He was required to sell not only his own shares in the family business to avoid a conflict of interest (Ferranti had extensive contracts with the ministry), but also other shares held in trust for his children. The latter proved impossible, and he resigned in October 1962.

Distressed by this experience, he left the Commons at the 1964 general election. Europe now became the focus of his political energies, which were directed in the consensual, non-partisan manner he had developed as an MP and which would later serve him well as an MEP. Like many others, he worried about the state of the Community which Britain joined in 1973. Progress had stalled; there was much talk of "Eurosclerosis".

De Ferranti made his first efforts to try to help overcome the deep-seated malaise before the first European Parliament elections, as president of the Economic and Social Committee of the Community between 1976 and 1978. He encouraged this slightly cumbersome, unelected body with 144 members representing employers and trade unions, to take greater advantage of the powers it possessed to press for change. In December 1976, the Economic and Social Committee declared emphatically that it was "convinced that a common European currency is necessary for a lasting economic stability to be achieved".

Greater monetary integration was one of the key objectives of the European Parliament's Committee on Economic and Monetary Affairs and Industrial Policy, of which de Ferranti became vice-chair in 1979 following his election as MEP for Hampshire West (after 1984 he represented Hampshire Central until his death in 1988). The committee was no less concerned to get the Community to fulfil another of its great original aims by completing the internal market. It was with this campaign that de Ferranti was to become most closely identified, working initially with other Conservative colleagues on the committee, Neil Balfour and Ben Patterson in particular.

The trio possessed a clear vision of a frontier-free Community and pressed vigorously for its realisation. A long-serving official of the Parliament, Francis Jacobs, later recalled that "they were among the most influential Members in campaigning for a much more systematic and less ad hoc approach to completing the internal market, arguing that far too little progress had been achieved over the previous 25 years". Pragmatism was their watchword. Jacobs stressed that "they were very cautious about unnecessary harmonisation and, where appropriate, pushed for alternative approaches such as mutual recognition of national standards". The committee was at this time under the overall chairmanship of Jacques Delors, who won the admiration of many Conservative MEPs as they worked with him to revivify the Community in its economic aspects.

Basil de Ferranti was indefatigable in calling for the end to all internal barriers. With parliamentary colleagues, he toured the capitals of the Community's nations in 1979-80 to make the case directly to ministers, running into difficulty only in Italy where an indignant senior civil servant overruled his minister after the latter had happily complied with the visitors' suggestions. De Ferranti kept up the momentum for reform through a permanent Community-wide campaigning organisation, which he set up in 1981 in partnership with two colleagues from other parties, the Social Democrat Dieter Rogalla and Christian Democrat Karl von Wogau, both from West Germany.

They decided to call their new all-party outfit the Kangaroo group, a name chosen to underline its commitment to leaping over national boundaries and to persuading all Community members to do so too. It described itself as "the movement for free movement". In his authoritative *Penguin Companion to European Union* (1995), Dr Timothy Bainbridge, a highly regarded Conservative Party expert, referred to it as "one of the most successful single-issue groups ever established at Community level … It played a very important part in providing the rationale and political impetus for the 1985 Single Market programme". That programme signalled clearly that the Community had finally put the malaise of the 1970s firmly behind it.

Much of the credit for the Kangaroo group's success lay with its principal founder. De Ferranti raised funds from sympathetic businesses to help finance its extensive range of activities throughout the Community. He advertised its work proudly, even bringing a toy kangaroo with him to his adoption meeting in Hampshire before the 1984 Euro elections. A few months later, as the programme for reform began to take final shape, he rejoiced at the prospect of a Community with "the single market that companies throughout Europe require if they are to compete with the Japanese and Americans in the marketplace".

At the same time, he was apprehensive about the future of his party in the Community. While he forged his own links with members of other parties, the Conservative group in the European Parliament worked only with the four Conservatives from Denmark. In a memorandum of 1 August 1984, he expressed deep concern about the bad relations existing between them and all the other centre-right groups which had come together as the European People's Party (EPP). "The stage has been reached now", he wrote, "where they are so suspicious of the British Conservatives that they might not allow us to join in their discussions, even if we wanted to". The acrimony seriously reduced the Conservative Party's influence in the Community. "Is there a danger", he asked presciently, "that Community countries on the other side of the Channel will always be 'them' to us?" If that was to be avoided, "British Conservatives really must spend more time with the European People's Party and the European People's Party really must understand that our interests are common".

A copy of this important memorandum was given to Mrs Thatcher by Charles Powell. She initialled it, signifying that she had read it but had no comment to make. De Ferranti's warnings went unheeded. Four years later, on 20 September 1988, she delivered her famous Bruges speech with a very different vision of Europe's future to his. Basil de Ferranti died four days later of cancer, at the early age of 58. He would not have enjoyed the post-Bruges era. He should be remembered always as one of the great progenitors of the European single market.

SOURCES

Timothy Bainbridge with Anthony Teasdale, *Penguin Companion to European Union*, 1995.

Rodney Brazier, *Ministers of the Crown*, 1997.

Alan Clark, *Diaries: In Power 1983-1992*, 1993.

Conservative Party Archive at the Bodleian Library, Oxford.

Iain Dale (ed.), *Conservative Party General Election Manifestos, 1900-1997*, 2000.

Francis Brendan Jacobs, "Contribution of British MEPs in the European Parliament: One EP Official's Perspective" at https://www.johnharperpublishing.co.uk/record-and-review, September 2016.

The Times, 26 September 1988.

The Times Guide to The House of Commons 1959.

Thatcher Papers at Churchill College, Cambridge (ref. PREM 19-1231).

Christopher Tugendhat, *The Worm in the Apple: A History of the Conservative Party and Europe from Churchill to Cameron,* 2022.

Laurent Warlouzet, *Completing the Single Market: The European Parliament and Economic Integration, 1979-89*, 2020.

4. John Hume
by David Harley

It would be hard to find another MEP, of whatever nationality, who made use of the European Parliament as effectively as John Hume to further their underlying political objective. In his case it was stopping the bloodshed and promoting peace and reconciliation in Northern Ireland. When the news came out that John had been awarded the Nobel Peace Prize in 1998, all those who knew him in Brussels and Strasbourg proudly claimed him as their own (as did, naturally, his thousands of friends and supporters in Derry, Belfast, Dublin – and Washington). The celebrations in London were slightly more muted. John was both tough as nails – he had to be, through the years of multiple death threats and ceaseless vilification by his political opponents – and great company over a jar when the day's work was done. A late night rendition of "Danny Boy" never needed much prompting.

The poet and fellow Nobel laureate Seamus Heaney also came from Northern Ireland and the two great men went to the same school, St Columb's in Derry. Heaney once complained when his poetry was included in an anthology of "British poets" without anyone asking his permission. Similarly, John Hume was not British but an Irish citizen, often referred to as "the greatest living Irishman". One of the few honours he declined was the invitation to stand for president of Ireland. He famously retorted to the colonel in the

Parachute Regiment in Derry, when asked to cease his peaceful protest, that he did not recognise the British government or their representatives. Yet he was elected under UK law and as such took his seat in the House of Commons – unlike Sinn Féin members – and in the European Parliament, as well as the Legislative Assembly of Northern Ireland. Hence his rightful place, not only in the pantheon of parliamentarians, but also in this volume dedicated to UK MEPs.

Despite his several elective mandates, Hume hardly ever missed the monthly sessions of the EP in Strasbourg. His work in Europe was as much an essential component of his overarching strategy as his regular visits to Washington, where Bill Clinton called him "Ireland's Martin Luther King". The years he served as an MEP from 1979 to 2004 led gradually, sometimes much too slowly for Hume's liking, through successive EU-generated and funded initiatives on cross-border and cross-community cooperation, to his secret talks with Gerry Adams (with the priest Father Alec Reid as intermediary) that created the conditions for the breakthrough ceasefires by the Provisional IRA and the loyalist paramilitaries in 1994, and finally the apotheosis of all Hume's efforts with the Good Friday Agreement on 10 April 1998. The award later that year of the Nobel Peace Prize, shared with Unionist leader David Trimble, was nothing less than a just reward and recognition for over thirty years of tireless work and campaigning for his beliefs, often risking his life, while at times being attacked by his own party and, at one stage, hung out to dry by the British government. As Gerry Adams put it: "When the news broke about him meeting with me, he was the victim of a tsunami of abuse and vilification – but he stuck with it".

Following his election to the first directly elected European Parliament in 1979, Hume became a member of the committee on regional policy and immediately set about developing his strategy to make maximum use of Parliament's processes and procedures. His initial objective was to broaden the context for discussions on Northern Ireland, and over time create a space where the British and Irish governments, together with the European Community, could cooperate on specific projects of practical benefit to the people of Northern Ireland, across all communities. Treading carefully and keenly aware of the sensitivities, on 15 November 1979 he tabled a motion for a resolution, on behalf of the Socialist group, calling on Parliament to draw up a report on the impact of Community membership on the six counties. At the time few, if any, and possibly not even Hume himself, realised that they were making history, or that this modest resolution, with its deliberately vague wording in order not to frighten off either the Commission or the UK government, marked the first step to involve the European Community in the conflict in Northern Ireland.

The subsequent report, under the name of the rapporteur, French liberal Simone Martin, but with significant input from the unlikely alliance of the three Northern Ireland MEPs – John Hume, Ian Paisley and John Taylor – focused on economic and social issues and the need for economic aid from the EC. The Commission reacted promptly and positively by designating Northern Ireland as an area for special assistance in the EC budget, later through the structural funds, as well as earmarking funds for housing development in deprived inner-city areas. So began a process over the next several decades which, going beyond financial assistance, saw the EU play a determinant role in promoting cross-border peace and reconciliation between communities in the region, remarkably with the three-pronged support of the Irish and British governments and the Northern Ireland Assembly. It is no exaggeration to say that the peace process began and took shape in the European Parliament, largely thanks to John Hume.

Peace brought new challenges. In 1994 the Commission president, Jacques Delors set up the Northern Ireland Task Force to examine ways of assisting the region and the border counties of the Republic and maximising the benefits of EU policies. In December of same year at the Essen summit – the last summit attended by Delors before standing down as president – the European Council approved a £240 million peace dividend. Ian Paisley wasted no time in insisting that the three Northern Ireland MEPs should have a systematic input into the implementation of the aid package. Then on 5 April 1995 the European Parliament adopted the Hume report on the Special Support Programme for Peace and Reconciliation in Northern Ireland, leading directly to the launch of the PEACE I programme three months later.

Hume's odyssey from Derry to Oslo (to receive the peace prize) via Strasbourg was exceptional. Few MEPs or politicians anywhere can boast of having changed their country and their community for the good as much as John Hume. Yet his success also revealed something significant about the workings of the European Parliament, and the freedom and scope for personal initiative that the institution provided for its elected members. An MEP, by comparison with a member of a national parliament, is relatively free of the occasionally negative partisan constraints of their party or home government (even if sometimes with a resulting downside in terms of lack of discipline or cohesion). Hume was nothing if not his own man, all through his life. John Hume and the European Parliament, with its culture of cross-party collaboration and pragmatic compromise, were made for each other.

Hume's many aphorisms or *bons mots* became legendary and accepted first principles for conflict resolution around the world. Among the best known was that "Difference is of the essence of humanity. Difference is an accident of birth and it should therefore never be the source of hatred or conflict. The answer to difference is to respect it. Therein lies a most fundamental principle of peace: respect for diversity". But the words he repeated time and time again during his 25 years as an MEP, as part of what became known as the "single transferable speech", and which he spoke once more when accepting his Nobel Prize on 10 December 1998, will forever be associated with John Hume and his vision:

"On my first visit to Strasbourg in 1979 as a Member of the European Parliament, I went for a walk across the bridge from Strasbourg to Kehl. Strasbourg is in France. Kehl is in Germany. If I had stood on this bridge 30 years ago after the end of the second world war when 25 million people lay dead across our continent for the second time this century and if I had said, 'Don't worry. In 30 years' time we will all be together in a new Europe and we will be working together in our common interests', I would have been sent to a psychiatrist. But it has happened and it is now clear that the European Union is the best example in the history of the world of conflict resolution."

Seamus Heaney, on hearing that Hume had been awarded the prize, caught the essence of the man with these words: "He never seemed to be in a hurry, never spent time scoring points and always trusted the capacity of his political opponents as well as his constituents to take an extra trusting step". Heaney went on to refer to the parable of the fox, who knows many things, and the hedgehog, who knows one big thing. In Seamus Heaney's view, John Hume was a hedgehog, a man who knew the preeminent truth that in the end justice had to prevail.

5. Henry Plumb

by David Harley

Henry Plumb, the only Briton to be elected president of the European Parliament, held office from January 1987 to July 1989.

He won the election by five votes in a surprise result against the Spanish socialist and former minister, Enrique Barón. The news was received in Margaret Thatcher's Downing Street with a mixture of bafflement and condescension, although the Foreign Office under Geoffrey Howe quickly adapted to this unexpected turn of events and saw an opportunity, if handled adroitly, to further advance UK interests in Brussels. With David Williamson (later Lord Williamson of Horton) installed as Commission secretary-general, several directors-general in key posts and now a British president of the European Parliament, the prospects of influencing the EC's agenda were looking positive.

The election had been a genuine contest, rather than the usual stitch-up between groups and self-appointed grandees acting under national pressure. Plumb largely owed his victory to the last-minute support of the Irish MEPs, who appreciated his farming background and generally conciliatory approach (which they considered unusual in a British Conservative), and the abstention and in some cases support of the French far right under Jean-Marie Le Pen. But Henry Plumb was elected president above all because people across the House liked and trusted him.

The bluff, affable, ruddy-cheeked exterior hid a canny pragmatist strongly committed to building bridges in the general interest and of the European project. He soon showed that he was not to be underestimated. An easy charm and the stamp of authority both came naturally to him.

It had been quite a journey for the boy who left school at fifteen to help on his father's farm in Warwickshire during the war. While raising his herd of dairy cattle, Plumb gradually progressed through the senior ranks of the National Farmers' Union to become its president in 1970, for which he received a knighthood, and the chair of COPA – the European Association of Agricultural Producers – before being elected as Conservative MEP for the Cotswolds in the first direct elections in 1979.

He quickly made his mark, becoming first chairman of the Agriculture Committee (in those days one of the most influential) and then leader of the group of British Conservatives. Once elected president, he appointed two experienced civil servants to his private office or cabinet: Robert Ramsay, who had risen to the highest ranks of the Northern Ireland civil service, and Emyr Jones Parry, who was on secondment from the FCO and went on to become UK ambassador to NATO and the United Nations.

Plumb's time in office coincided with a significant extension of the European Parliament's competences and powers, with the entry into force on 1 July 1987 of the Single European Act, the first major revision of the Treaty of Rome. The original white paper leading to the act was drawn up by the British commissioner and Thatcher nominee, Lord Cockfield. Its call for the creation of a single market by 1992, accompanied by a reform of the Community's legislative process with the introduction of cooperation and assent procedures, meant that it was in the European Parliament's interest to be closely involved in preparations for its implementation. This watershed moment and its political implications for the balance of power between the institutions were not lost on Lord Plumb – he was elevated to the peerage in April 1987 – and the leaders of the main political groups. From now on Parliament's role was to become much more than consultative and would develop into that of co-legislator. As a consequence, in addition to the day-to-day management of the House, an important part of Plumb's duties that had not been in the original job description was to project, through his presidency, the image of a Parliament that worked effectively and responsibly together with the Commission and Council.

This new spirit of inter-institutional cooperation was given concrete form on 29 June 1987 when, at the invitation of the Belgian presidency and largely on the initiative of the then foreign minister Leo Tindemans, Lord Plumb became the first president of the European Parliament to address the European Council, a tradition that has continued ever since. One prime minister, in particular, was less than delighted at this innovation: in the anteroom awaiting the start of the summit with the assorted heads of state and government, he was greeted by Mrs Thatcher with the words "Henry! What are you doing here?". Chancellor Helmut Kohl quickly took Plumb aside, and with a twinkle in his eye told him sternly, through an interpreter, that if he wasn't careful he would be sent to the Tower of London on a diet of stale bread and water.

Relations with Mrs Thatcher were to become further complicated with her infamous Bruges speech the following year, which many saw as the start of the unravelling of Britain's European policy, and which served as a "lightning rod" for Euroscepticism in the Conservative Party. Whatever his personal views, given his institutional position Plumb was careful not to become directly embroiled in the ensuing battle. Nevertheless, despite his best efforts to remain aloof, the Independent newspaper reported that "Lord Plumb will criticise almost every aspect of Mrs Thatcher's Bruges campaign, reserving particular poison for the suggestion that Brussels is wilfully creating unnecessary red tape. 1992 is blowing the whistle on red tape, not creating it". No denial was issued from Plumb's side.

Another "first" of the Plumb presidency was the creation in 1988 of the Sakharov Prize for Freedom of Thought, following an initial proposal by the British Conservative MEP Nicholas Bethell. The awarding of the prize in December each year remains an important event in the European Parliament's calendar to this day. The first winners were jointly Nelson Mandela and Anatoli Marchenko, the Soviet author and dissident. Plumb was no longer president when

Mandela, after his release from prison, came to collect his prize in Strasbourg the following year. Plumb was however still an MEP and hosted a lunch in Mandela's honour. Over coffee, in an expansive mood, Mandela recounted his clandestine visits to London in the 1950s under an assumed identity to purchase arms for the ANC and the armed struggle. He had enjoyed telling Mrs Thatcher about these secret trips to buy Kalashnikovs when he had visited Downing Street the previous week. Apparently the prime minister was not amused.

In terms of media coverage of Henry Plumb's presidency, one incident surpassed all others – when he expelled Ian Paisley MEP from the chamber during the visit of Pope John Paul II on 12 October 1988. After Paisley had held up a poster denouncing the pope while shouting "I refuse you as Christ's enemy and Antichrist with all your false doctrine", he was quickly and summarily bundled out of the chamber by security staff. His holiness remained unperturbed during this incident. Paisley claimed after the event that he had been grievously mishandled, and that Plumb should have never allowed a vicious attack on a member of Parliament exercising his right to free speech. In fact, the reaction to Paisley's rant and his ejection had been carefully planned in advance and stage-managed by Plumb's cabinet, moreover with the Vatican's full agreement.

Shortly before the end of his mandate, as something of a swansong, Henry Plumb visited Argentina in February 1989 with the discreet blessing of the British foreign secretary. There he met President Raoúl Alfonsín in the Casa Rosada – the presidential palace – in Buenos Aires. He was the first British politician to meet the Argentine authorities since the Falklands War six years earlier, and diplomatic relations were still suspended, with all communications having to go through the Swiss consulate.

Somewhat to Plumb's surprise, Alfonsín, an erudite if slightly eccentric social democrat, seemed genuinely pleased to see him. After thanking the European Parliament for its support for human rights in Argentina and Latin America generally, he then appealed for help from the EU and the European Parliament, asking Europe "to show generosity of spirit" to help tackle Argentina's grave economic problems and crippling levels of debt. Although it was still too early to discuss questions of sovereignty over Las Malvinas, surely the two sides could start by sitting round a table to discuss economic and trade issues? Plumb replied that perhaps the European Parliament could be the vehicle to make that happen, and he would convey Alfonsín's message to Brussels and London. As it turned out, almost exactly one year later, on 15 February 1990, diplomatic relations between Britain and Argentina were re-established.

By that time Lord Plumb had been succeeded as president of Parliament by his opponent in 1987, Enrique Barón MEP. As he exited the chamber for the last time as president, MEPs across the House gave him a standing ovation, shouting their thanks and congratulations to "Henry" in various languages. Proudly calling himself "semi-bilingual", Plumb didn't understand all the words but got the gist and smiled broadly.

If the moment was not exactly the end of an era, at least it marked the closing of a significant chapter in the European Parliament's development, under the firm and effective stewardship of "the farmers' man".

6. Christopher Prout

by Brendan Donnelly

Brendan Donnelly is the director of the Federal Trust for Education and Research. He was elected as a Conservative MEP in 1994 but subsequently sat as an independent; he ran in 1999 as an independent pro-European conservative but was not elected. He had previously worked for the Foreign Office, the European Commission, the Conservative group in the European Parliament, and as a political adviser to Lord Cockfield.

Christopher Prout entered the first directly elected European Parliament in 1979 as the Conservative member for Shropshire and Stafford. Until his unexpected defeat in the European elections of 1994, he was one of the best known and respected among the British MEPs, becoming leader of the Conservative group in 1987. Although his first degree was in economics, by 1979 he was an academic and practising lawyer. These legal skills shaped all his political activity and were at the heart of his most important legacy, the rewriting of the European Parliament's rules of procedure in 1986.

Before becoming leader of the Conservative group in the EP, Prout had been for five years the group's chief whip, serving under the then leader Sir Henry Plumb. Although the two men worked amicably and constructively together, there was a striking contrast in their personal and political styles. Plumb was affable, expansive and easy-going. Prout was more reserved, rigorous and intellectually demanding. Plumb's popularity within the Parliament, reinforced by his agricultural background, opened the way for him to become the UK's only president of the EP in 1987. Prout succeeded him as leader of the Conservative group, beating (to the surprise of some) two prominent British colleagues – Lady Diana Elles and Sir Fred Catherwood.

Prout's leadership coincided with a turbulent period in the Conservative Party's modern history, turbulence in which European policy played an important part. It was no secret that in the latter years of her premiership Margaret Thatcher's relationship with her MEPs had become increasingly distant. Very few of Prout's colleagues had anything but disapproval for her 1988 Bruges speech. This disapproval was bluntly conveyed by Prout to the 1922 committee of Conservative backbenchers during the leadership election of 1990. Against the advice of some of his colleagues, he told the committee that the great majority of Conservative MEPs wanted to see Mrs Thatcher replaced. Given the centrality of European issues to the Conservative leadership debate, this was not an insignificant intervention. Like the great majority of his colleagues, Prout was relieved by the end of the Thatcher premiership. He would have personally preferred Michael Heseltine to succeed her, but welcomed the opportunity of working with John Major, with whom he had a cordial, even if not especially intimate, political relationship.

One important fruit of this more relaxed political climate after 1990 was the renewal, with John Major's approval and that of party chairman Chris Patten, of negotiations with the European People's Party (EPP) intended to establish a parliamentary alliance between the EPP and the Conservative Party in Strasbourg. Since 1979, Conservative MEPs had belonged to a parliamentary grouping, the European Democratic Group (EDG), which they dominated numerically. As the number of Conservative MEPs dwindled in successive European elections, the attractions of the autonomy given by the EDG dwindled correspondingly. More and more Conservative MEPs came to think they would be personally and politically better located in the European People's Party group, in which German and Italian Christian Democrats were then the most numerous. This analysis was reinforced by the decision of the Spanish Partido Popular, which had been a member of the EDG since 1986, to abandon their Conservative colleagues after the 1989 elections and join the EPP in the Parliament.

While Margaret Thatcher was prime minister it would have been difficult, if not impossible, for any headway to be made on this issue. Her successor proved himself more flexible. He may well have believed that a closer association in Strasbourg between the Conservatives and EPP would go some way to restoring the goodwill towards the UK in continental Europe which Margaret Thatcher's later years in power had compromised. In particular, he was probably hoping to reinforce a relationship to which he attributed great importance, namely that with Helmut Kohl and his Christian Democratic party. But whatever reinforcement Major may have thus achieved in his relationship with Kohl was to be more than reversed seventeen years later, when a subsequent British Conservative leader and German chancellor fell out over the Conservative decision to break its European Parliament ties with the EPP.

It was not until 1992 that the Conservative MEPs became "allied" members of the EPP parliamentary group. This ambiguous status was convenient to both sides. There were many in the EPP who were unenthusiastic about taking the Conservative cuckoo into their Christian Democrat nest. Prout and his chief whip, Amédée Turner, who conducted the negotiations, had also to tread warily, knowing that many Conservatives in London were suspicious of closer links with the EPP. Prout and Turner were always careful to explain to Conservative audiences that Conservative MEPs had not joined the EPP but had simply entered into a parliamentary alliance with MEPs from the EPP. This was not a distinction that always commended itself to these Conservative audiences.

The years after 1992 were the beginning of the bloody Conservative civil war over Europe. The alliance with the EPP in Strasbourg was one surprisingly active theatre of operations in this civil war. Conservative MEPs were depicted in the Eurosceptic media as traitors to true conservatism, seduced and turned "native" by the fleshpots of Brussels. The EPP was denounced in these same media as federalist, quasi-socialist, corrupt and corporatist. As the Conservative Party became less interested in making a success of British membership in the EU, its interest in making a success of its European Parliamentary activity also waned. The argument that the Conservative Party was stronger in Brussels and Strasbourg because of its association with the EPP fell on deaf ears. It was alleged by some in Conservative Central Office that Prout had not kept the party in London fully informed of his negotiations with the EPP, an allegation he denied. The fate of the European Parliamentary alliance between Conservatives and the EPP was casually settled by an uninformed David Cameron, who thought his leadership campaign in 2007 would be helped by banging the anti-EPP drum. His later attempts to escape from his wanton commitment to break the association between his party and the EPP were unavailing, and foreshadowed his historic and unforgivable fecklessness of 2016.

By a sad irony, Christopher Prout died at the age of 67 in the same year (2009) that an end was definitively put to his project of bringing the Conservative Party and the EPP closer together. Before the European elections of that year, William Hague informed the EPP that the Conservative MEPs would not be sitting in the EPP after these elections. But if he harboured regrets about the termination of the Conservative liaison with the EPP, Prout had every reason to look back with pride upon an infinitely more important legacy he left the EP. In 1986, Prout produced, largely through his own efforts, a report rewriting the rules of procedure of the European Parliament in the light of the Single European Act. It is no exaggeration to say that this report and its implementation changed forever the workings and even self-understanding of the European Parliament. It was wholly fitting that the political and legal aspects of Christopher Prout's political personality came so harmoniously together in this report.

Prout was always a firm believer that the European Parliament had a crucial role – probably *the* crucial role – to play in filling whatever democratic deficit might afflict the European Union. In this respect he was an orthodox "federalist" although he understandably avoided using the term. Prout was the first MEP to realise that the 1986 Single European Act, and particularly its new cooperation procedure between Commission, Council and Parliament, could be implemented so as to augment the power of the Parliament in legislative procedures. This, for Prout, was an unalloyed reinforcement of the democratic legitimacy of the European Union as a whole. In its form, his 1986 revision of the Parliament's rules of procedure was technical, even prosaic. In fact, the revision served the highly political purpose of enhancing the Parliament's standing within the institutional architecture of the Union. After 1986, the Commission in particular would find it much more difficult to ignore the wishes and preferences of the Parliament. Generations of MEPs have benefitted from the efficient ratchet effect set in motion by Prout.

At every amendment to the European treaties since the Single European Act, the European Parliament now reflexively reaches for its rules of procedure and asks how they can be revised in the light of any new powers given to it by the latest treaty. In doing so, it follows consciously or otherwise the trail first set out by Christopher Prout. If critics are sometimes tempted to claim that the British membership of the EU was an entirely negative and unconstructive experience, Christopher Prout's legacy is a firm rebuttal of that proposition. The Proutian method has outlived not merely its originator, but British membership of the European Union as well. He would have been pleased by the first of these facts. He would have been appalled by the second.

7. David Martin

by David Gow

David Gow was the Guardian European business editor in Brussels from 2004-12, having previously been the newspaper's political editor. He was the co-founder and co-editor of sceptical.scot (2015-22) as well as a consultant editor for Acumen PA (Brussels), Bertelsmann Stiftung, and the Jacques Delors Centre in Berlin. He lives in Edinburgh.

"I like to think of myself as having been a major peripheral player," David Martin says modestly. An understatement, given that he was an MEP for 35 years (1984-2019) – the second longest serving Euro-parliamentarian after the German Christian Democrat Elmar Brok (39 years). Martin is also the longest serving vice-president of the Parliament (1989-2004), though he wryly admits he regrets never achieving his ambition of becoming president.

In fact, Martin exercised considerably more influence over the European Union's development, both at home in the UK and across Europe, and also in the wider world, than his self-assessment suggests. A substantial reason is that he honed his skills as a conciliator; he brings people with opposing views together rather than pushing them asunder; he works with others, including those of a different political persuasion, to achieve shared goals; he thinks as a European and, *pace* Theresa May, as a citizen of the world.

The thread running through his sustained work as a pro-European and internationalist is one of ensuring that a social, environmental and rights dimension is integral to European policies that hitherto put a primacy on market solutions, and that trade policy is driven not simply by mercantilism but by European values such as fairness, justice and human rights. At the height of neo-liberalism (aka the Washington consensus) Martin was a co-architect of social Europe.

"I did fall in love with being in Europe"

David Martin first entered politics in 1982, not on the European stage but as a local Labour councillor in his native city of Edinburgh. His goal as an up-and-coming young politico was to take a seat in Westminster: Edinburgh South, a seat where Gordon Brown came second in 1979.

When he didn't win the Labour nomination for the 1983 general election, Martin embarked on his career in European politics, winning the Lothians seat in the European Parliament from the Conservatives in 1984. Three years later he briefly became Labour group leader (on a 16-15 vote, with one abstention), at the relatively tender age of 32 – a largely dispiriting experience he recounts now, given the splits within the group between the pro- and anti-Europe wings that brought his leadership to an early end.

In 1988 he wrote a Fabian pamphlet, *Bringing common sense to the common market: a left agenda for Europe,* that may have sealed his fate as group leader but, arguably, swung Labour as a whole into standing as a pro-European party. It came with a foreword by Neil (now Lord) Kinnock, the then Labour leader who went on to become a European commissioner, which wholeheartedly backed Martin's stance. "It was the moment he [Kinnock] decided Labour had to be pro-European if it was to win the election" Martin now says.

The pamphlet's core message – one that retains compelling relevance today – is that the EU's single market cannot be driven by market forces alone. Martin's analysis of the Single European Act, which was in force from July 1987, argued the case for co-ordinated reflation, using Europe's combined economic muscle to put the 16 million then unemployed in the EU-12 back to work; root-and-branch CAP reform; restructuring of global economic, trade and financial relations to enable poorer nations to share and catch-up on greater prosperity; sustained growth at home; and, critically, support for progressive socio-economic legislation ("openings").

It enshrined what he called a "positive optimistic vision of how Europe should develop," including leadership of the pro-environment lobby. And, in a prescient foretaste of today's €750bn "Next Generation EU" programme, it called for greater industrial planning at EU/regional levels and a stronger regional policy dimension. "Important democratic socialist objectives can no longer be accomplished within the boundaries of a single country," Martin wrote.

Domestically, Martin's conclusion, backed by Kinnock, was crucial:

> "The British Left must accept that if we are going to achieve our objectives of 'Jobs, Peace and Freedom' there is no substitute for international cooperation. This means working within the institutions of the European Community. The EC is here to stay. Our task is to use it to our own ends".

Withdrawal from the EU, "once a totem around which the left was expected to dance", was no longer an option that was obtainable or desirable.

A tangible result of this fresh approach was RECHAR, a regional policy programme set up in 1990 to accelerate the economic conversion of coal-mining areas such as those in the UK ravaged by pit closures, which was co-piloted by Martin with Bruce Millan, former Scottish secretary and then EU regional policy commissioner. It brought hundreds of millions to deprived areas and, Martin claims, "there are some villages in Scotland that would not exist today without RECHAR".

In the 1990s Martin spread his wings and played a critical role in the creation of "social Europe". The over-arching mastermind of that concept was, of course, Jacques Delors, the former French finance minister, who served as European Commission president from 1985 to 1995. If Martin helped swing Labour to a pro-EU position, so too did Delors, who electrified the 1988 TUC conference in Bournemouth with his socialist argument for the European project. The two worked closely together in making (and remaking) that case.

Maastricht and more

His contribution to the Maastricht Treaty of 1992 setting the path towards economic and monetary union, including the euro currency, represents for Martin his biggest achievement. He was the EP's rapporteur, which meant visiting all 12 of the EU's heads of state or government, including François Mitterrand, Helmut Kohl, Giulio Andreotti and John Major, in their national capitals to put Parliament's case for what should be in the treaty.

This heavyweight dozen, plus Delors, approved the treaty at a sumptuous dinner in a chateau outside Maastricht in December 1991. However, Martin recalls little wining and dining – apart from at the Elysée where Mitterrand merely exchanged a few pleasantries before moving to the drinks table. Kohl gave him a lecture standing at his desk in Bonn. Ironically, his "most fascinating" interlocutor was Major who, he says, was exceptionally well-briefed on each and every topic and could argue his case extremely well.

As Martin sees it, the European Parliament managed to persuade Major (and others) to give MEPs a bigger role, not least in having an effective veto over the choice of Commission president, en route to its current co-decision powers. The treaty expanded structural fund aid to deprived regions and, in a social policy protocol from which Major secured an opt-out for the UK, set out minimum social and employment protections.

This was manna for Martin as a European. What's more, he claims to have persuaded Delors over dinner in Bruges to give the green light for establishing the Committee of the Regions alongside the European Economic and Social Committee (despite the Frenchman's initial resistance). This he sees as giving substance to the principle of subsidiarity which was meant to run like a thread through all EU institutions. As he now says:

> "By and large I think the treaty was a success ... Europe would have much less credibility with the general population [i.e. of the EU-27] if it didn't have an element of social and environ-

mental policy ... a pure single market without flanking policies would have been much less popular and might have been at risk".

Martin went on to be rapporteur for what became the Nice Treaty of 2001 and worked closely with Julian Priestley, the Parliament's British secretary-general, on the members' statute and professionalising the secretariat (a process he thinks has gone backwards in recent years). But, after losing the 2002 election as Socialist group nominee for the Parliament's president to Pat Cox who stood for the Liberals, Martin focussed his attention during his final 15 years on trade policy.

Trade policy for a new age

As Socialist group spokesman/co-ordinator on the international trade committee (INTA), David Martin played arguably as impactful a role as he did over Maastricht and other EU treaties. He worked on the CETA and TTIP proposals for trade agreements with Canada and the USA, helping to secure protection for European public services and high social and environmental standards, and, as rapporteur, piloted the Singapore free trade agreement through Parliament against strong opposition. He met (and overcame) equally strong opposition in extending (Generalised System of Preferences) GSP-plus status to Pakistan despite its record on human rights – largely on the grounds that it needed to be encouraged on a reform path.

But his biggest coup was in marshalling opposition among MEPs to the Anti-Counterfeiting Trade Agreement (ACTA) of 2012 on the grounds that it could discourage generic drug supplies to low-income countries and, anyway, rested on an outdated concept of intellectual property rights (IPR). "We have to modernise our approach to IPR. There is a risk that ACTA will freeze it in its current form", he said at the time. MEPs backed his stance by 478-39, with 165 abstentions – the Commission's biggest ever defeat at Parliament's hands.

EU trade policy is constantly under re-evaluation (its latest iteration is designed to make it "open, sustainable and assertive") to inject more social equity – a process wholly endorsed by Martin who worked to make the policy reflect European values. He admits that process is incomplete and, of course, that is inevitable in what remains the world's biggest trading bloc. Indeed, Martin is a classic gradualist reformer, a realist not a radical revolutionary.

Looking forward and back

It was that realism and ability to conciliate and compromise which won David Martin the cross-party respect that remains in place today. In Scotland he caused controversy within Labour by joining the (SNP) first minister's standing council on Europe and arguing for a potential coalition with the Scottish National Party which, in turn, chose him as (a short-lived) co-chair of the first citizens' assembly (on the country's future and ability to meet 21st century challenges).

Nevertheless, he accepts that the European project – to which he has dedicated four decades of his career – is over for the British. "I think we're talking about 20 years," he says, insisting re-entry would be too divisive at home and, moreover, too traumatic for an EU-27 still digesting Brexit on top of an over-hasty enlargement.

Martin also accepts that his own political career is over after what many view as considerable achievements. The EU remains work-in-progress, moving forward slowly despite setbacks, acquiring new powers despite nationalist opposition, and acting by and large as a force for good in the world. Martin can be proud he helped move its dial.

8. Pauline Green

by Dianne Hayter

Born in Malta (of a Maltese mother) and now in proud possession of a Maltese – hence EU – passport, this former police officer rose to be the most senior woman in the EP, the first female leader of the Socialist group, and – after Barbara Castle – perhaps the best known of British Labour MEPs.

Pauline's first parliamentary duty was, wearing white gloves, as part of the Met police detail at a State Opening (after which, back in plain clothes, she was visiting prostitutes under a London arch, seeking information on a notorious male attacker).

This public service role, allied to her father's military and police career, showed her both the "levers of power" and also how to enable change, in addition to introducing her to internationalism. Coincidentally, both she and I were at military schools in West Germany at the same time in the 1950s, our fathers stationed respectively in Celle and Brüggen. In growing up, Pauline was aware – if only because of the ban on fireworks – of the 1956 Hungarian uprising, and of the division of Cyprus and of Germany.

Leaving the police force to raise two children provided the time and space for political activity, when she became an active party member and fought (unsuccessfully) a council seat in Barnet. She was then chosen as the Labour candidate for the London North seat in the 1989 European elections, where she dislodged the Conservative John Marshall.

Selected in the days of constituency-based representation, she cherished her relationship with her local communities, particularly the Greek Cypriots, but also with the growing bank of Labour MPs in her patch – from just one out of 9 (one seat being Margaret Thatcher's) in 1989 when she was elected, to 7 out of 8 by 1997.

1989 proved to be the start of perhaps the most exciting and constructive decade in the EU's development, right from the 9 November toppling of the Berlin Wall just months after her election, after which the Socialist MEPs were the first political group to walk through the Brandenburg Gate, led by their then leader, the French MEP Jean-Pierre Cot.

This was followed not just by the 1990 German reunification, and preparation for the entry of into the EU some 15 years later of several former Soviet bloc countries, but also the 1995 accession of Austria, Sweden and Finland during her period of leadership, the adoption of the single currency in 1999 and increased EP powers through the 1992 Maastricht Treaty.

It was a breathless decade therefore but, despite the potential for Labour to play a central role in these developments (as Alan Donnelly was to do in relation to German reunification, and Gary Titley in relation to Finland), Pauline Green initially found the EPLP (which still contained some Euro-wary MEPs) divided, uncooperative and performing well below its numeric strength. She judged its leader, Glyn Ford, to be unable (or unwilling) to bring the then 45 members together into an effective, purposeful and agenda-led whole. She therefore challenged and beat him to become the EPLP leader in 1993 and set about welding a more coherent and positive parliamentary party.

However, in 1994, soon after the June European elections, the normal five-yearly rotation of EU positions was due (when Commission, Council and Parliament places are re-shuffled, the juggling guided by the election results across the member states). Labour having won an unprecedented 62 seats, it was clear that the party could ask for a major position: leader of the Socialist group. Just before his death, Labour leader John Smith MP agreed

Pauline Green should be the candidate, though it was left to his pro tem successor, Margaret Beckett MP, to negotiate with fellow Socialist leaders (much of the negotiations taking place around a hotel swimming pool in Corfu). The deal done, Green was elected unopposed, becoming a major player in the EU firmament as leader of the Parliament's largest political group. She was virtually unknown in the UK even in the Labour Party before her surprise election.

The former Labour deputy leader Roy Hattersley described Green as "radiating blunt practicality, guided by common sense and an antagonism (almost amounting to contempt) towards the superficialities of political image-making". Along with Julian Priestley (the Parliament's British secretary-general, who turned down an offer to become Tony Blair's chief of staff), she worked closely with the EPP group leader, the former Belgian prime minister Wilfried Martens, to increase Parliament's standing vis-à-vis the Commission and the Council. Within the Socialist group, she sought to increase cross-EU solidarity and build greater cohesion amongst the social democratic family.

The timing of her election matched what was happening across the 15 member states. Early on she had met the social democratic leaders of the four Nordic countries. Then in May 1997 Labour's Tony Blair was elected in the UK, closely followed in June by Lionel Jospin in France and Gerhard Schröder in Germany in October 1998, giving not just 12 of the 15 countries a centre-left government but, significantly, in the three largest countries.

However, Green became disappointed by what she saw as Tony Blair's failure to play the role the progressive left had envisaged. His first meetings, prior to the June and October elections, were with the conservatives Kohl and Chirac rather than center-left leaders. Even worse, at a major socialist congress in Malmö in June 1997, where the expectation had been that the left victories and the position in the EP would herald a new future for the European Union, Prime Minister Blair rejected a planned joint platform appearance with the French socialist prime minister, Lionel Jospin and SPD chancellor-candidate Gerhard Schröder. Instead, he alienated some by a speech which, rather than championing a new social Europe, was a call to the left to "modernise or die" (see also Part II, chap.2 by Roger Liddle). Others present at Malmö, however, perhaps new to Blair's charisma, judged that Tony "stole the show".

Green's disappointment over what she saw as his lack of leadership at Malmö wasn't helped as the UK prepared to take over the six-monthly rotating Council presidency in January 1998. The Council presidency provided the opportunity to drive progress on significant projects. Felipe González, as Spanish prime minister (1982-96), had launched the Mediterranean initiative (to consolidate Southern European democracy through economic regeneration). So when Pauline Green met the UK Europe minister, Doug Henderson, to discuss how the EP could facilitate Labour's equivalent vision, she was stunned to find a complete dearth of ideas (outside of a school competition for a logo for the presidency). Thanks to Maastricht, the EP had gained more powers, so a left-led Council together with a dominant Socialist group in the EP, created the possibility of a major boost for the EU's progressive role. Green's judgement that Labour did not make the most of this potential was not universal, however, others rating the UK presidency far more favourably.

Blair had worked to improve dialogue with fellow social democratic prime ministers and heads of state, organising via the Party of European Socialists pre-Council summit dinners which included the socialist commissioners along with Pauline Green (sometimes the only woman in such meetings). Her inclusion recognised her significant role over major issues, such as her support for the customs union with Turkey and greater transparency over MEPs' expenses – though this did not find favour with many, if not most, in the Parliament.

A major issue in which she led the charge was the use of new powers to sack the Santer Commission. In 1999, following allegations of financial mismanagement from the EPP group against two socialist commissioners, the Socialist group sought to sidestep this by agreeing to an independent committee to investigate the claims – but only after Pauline Green had first proposed and then withdrawn a motion of censure, handling the highly charged issue with a less than steady touch. The committee's subsequent conclusion that "It was increasingly difficult to find anyone who had the slightest sense of responsibility" in the Commission left the position of its president, Jacques Santer and his whole Commission untenable, with no choice but to resign, plunging the institution into chaos, and worsening the reputation of the Union. For some, the rather botched use of new powers did no favours for Green's reputation.

Despite such drawbacks, her role as the leader of the largest group gave her a ring-side seat at major European events: nominating John Hume for the Nobel Peace Prize, and – together with Mo Mowlam MP – encouraging Santer to provide substantial funding after the Good Friday Agreement to bed in the changes.

Within the UK, a major disappointment was that proportional representation and the vast regional constituencies broke the link with constituency activists and communities. Perhaps partly because of this, Green witnessed the growing public disenchantment with the perceived remoteness from Brussels, leading to Brexit. She also regrets that a workable solution was not found for the problem of the division of Cyprus, to which she devoted so much time.

Despite the customary rotation of positions in the EU institutions every five years, and Labour's loss of MEPs (from 62 to 29), Green somehow hoped for a second term as Socialist group leader – an unlikely outcome, but its failure to happen left her deeply disappointed. When Tony Blair supported Robin Cook for the presidency of the Party of European Socialists, there were no senior posts left that Pauline could realistically aspire to. She resigned as an MEP in December 1999 only six months after her re-election and was appointed chief executive of Cooperatives UK and later president of the International Cooperative Alliance. Fourteen years later she was appointed a Dame of the British Empire, a belated recognition of her loyal service to her party and her country.

From police office to a major female player in Europe, from the streets of London to the highest councils on the continent, this daughter of a soldier served the public devotedly, though with little public credit or acknowledgement. She remains firmly rooted in her locale and in Labour, even as her heart remains firmly European and her passport purple.

9. Graham Watson

by Giles Merritt

Giles Merritt arrived in Brussels as a Financial Times journalist in 1978, vowing to stay for no more than two years before resuming his peripatetic FT career, but has been an EU watcher ever since, as an op-ed columnist for the International Herald Tribune and founder of a leading think tank called Friends of Europe – "of Europe" he insists, "but not necessarily of the EU institutions".

It's Christmas time in Brussels and the lights shine brightly on wet pavements. The "capital of Europe" is *en fête* and one of the livelier Xmas parties is in full swing at Rita and Graham Watson's house not far from the European Parliament. The hubbub can be heard several streets away.

You can tell a lot about people from their friends, and that's particularly true of the Watsons. Their Christmas gatherings attract Brussels' *"gratin"* (the French version of *crème de la crème*) of top Commission and Parliament officials, fellow MEPs, international legal talent and a sprinkling of journalists. As you'd expect, it's a multi-lingual, multi-cultural crowd – Italian friends and family of Graham's lawyer wife Rita Giannini mingle happily with guests drawn from the nooks and crannies of the EU's institutions.

Graham Watson is almost as much a Bruxellois as he is a Scot. He arrived in 1994 as the first of the UK's Liberal Democrats to be elected as an MEP, and his political fortunes as a shaper of European policies have since then waxed and waned along with those of his party.

Graham soon became prominent within the body of British movers and shakers in Brussels who did so much to push forward the project of European integration. In the wake of Brexit, it's easy to forget that senior Commission officials who either were or would have been marked out for the top in Whitehall played, along with committed British MEPs, vital roles in achieving the EU's goals.

Elected for Somerset and North Devon at the comparatively early age of 38 after a spell in banking at HSBC in Hong Kong, Graham found himself in a new political environment convulsed by the collapse of the Soviet bloc and uncertainty over how to deal with formerly communist countries now clamouring for EU membership.

The European Parliament was itself flexing the new muscles of co-decision it had gained in the Maastricht Treaty. As well as creating the European Union, as distinct from Community, this landmark agreement opened the way to the euro as a common currency, so Graham's role on the Parliament's Economic and Monetary Committee placed him at the heart of the action.

At that point Graham was one of only two Lib Dem MEPs. The 1999 European elections, though, were to dramatically change that. Surging support for liberal parties across Europe saw the number of the UK's Lib Dems rise to ten, with Graham taking the role of party leader. The next five years were to see a remarkable transformation of liberal politicians' influence and powers at EU level, with Graham Watson playing a significant part. In January 2002, Irish liberal Pat Cox was narrowly elected to the presidency of the Parliament, enabling Graham to succeed him as leader of the ELDR group of European liberal democrats.

In the weeks before Christmas that year Graham gleefully seized on a colleague's idea and sent out packs of commemorative playing cards featuring photos of the ELDR's 52 MEPs. That they in fact numbered 53 was solved by featuring Pat Cox as Joker.

Europe's liberals were on a roll; the 2004 elections saw the ELDR's ranks rise to 67, and those of Britain's Lib Dems to 12. The "big bang" enlargement that brought 12 new member countries into the EU had favoured not only the ELDR but also other political parties of similar persuasion. Graham seized the moment and brought them together into a wider parliamentary grouping to be called the Alliance of Liberals and Democrats for Europe – ALDE – which with 106 MEPs became the Parliament's third largest group behind the EPP's Christian Democrats and the Socialist group.

These were heady times for members of the European Parliament, although far from straightforward. The bigger and more muscular EU now wielding the powers of a common currency was also beset by the many uncertainties that followed 9/11 and the US-led invasion of Iraq. The global financial crisis of 2008 inevitably made itself felt in the following year's elections. Europhiles in Brussels and throughout Europe began to sense that the tide of political fortunes was turning against them.

The shifting mosaic of European politics has been well-described by Graham himself. Following the reverse suffered in those 2009 elections, he sat down to chronicle ALDE's ups and downs in a book entitled *Building a Liberal Europe: The ALDE Project* (John Harper Publishing, 2010). This sets out to answer the question he himself poses – "Little has been written about political parties and ideology at European level. Why?" Whether intentionally or not, Graham Watson's account of life as a Euro-politician offers outsiders some troubling insights. Although the broad thrust of achieving a stronger and more united Europe is shared by most of his dramatis personae, the reader inevitably finds that short term interests and the tactics to achieve these are dominant themes in his account.

German Chancellor Helmut Kohl's use of the Konrad Adenauer Stiftung to "seduce" Valéry Giscard d'Estaing's liberals into joining the EPP group is but one of the grubbier moves described. For students of behind-the-scenes politicking, Graham's account is absorbing reading. Watching the deals and understandings between the factions and ideologies that make up the spectrum of European politics is like seeing amoeba changing shape. Graham Watson's pen does the topic full justice and presents a vivid picture of the personalities involved as well as the issues they championed.

Whether Graham would have chosen to find the time to record the intricacies of life in the EP from 2002-2009 is moot. The ALDE's loss of 22 seats in 2009 saw his decision to step down from the leadership and instead declare a very public candidature for the European Parliament's presidency. He eschewed the usually secretive nature of such bids, saying "I saw no reason why these decisions should continue to be made behind closed doors".

Because the ALDE group no longer had enough seats to be a kingmaker through alliance with either the EPP or the Socialist group, Graham's bid was probably doomed from the outset. He withdrew from the race to resume the role of a rank-and-file MEP. In 2011 his contribution to Europe's political development, and the UK's hand in that, was recognised with a knighthood.

The tide of politics had not only turned but was ebbing fast. The 2014 election was the fifth that Graham contested, and the last. In a portent of the Brexit referendum to be held exactly two years later, Graham lost his now enlarged seat of South West England by a narrow margin. Of 1.5 million voters, he was 6,000 ballots short of remaining an MEP.

Like many politicians, Graham displays an admirable resilience to setbacks. He is to this day a relaxed and positive part of the Brussels intelligentsia, representing until recently the EU-related interests of Gibraltar, which had been tacked onto his West of England constituency until Brexit intervened. Like so many of us "Euro-Brits", though, he finds it hard to hide his nostalgia for the days when Britons had a major hand in determining Europe's future.

10. Glenys Kinnock

by Neil Kinnock

Neil Kinnock married Glenys on 25 March 1967. He was first elected to Parliament in 1970 and was leader of the Labour Party from 1983 to 1992. He became a European commissioner in 1995 and vice-president of the Commission from 1999 to 2004, before being appointed to the Lords in 2005, where Glenys joined him in 2009.

Early in October 1992, we were driving to Bristol to visit our daughter, Rachel, who had just started her degree course at the University of the West of England. As we chatted, Glenys asked me who was likely to succeed Llew Smith as the Labour candidate for South East Wales in the 1994 European Parliament election. I gave a list of assumed runners and riders and then, after a ruminative silence, Glenys astounded me by saying "Dammit, I'm going to run!".

My astonishment was natural. For decades Glenys, the inveterate campaigner and dedicated primary school teacher, had been my permanent political ally and had repeatedly declined offers of support for candidacy by Labour Party members in various parts of the UK. Now she had decided, obviously after typically thorough but private thought, that election to the EP – "less nasty than Westminster, and more aware of the future" – was her aim. "The kids have gone to university and Europe offers a better chance of development action in Wales and the world," she explained with her usual directness. Within days, she was on the campaign trail again – for the first time since she'd won the chair of the National Union of Students branch in Cardiff University – asking people to "vote for Glenys".

The selection battle against politically experienced men, some with established support, was tough, not least when some opponents managed to get the "she's doing his bidding" line running in parts of the press. It was cheap, nasty – and absurdly wrong. My advice was welcomed (and occasionally taken), my direct involvement (except as a driver and bag carrier) was discouraged: "I'm proud to be your wife," she said, "but I have to make my own way – I must never be regarded as 'your' candidate". With some reluctance, I recognised the wisdom of that. Surrogacy can have great value – but not in democratic politics. So, with some long-cherished comrades and friends, Glenys slogged around the 10 parliamentary seats that then made up the European constituency. She won nominations from four of the constituency Labour parties, narrowly losing in another three, and secured the candidacy in the third round of voting in the selection meeting. I waited outside like an expectant husband near the labour ward. Her phone call said: "It's a girl – ME!"

A year of itinerant campaigning followed, with continual visits to the multitude of communities across the constituency – with particular frequency and intensity in Monmouth, the only Tory-held parliamentary seat, where party members warmly welcomed the chance to get stuck in. Primary schools, choirs, retirement homes, factories, sixth form classes, rugby clubs, shopping centres and anywhere that people were likely to gather drew Glenys like a magnet. She thoroughly enjoyed the whirlwind.

The result on 12 June 1994 was a triumph with Labour gaining 17 seats to finish with 62 and Glenys winning a Guinness Book of Records-entry majority of nearly 130,000. Joy was unconfined – and so was the busy-ness. Within weeks, a disused main road shop had been rented and redecorated in Cwmfelinfach in the Sirhowy Valley, assistants had been hired, a second hand (red) Montego bought, and a "things to do" list drawn up. At the top of it was an early meeting with Bruce Millan, the UK (Labour) member of the European Commission with the regional development portfolio.

Brussels and Strasbourg came next. It brought brief, slight deflation: after years of being referred to in Holyhead as "Cyril's daughter" and more widely as "Neil's wife", within hours at the EP she was being introduced as "Steve's mum" by young Socialist group aides who had known our son for the months in which he'd been working for a Labour MEP.

Making her "own way" then resumed in earnest. For Glenys, it meant immediate membership of the Development and Cooperation Committee. As an experienced campaigner and commentator on world poverty and women's rights, with four books on relevant issues published, she was soon leading activity in parliamentary sessions and international visits, and earning respect and support – vital, as she quickly realised – from well-motivated non-socialists as well as comrades.

Recognising the significance and potential of the Africa, Caribbean and Pacific (ACP)–EU Joint Parliamentary Assembly, she immersed herself in its operations. The Assembly brings together parliamentary representatives from the EP and from (then) 78 countries (mainly former colonies) in the other continents, first under the 1963 Yaoundé Convention, later the 1975 Lomé Convention and, since 2000, the Cotonou Agreement. The consistent aim has been the reduction and abolition of poverty and to give a political dimension to trade and development cooperation relations. Over the years (and with urgings from Glenys and international colleagues), the scope of that association has been extended to migration, security and peace, the arms trade, and "good governance" including combatting corruption and the impunity of delinquent, often murderous, leaders. Clearly, those purposes require active improvement of democratic and human rights, with particular and necessary focus on the advancement of opportunity, care and security for women and children.

Glenys had been involved in campaigns, NGO activities, research and advocacy in all of those areas throughout her adult life and she engaged relentlessly in the work of the JPA. "We who are free have the elementary duty to sustain those who yearn and strive for liberty" she declared to all who would listen – and some who wouldn't. By 1999, she had been elected co-president of the Assembly and, in 2002, became the first EU co-president ever to be re-elected.

For Glenys, the role was deeply fulfilling. She struck up very close relationships with fellow MEPs and with colleagues from the ACP member states, particularly Botswana, Mauritius and the Caribbean democracies, in efforts to energise the Assembly, assert the trading interests of the underdeveloped member states – 40 of which were Less Developed Countries (LDCs) – and give prominence to health and education priorities. Her characteristic forthrightness and reluctance to concede to vested interests meant tussles (usually friendly, sometimes not) with formality in the European Commission and Council and the notoriety of being *persona-non-grata* in Mugabe's totalitarian Zimbabwe, junta-ruled Nigeria, and Afwerki's ruthlessly oppressed Eritrea.

To balance all that, she spoke at the General Assembly of the UN in New York and to UNHCR meetings in Geneva, delighted in meeting countless school classes in just about every ACP member state, visited innumerable health and maternity projects, earned the title "Madame La Banane" in the Caribbean as she sought to secure improved trading access to the EU when the vital sugar and fruit protocols were being renegotiated, could count Nelson Mandela and Graca Machel among her friends, and got a new EU budget line to finance the operation of the anti-Mugabe Radio Free Zimbabwe from a neighbouring country.

I used to become (fruitlessly) alarmed when her colleagues told me how she had confronted "gigantic" heavily armed border guards in the Democratic Republic of Congo (to the consternation of Sir Henry Plumb, the kindly Tory who was with her); left detention in her hotel room to intervene with the leaders of the violent 2000 coup in the Solomon Islands to secure the release of the injured prime minister; was given a luxury tent by a considerate French army general when she strayed over the border into Chad and avoided the marauding Janjaweed in Darfur; undertook election observation in war-ravaged Cambodia and Rwanda (controversial when she refused to recognise the voting as "free and fair") and in newly democratic South Africa; and as Chief Guest in Mali she ate the egg which had been baked – in the hot desert sand – inside a chicken, inside a goat, inside a camel.

All of these adventures (and many more) were accomplished with "regal aplomb and dignity" according to the tributes at her last Joint Assembly meeting in Prague in 2009. She was described as "indefatigable, irresistible, irrepressible, unsinkable" by a Caribbean deputy prime minister at that gathering and, although that was very gratifying, she seemed to be most pleased by those who spoke of her "invariable elegance, even in the worst physical conditions after little sleep". I could certainly join that applause. Glenys could get more crease-resistant clothes into a tiny wheelie case – it was called "the Tardis" – than ever seemed possible and, from schoolgirl Eisteddfod soloist to TV light entertainment show guest to speech-making, cause-rousing MEP (and, later, minister) she had always masked her terror with cheekiness.

That seems to have worked. In a book of retirement tributes from Josep Borrell (now the EU high representative for foreign and security policy), Wole Soyinka, Sharon Webster and a host of parliamentary colleagues and staff from across the EU and ACP, there is a stream of declarations of affection and respect with a continual emphasis on her practical and audacious commitment to development, human rights, freedom and democratic socialist values. As she said, "I've never deliberately made enemies, but when they have come I haven't avoided them either. Friends and true comrades, of course, I love and cherish always". In a moving ceremony, the ACP-JPA, "as an exceptional case", conferred on her "the Title of Honorary President for Life".

In the UK, the 1999 EP election under the bizarre new Labour-sacrificing, constituency-abolishing, worst-available form of PR meant that Wales became one "regional" constituency with a resulting fall in Welsh Labour MEPs from 5 to 2. Glenys and the young Eluned Morgan had a famously friendly and fruitful partnership and, operating from their new base in Cardiff, established an additional office in North Wales and set about continuous campaigning on everything from infrastructure needs and women's rights to agricultural fund reform and unwanted refuse tips. They were well-equipped for the task: Eluned was a multilingual, school-taught Welsh speaker from Cardiff; Glenys a native Welsh speaker raised in Holyhead. Both had multiple contacts all over the country. With excellent young staff they made a formidable team of representatives and, as a bonus, their uproarious duets – accompanied usually by the brilliant Hennessys folk group – delighted every Labour conference *Noson Lawen* (Happy Night).

Glenys considers her crowning achievement to have been to secure the EU funding for the new ferry terminal in Holyhead (which, at the invitation of the Stena Line, she was thrilled to formally open); but insistent lobbying of regional development commissioner Monika Wulf-Matthies, which helped to gain Objective 1 status for most of Wales, the EU support which saved the Big Pit industrial museum in Blaenavon, built the Ystrad Mynach by-pass, and secured the Ebbw Vale–Newport passenger rail line, all testify to avid constituency advocacy. Alongside all that, there were the annual International Women's Day celebrations that she organised with guest stars including Ruby Wax, Dawn French, Helena Kennedy, Barbara Castle, Emma Thomson, Cherie Blair and other women of distinction. A new enterprising and enlightened editor of the Western Mail established the Welsh Women of the Year awards with Glenys as advisor and compere. Later, as retirement from the EP in 2009 approached, that newspaper – for most of its history a critic of most things Labour – published an editorial by a different editor which spoke of her as "a citizen of Wales and the world" in the "great tradition of Welsh politicians" who were tirelessly committed to "the greater global community of men and women who want to live free from hunger and war". It was headlined "Glenys's record should inspire a new generation".

Some young women and men have already testified to that inspiration by working for the greater good in ways that emulate Glenys in word and, vitally, in deed. If that continues, Glenys will be very pleased.

11. Richard Corbett

by David Harley

He was Labour's last leader in the European Parliament, and none was more committed to the European ideal. He had been one of the first to arrive and was now among the last to leave, after a political career in Europe spanning over four decades. Probably more than anyone else either present or watching, at the end of the last plenary session attended by British MEPs on 29 January 2020, as the tearful MEPs held hands and sang Auld Lang Syne, Richard Corbett personified the crushing disappointment felt by the majority of his colleagues in Brussels that day. He had given his all; nobody could have worked harder as an MEP to further the interests of the institution he served. And now it was all over.

He was the leader of a dwindling band, with Labour having won only 10 seats in May the previous year, against the Brexit Party's triumphant 29 and the combined 23 for the Lib Dems and the Greens. But Corbett's reputation and the respect in which he was held by his colleagues went way further than the size of his troops. Fighting for increased powers for the Parliament, and thereby, as he saw it, making the EU more democratic, had been the focus of his entire professional and political life. From 1979 to 1981, after leaving Oxford, he was president of the Young European Federalists and helped set up the Youth Forum of the European Communities, the predecessor of the European Youth Forum. He then spent a brief period as an EU official before becoming political advisor and deputy secretary-general in the Socialist group. He was elected as an MEP in 1996, 1999 and 2004 and again from 2014 to 2020. During the four years following his defeat in 2009, he worked as an advisor to the president of the European Council, Herman Van Rompuy.

Corbett had thus experienced the Parliament from many different perspectives; his personal achievements were exceptional, and his knowledge of institutional and procedural questions unrivalled. No single MEP did more to significantly increase its powers, standing and efficiency. It would scarcely be an exaggeration to suggest that statues of Richard Corbett should be erected in town squares all over Europe. He helped draft the treaties of Maastricht, Amsterdam and Lisbon, and was familiar with every sub-clause, dot and comma. In particular, he worked on drafting the parts of the treaties that increased the powers of Parliament, notably the co-decision procedure which now applies for adopting EU legislation through successive readings of Parliament and the Council of Ministers. In parallel, as rapporteur for the Rules Committee, he led the continuous updating of Parliament's rules of procedure in order to extract maximum practical and political advantage from its newly acquired treaty competences by appropriately adapting its working methods. (His general knowledge was not limited to arcane Euro-matters: Richard is also a fearsome opponent in any pub quiz and would probably be unbeatable in Mastermind on the subject of the history of Liverpool Football Club.)

The plaudits and tributes rained down in Brussels from all sides. In the UK, not so much, although Corbett was eventually awarded a CBE in the 2021 New Year's Honours for European parliamentary services. After all he had achieved in Europe, he deserved no less – and possibly more. The ultimate EP insider – despite the affection with which he was held by so many of his constituents in Yorkshire and the Humber – Richard Corbett was an example of the biblical dictum that no man is a prophet in his own country. In the microcosm of the European Parliament, among his fellow members of the Constitutional Affairs Committee, the Rules Committee, and within the Socialist group, Corbett was the go-to member for anyone seeking clarification on institutional and procedural matters, on account of his deep understanding and elephantine memory of the history of the institution and the evolution of its powers and competences. That respect transcended boundaries of political affiliation or nationality. But did it extend to London and the upper reaches of the Labour Party? Or were the two worlds and political cultures too different and far apart?

The BBC journalist Mark Mardell described Corbett as "A decent and a thoughtful man, one of the few who understands how the European Parliament actually works and explains it well". That much is undeniable. His occasional appearances on Newsnight during the Jeremy Paxman era were a master class in delivering polite putdowns in the face of ignorance and prejudice. He had proved himself both strong on substance and a competent communicator. Yet the broader question of how much Corbett, with all his experience and knowledge, or any MEP could hope to influence the European debate in the UK and the Labour Party was far from clear. Other political parties in certain EU countries, such as Germany and France, made greater use of their MEPs' European expertise and integrated them into their internal decision making. In the UK the degree of dissonance seemed more acute. Perhaps a greater emphasis on practical outcomes rather than process might have made communications easier.

In October 2017, as the newly elected leader of the EPLP, Corbett took up his seat on the party's NEC. He immediately realised – although was not at all surprised – that the NEC's mode of operation was "highly factional", with all key votes prepared in advance by the leadership. The Corbyn camp moreover was riding high after the Conservatives had lost their majority in the election imprudently called by Theresa May in June that year. The Mephistophelian coincidence of the chaotic aftermath of the Brexit referendum and Jeremy Corbyn's leadership had dramatically reduced the chances of formulating a clear and coherent Labour policy on Europe. The distance across the Channel and the North Sea was gradually but inexorably increasing.

In conversation with the author, Richard spoke frankly about the weaknesses of Labour's contribution to the Remain campaign:

"It's too simple to blame everything on Jeremy. His position was more one of indecision. Europe had never been his career focus: he was suspicious of the EU, but never really had a grasp of its details. Consequently, something like 40% of people who said they normally voted Labour didn't know what the party position was. If we had had a leader who was really engaged in the campaign, making clear arguments and knowledgeable enough to engage in these arguments, that in itself could well have swung the difference between the 51.9% and the 48.1%."

Those few lines are typical Richard Corbett: clear, articulate, polite almost to the point of excess – even when talking about an outcome that was nothing short of calamitous in terms of everything that he had campaigned and fought for during more than forty years. Others might not have showed such understanding in their assessment of Jeremy Corbyn's direct responsibility for Brexit, for not sufficiently opposing the deeply unsatisfactory terms of withdrawal, and for the ambiguities surrounding Labour's belated endorsement of a new referendum, causing it to lose support among both committed Leavers and Remainers and contributing to a defeat for which Labour is still paying the price. Like many Remainers, Corbett marched in the streets and held out the hope for as long as possible that a parliamentary majority might be found for a second referendum. But once Johnson's Conservatives won a crushing majority of seats on 43% of the vote (despite 53% going to parties demanding a new referendum), the gates came clanging down on all escape routes, sounding the final death knell for those of Britain's remaining MEPs who still believed, some passionately, in Britain's continued involvement in the European project.

The referendum result and Britain's effective withdrawal was not the first political setback that Richard Corbett had suffered. Losing his seat to the BNP in 2009 was a particularly bitter pill. He showed great resilience in preparing the ground for his successful return five years later. Similarly, he was far from idle following Britain's withdrawal, representing the European Parliament in the common secretariat running the Conference on the Future of Europe and occupying a senior post in the cabinet of Parliament's secretary-general, Klaus Welle.

Asked what gave him his greatest satisfaction as an MEP, Richard replied:

> "The pleasure of working in a Parliament with colleagues from so many countries, where you learn something new every day, and of being in a Parliament that is not a rubber-stamp where ordinary Members are just lobby fodder, and where majorities are built issue by issue by explanation, persuasion and negotiation, meaning that if you roll your sleeves up, you can have real influence".

12. Nigel Farage

by Michael Crick

Michael Crick has been a broadcaster for forty years, reporting for Channel 4 News, Panorama and Newsnight. His several books include biographies of Arthur Scargill, Jeffrey Archer, Michael Heseltine, Michael Howard and, in 2022, "One Party After Another: The Disruptive Life of Nigel Farage".

Of all the British MEPs to sit in the European Parliament between 1979 and 2020, Nigel Farage was probably the most famous – and historically the most influential – yet was despised by most of his British colleagues for his crucial role in bringing Britain's 48-year membership of the European Union to an end.

Yet the great irony of Nigel Farage's career is that Brexit might never have happened without the platform and resources provided to him and his parties by the European Parliament, and the regular boosts in support and attention supplied every five years at European elections. He owes especial thanks to the Blair government's decision to adopt proportional representation for European elections in the UK, in compliance with EU policy.

PR was a Labour manifesto pledge in 1997 but it almost didn't happen. The House of Lords blocked the legislation six times because peers thought the proposed "closed list" system would give party officials too much power. Home Secretary Jack Straw – never a fan of PR – wanted to ditch the bill, but Tony Blair insisted they override the Lords by invoking the Parliament Acts for only the fifth time since 1911. Blair was under pressure from the Liberal Democrat leader Paddy Ashdown, having reneged on his secret promise to Ashdown before the 1997 election to bring Lib Dem MPs into a Labour government.

UKIP, initially called the Anti-Federalist League, had been founded in 1991 by the academic historian Alan Sked. When the party contested the 1994 European elections, Sked insisted that any UKIP MEPs elected would not take their seats – rather like Sinn Féin MPs at Westminster. Then Farage, having spotted well before 1999 that PR could suddenly put UKIP on the map, led the fight within his party to overturn this "abstentionist" stance.

Farage – in the South East, the biggest UK region, with 11 seats – was one of just three UKIP MEPs elected in 1999 (the others were the party's then leader Michael Holmes in the South West, and his successor Jeffrey Titford in the Eastern region). UKIP's delegation to Brussels and Strasbourg would rise steadily to 12 MEPs in 2004; 13 in 2009; and 24 in 2014 when, remarkably, the party topped the poll in Britain.

Forty-one people served as UKIP MEPs at one time or another between 1999 and 2020. It was a motley crew, which included the celebrity TV presenter Robert Kilroy-Silk; a former European Commission accountant and whistleblower, Marta Andreasen; and Britain's first ever transsexual parliamentarian, Nikki Sinclaire. All three would fall out with Farage and quit the party well before the end of their parliamentary terms. Two UKIP MEPs, Ashley Mote and Tom Wise, were jailed for fraud.

Farage and his colleagues enjoyed the high life of Brussels and Strasbourg: the haute-cuisine, the Belgian beers and French wines, the incessant invitations to champagne receptions, and the physical temptations too. They hadn't become MEPs to spend hours poring over EU directives, or reading incomprehensible Commission reports, or serving on boring committees. Farage and his team did not participate much in parliamentary business. Early on, he himself joined the Fisheries Committee, attended just one meeting, and was never seen again. UKIP had the worst record of any party in Europe for attendance and voting. Instead, the goal was to achieve withdrawal from the EU by exploiting the considerable advantages of being an MEP.

The most obvious asset was money and staff. In the 1999 elections, UKIP candidates pledged to deploy their lavish parliamentary allowances (as directed by the party's national executive), to publish regular accounts of where their EU money went, and to devote any surplus on their expenses to a trust fund for "the defence of victims of EU regulations". But the parliamentary authorities declared it was against the rules to use such funds for party political and campaigning purposes, and over the two decades they would regularly penalise Farage and other UKIP MEPs for misusing EU money. UKIP was also blatant in using its parliamentary employees, who were meant to work solely on European matters, as its core staff as a British political party. UKIP was not alone, of course, in abusing the allowance and staffing systems for electoral purposes. Most British parties – and no doubt many from other EU states – broke the rules too, though rarely so openly.

In 1999, the three UKIP MEPs joined the Eurosceptic parliamentary grouping, the Europe of Democracies and Diversities, but were only minor players. After 2004, however, with twelve MEPs, Farage became co-leader of the similar Independence/Democracy group, whose 37 members included parties from Greece and Poland which were tainted by anti-semitism, plus MEPs from the Italian Lega Nord, two of whom were convicted of violent offences.

After each European election, Farage was skilled at forging new alliances of Eurosceptics, aware that parliamentary groups got extra funds, speaking time, staff and other perks. But Farage blocked Alessandra Mussolini (granddaughter of the Italian dictator) and Marine Le Pen from ever joining his group. Their names were simply too toxic back home. Farage was also careful to avoid dealings with Nick Griffin, one of two British National Party MEPs elected in 2009, again thanks to PR.

Farage may have been one of the EU's greatest critics, yet he enjoyed the trappings, status and access which group leadership conferred. He had a front-row seat in the hemicycle, sitting at an adjacent desk to the president of the Commission. He enjoyed especially good relations with Jean-Claude Juncker, and only five days after the 2016 Brexit referendum, the two men even hugged in the chamber.

Farage's early speeches in the Parliament's plenary sessions were dull and unremarkable, often about fishing, agriculture and environmental matters, with little of the bombast and wit heard later on. After 2004, however, he became a master at using his parliamentary performances to make an impact outside. In his very first speech as group co-leader, Farage attacked several of the commissioners proposed by the new president, José Manuel Barroso. These included a nominated vice-president, Jacques Barrot, a French politician who had received an eight-month prison sentence in 2000 for embezzling £2 million of public money, only for his penalty to be quashed thanks to an amnesty on political funding by President Chirac.

Perhaps Farage's most memorable intervention was his attack on the first appointed full-time president of the European Council, the former Belgian prime minister Herman Van Rompuy. "You have the charisma of a damp rag and the appearance of a low-grade bank clerk," Farage taunted. "Who are you? I'd never heard of you. Nobody in Europe had ever heard of you. I would like to ask you, President: 'Who voted for you?'" Farage subsequently apologised, but only to "bank clerks the world over". He was fined ten days' worth of parliamentary allowances – around €3,000.

It was worth it. The session had been sparsely attended, but Nigel Farage's 90-second onslaught rapidly went viral. Farage had learnt to turn strict time limits to his advantage, honing punchy soundbites and questions which made his name across Europe – and also in America, where his YouTube clips were enjoyed by the property tycoon Donald Trump.

Yet Farage also fell victim himself to a well-crafted question. In 2004, UKIP MEPs had agreed to ban their spouses from serving on the European payroll. Farage ignored the edict and employed his wife and at least one girlfriend from parliamentary funds. So, in 2014, the former UKIP MEP Nikki Sinclaire asked in the chamber whether Farage thought it "a fair use of taxpayers' money – namely his secretarial allowance – not only to employ his wife, Kirsten, but his former mistress Annabelle Fuller?" For once, Farage was silent.

After the referendum result in 2016, it was assumed that Britain would leave the EU, and give up its MEPs, before the 2019 European elections. But with delays in reaching a withdrawal deal, Farage soon spotted that Britain might have to participate in the 2019 contest after all. By now, Farage was estranged from UKIP, the party he'd led on and off for ten years, and in late 2018 he helped establish the Brexit Party.

The 2019 Euro election was his greatest electoral success, the Brexit Party topping the poll in the UK with 30.5% of the vote and 29 MEPs, more than any other party in the EU. Nigel Farage was the first man in history to lead two different parties to success in UK elections. The Conservatives were pushed into fifth place with less than 9% of the vote, and the Tory prime minister, Theresa May was forced from office before the results were announced. Almost close to panic, the Conservatives replaced May with Boris Johnson, their answer to Nigel Farage.

The Brexit Party delegation was substantially more able than Farage's previous European teams, but only served for seven months, until Johnson ensured that Brexit finally took place in January 2020.

Over the twenty-one years since 1999, Farage and the 67 UKIP and Brexit Party MEPs had ruthlessly exploited the European Union and its generous parliamentary structure to achieve the greatest split in the Union's history.

13. Daniel Hannan

by Dianne Hayter

Arguably the most single minded and focused of any MEP, Dan Hannan entered Parliament in 1999 at the tender age of 28, clear that this would provide the platform for his already-formed views about the European Union and Britain's part in it. Just as an earlier cohort of MEPs, formed by the experience of the Second World War, saw the project in its historical context of ending European wars, so Dan Hannan's teenage experience of the fall of the Berlin Wall, and the emergence of democracies in Eastern Europe, formed his judgement of the EU. He used his pre-university gap year to visit academic dissidents in former satellite states of the Soviet Union: Czechoslovakia, East Germany, Poland, Hungary and Romania. These were, as he describes them, "Mitteleuropa" thinkers who wanted a return to independent governments. He took from them their abhorrence above all of occupation, of rules decided by others and the lack of national democracy. He even came to see the EU's cross-national decision-making as being imposed in the manner of Soviet diktats, and he took his belief in national sovereignty into all his subsequent Brexit campaigning.

This aim for his own country to break free from the EU project became his life's motif. Straight from university, he became the first director of the European Research Group, an organisation for Eurosceptic MPs, where he stayed until 1999, meanwhile becoming a leader writer at The Telegraph which offered him an outlet for such views. He worked closely with the Conservative Party, including as a speech writer for Michael Howard and William Hague and, in 1999, was elected a Conservative member of the European Parliament, his Eurosceptic views being already well known.

He immediately started to make himself unpopular with some colleagues, both by his exposure of misuse of expenses but even more by supporting the Danish campaign against joining the euro, the first of his involvements in referendums. Having believed Blair's promise of a referendum on the proposed new Constitutional Treaty (which, after referendum defeats in France and the Netherlands was ultimately replaced by the Lisbon Treaty, approved in the UK by Parliament and not in a referendum), his campaign for a public vote was to continue and finally bear fruit. Indeed, his hostility to the Lisbon Treaty took the form of a demand for a referendum.

Having learnt a useful technique of employing the permitted one minute "explanation of vote" in the European Parliament, together with his 70 cross-EU Eurosceptic MEPs – the "SOS Democracy" group – he used this and any other speech (regardless of the subject) to finish with a call, in Latin, for the Lisbon Treaty to be put to the vote: *Pactio Olisipiensis censenda est,* an echo of Cato the Elder ending every speech with a call for Carthage to be destroyed: *Carthago delenda est.* None of this found favour with the (then) majority of Conservative MEPs, let alone Labour or the vast majority across Parliament, especially as he was adept at publicising his interventions via his weekly Telegraph column and getting them picked up in the British media.

Perhaps his main impact, however, was within the Conservative Party. When David Cameron was seeking the leadership, Hannan and some other MEPs extracted a promise that the Conservatives would leave the EPP political group. They also obtained a promise from him to hold a referendum on EU membership – a promise which Cameron made publicly in his Bloomberg speech in January 2013. Hannan was a founder member of the Vote Leave campaign, helping steer this towards the national sovereignty issue: "Take Back Control".

Looking back, Hannan thinks that had Cameron recognised the importance of the issue of national sovereignty, he might have been able to achieve some repatriation of decision-making in his negotiations with the EU, instead of focusing on migration, and perhaps then won the referendum. More surprising, perhaps, is Hannan's contention that he had never expected a "hard" Brexit and would have favoured something akin to re-joining EFTA, with a continuing relationship with the EU. Had a Leaver taken over from Cameron, instead of the Remainer Theresa May seeking to prove her acceptance of the referendum result, then he thinks such a closer relationship could have been obtained by a PM with nothing to prove.

In June 2022 Hannan wrote that "Staying in the Single Market, or large parts of it, would have saved us a lot of trouble" – a comment which led Boris Johnson to tell this author that Hannan was "a paladin of principle except for his strange views about the single market".

Today Hannan says he is still slightly taken aback as to how bitter – and tribal – the arguments post-referendum became within the Conservative Party. Others might raise an eyebrow at someone who had so single-handedly pushed for withdrawal to be surprised at the depth of division that resulted. Whether or not known at the time to fellow colleagues, or only on the publication of Michael Crick's opus on Farage, loyal Conservatives will have been somewhat shocked to learn of Hannan's secret encouragement to the Conservative MP, Douglas Carswell, to defect to UKIP as part of their shared Eurosceptic strategy, a deliberate attempt as they saw it to detoxify the UKIP brand. The two had long worried about the challenge of reaching 50% in a referendum if the main Exit party was the unpopular UKIP whilst also losing faith in whether Cameron would honour his Bloomberg speech. By any measure, an elected Conservative engineering a colleague's defection would hardly have attracted bouquets from anywhere in the party.

Pro-EU Conservative MEPs see his role even more negatively, especially in the light of his success. They disapproved of his "usurping" of procedures and his near obsessive pursuance of withdrawal which they saw as contrary to both UK and Conservative interests. They also recall his internal party maneuverings over officer elections and the move of the party out of the EPP and into the ECR effected under Cameron, to the detriment, as they see it, of their relations within the Parliament and the prime minister's with his fellow heads of government.

Tim Kirkhope, whom Daniel replaced as leader, still finds Hannan's way of doing politics and his near absence from core parliamentary and group work distasteful. By contrast, his long-term colleague both in the EP and now in the Lords, Martin Callanan, told the author:

> "Hannan made a big impact within the Parliament for his exposure of the egregious abuses of expenses, but his main impact was using the platform provided (including his attack on Gordon Brown) to promote his views. His South East Region seat gave him full access to about 100 constituency parties within the largest Tory area in the country."

Nigel Farage, whilst calling Hannan the "high priest of Euroscepticism" is critical only of his failure to join UKIP.

Asked how he himself views his time in the European Parliament, Hannan says this is (positively) coloured by the happy four years he lived in Brussels with his wife and two daughters, and he even now hates "Brussels" being used as shorthand for the much-disliked EU. It's unclear what his next challenge will be. Still only just past 50, it's hard to believe that only journalism and the occasional Lords speech will keep this campaigner happy, much as the UK's Remainers would have liked to see him sidelined many years ago. He sits on the Parliamentary Partnership Assembly, which brings together EP and UK parliamentarians, so hasn't put that part of his life behind him just yet. He has been active in support of Ukraine and in attacking Russia's aggression, and he retains a strong interest in European history and culture. What a shame, some might say, that his fluency in Spanish and French, and his energy, hadn't been used to build and fashion a new EU rather than to extract us from our continental friends and partners. A great big "What if ...?" is left.

14. Malcolm Harbour

by David Harley

Malcom Harbour's enthusiasm for the European single market was a constant theme of his professional and political life, even before becoming an MEP. In his early career designing cars and vans, he saw the unnecessary and costly complexity of different national regulations. Later, when he ran sales and marketing operations, he saw at first hand the real benefits of barrier-free markets.

When he arrived in Brussels in 1999 as a newly elected MEP, he joined the EPP-ED, the largest political group in the Parliament, thanks to an agreement on continued Conservative support for a centre-right alliance reached by his party leader, William Hague. Harbour was allocated a place on the Legal Affairs and Internal Market Committee and was soon appointed rapporteur for his first legislative report, on the safety of motor vehicle fuel tanks.

Acting as rapporteur on this issue was a useful introduction to how MEPs could shape the legislative process, and the influence wielded by the political group co-ordinators in the various parliamentary committees. The subject of the report was highly technical, but Harbour soon discovered that every aspect of the single market had both political salience and practical consequences for the sector concerned. Harbour was immediately approached by the European Motorcyclists' Federation who were extremely concerned about accidents to their members caused by diesel spillage. His first contribution to EU legislation was a short additional clause highlighting their concerns, and he subsequently retained positive links with the motorcycling community throughout his time as an MEP.

Over the following five years, the committee approved landmark legislation around the emerging digital market, the growth of the internet and the development of mobile communications. Harbour was rapporteur on electronic communications, shaping the competitive and consumer legislation which laid the grounds for investment and market expansion. On his return to Parliament after the 2004 elections, he was elected EPP co-ordinator for the newly formed Committee on the Internal Market and Consumer Affairs (IMCO).

A crucial dossier for the incoming Barroso Commission was a directive to create a single market for services, which was also a long-standing priority for the British government. In 2002, a report drawn up under the Prodi Commission had set out a long list of barriers that service companies were experiencing. In 2004, Commissioner Frits Bolkestein launched an ambitious and wide-ranging services directive to remove them. Harbour had been appointed "shadow rapporteur" for the EPP-ED on this dossier before his re-election in 2004 and continued with this responsibility under his new mandate.

In the run-up to the 2004 elections, strong opposition to the proposal – now colloquially known as the Bolkestein directive – was stirred up by some left-wing parties. The Commission came under severe pressure from some member states to withdraw the proposal. Antagonism to "Bolkestein" was seen as one of the factors contributing to the rejection of the Constitutional Treaty in the 2005 French referendum. Within the EP there was broad opposition among the centre-left groups, on the grounds that the proposed directive, if not substantially amended, would lead to "a race to the bottom" between workers in different member states and result in social dumping.

When the new Parliament started work, the directive had few vocal supporters. The EPP-ED group had done well in the 2004 elections, and as their leading player on single market issues Harbour was determined to deploy the group's political strength to make a significant advance for the single market. In seeking to build the necessary consensus across the group, Harbour was encouraged by strong support from MEPs from the new member states who saw services liberalisation as a significant opportunity for underpinning economic growth.

The EPP-ED group tabled amendments to restructure the directive without diluting its effectiveness. In November 2005, with support from the Liberals and other centre-right parties, the committee supported the revised text by 25 votes to 10. The success of this approach was reflected in the fact that there were only 5 abstentions, including that of the rapporteur, the German socialist member, Evelyne Gebhardt.

In February 2006 the full Parliament approved the changes at first reading by 391 votes to 213 with 34 abstentions. Commissioner McCreevy, who had inherited this controversial proposal, declared that he would use this as the basis for a fresh proposal which he tabled for a second reading in April 2006.

To be successful in co-decision, MEPs had to work with the member states who negotiated with them in the Council of Ministers. Harbour frequently briefed national officials in Brussels, and sometimes their ministers, on issues falling within the competence of his committee. Support from the country holding the Council presidency, who chair the negotiation meetings, was crucial. In early 2006, there were worrying reports from Austria, the incoming presidency, that their support might be wavering. In the margins of an EPP-ED meeting, Malcolm Harbour was able to secure a meeting with Chancellor Wolfgang Schüssel and his industry minister, Martin Bartenstein, where he managed to persuade them that an agreement was within reach on the basis of Parliament's comprehensive proposal.

Bartenstein was enthusiastic and took the unusual step of inviting a small delegation of MEPs to an informal Competitiveness Council to make their case. Harbour took the lead for the EPP-ED in presenting Parliament's position at this meeting, on a sunny May morning in Graz, after which Bartenstein skilfully opened the way to the final agreement. It was formally agreed by the Council in May 2006 and adopted by Parliament in November.

The services directive outcome demonstrated the ability of Parliament to produce workable compromises, and its effectiveness in brokering agreement across EU governments. A Financial Times editorial in February 2006 noted:

> "That is where the European Parliament has suddenly come into its own. It marks another shift in power between the three central EU institutions. Last week's vote suggests that the directly elected MEPs, in spite of their multitude of ideological, national and historical allegiances, have started to coalesce as a serious and effective EU institution, just as enlargement has greatly complicated negotiations inside both the Council and Commission."

In 2009 the British Conservatives, following a pledge made by David Cameron on his election as leader, left the EPP and joined a new parliamentary alliance. Re-elected, Harbour returned to the IMCO committee as a member of the European Conservatives and Reformists, which nominated him as chairman of the committee. His first task was to work with the co-ordinators to introduce a more strategic approach, using political initiative reports to shape policy positions well ahead of receiving legislative proposals. They gathered information from public hearings and meetings with national parliamentarians. This was appreciated by external stakeholders, and members valued the opportunities that were created for them to be more influential.

The IMCO committee successfully scrutinised, improved and achieved agreement with Council on a wide range of measures covering many of the foundational single market rules. These included mutual recognition of qualifications, consumer rights, European standardisation, and public procurement. They advocated a market relaunch that pulled together a range of legislative and non-legislative actions. Commissioner Michel Barnier was enthusiastic and chaired a team of 10 commissioners who presented "The Single Market Act – twelve levers to boost growth and strengthen confidence in the economy" in April 2011. It was followed up with the Single Market Act 2 in October 2012.

Malcolm Harbour retired as an MEP in 2014 and was awarded a CBE in 2013 for 'Services to the British economy'.

President of the Parliament Henry Plumb (second from right), meeting members of an Icelandic delegation. His adviser, David Harley is on the right of the picture.

(l-to-r) David Harley, by now secretary-general of the Socialist group; Martin Schulz, leader of the Socialist group; and Julian Priestley, the secretary-general of the European Parliament, in London in June 2005.

Photo courtesy of and © Susanne Oberhauser

A newly elected 32-year-old Alan Donnelly in October 1989. He was pitched straight into a key role for the Parliament on German reunification.

Claude Moraes, longstanding chair of the influential Committee on Civil Liberties, Justice and Home Affairs, pictured in 2018.

Caroline Lucas, one of the first two UK Green MEPs, who went on to become the first Green MP at Westminster.

Two of the leading pro-European thinkers and advocates among British MEPs. Above: Brendan Donnelly, elected for the Conservatives in 1994 but who left the party over its increasing Euroscepticism and went on to become director of the Federal Trust. Below: Andrew Duff, Liberal Democrat MEP from 1999 to 2014 and co-founder of the federalist Spinelli group. Here, looking suitably sombre, he is seen at a hearing of the EP Constitutional Affairs Committee on "lessons to be drawn from the 2019 elections".

Graham Watson speaking in plenary in 2013. He led the Liberal group in the European Parliament from 2002 to 2009.

Edward McMillan-Scott: leader of the Conservative MEPs who left the party over its Eurosceptic drift and subsequently sat for the Liberal Democrats. He was a longstanding vice-president of the Parliament.

Ken Collins in 1984: the ultimate example of an MEP who exercised influence as a longstanding committee chair, in his case of the Environment Committee.

Malcolm Harbour in 2014: Conservative who helped shape the single market.

Voices of the coming Eurosceptic tide: Christopher Heaton-Harris (left) and Roger Helmer in 2004; both were then Conservatives, but Helmer later switched to UKIP.

Conservative MEP Daniel Hannan: Nigel Farage called him "the high priest of Euroscepticism".

James (Jimmy) Goldsmith: his Referendum Party was a forerunner of UKIP, though Goldsmith himself sat as an MEP for a French constituency from 1994 until his death in 1997

29 January 2020: mission accomplished. Nigel Farage speaking in plenary on British withdrawal, with two days left to go.

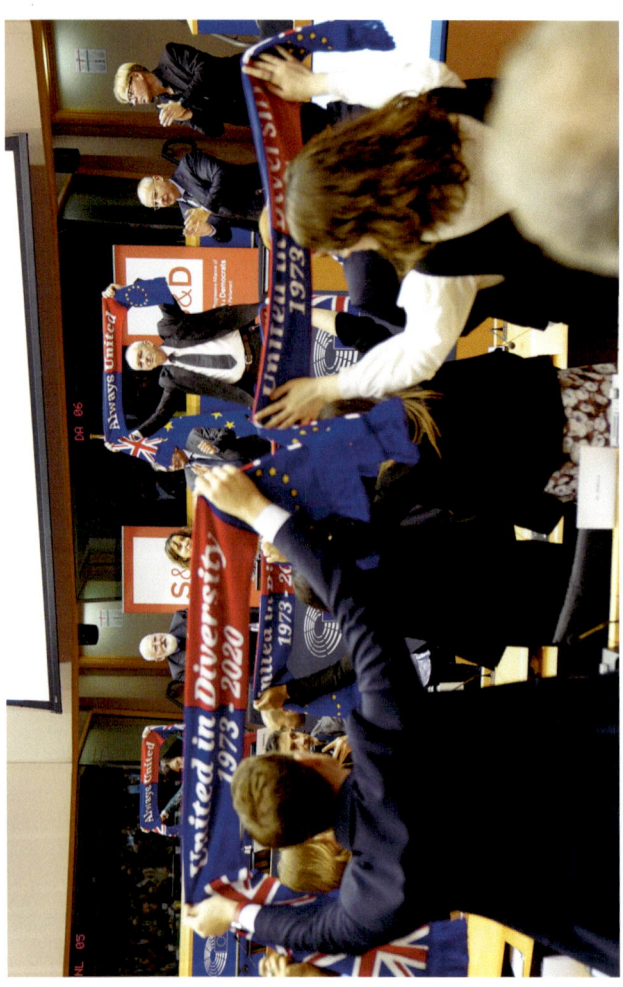

29 January 2020: defeated but defiant. Richard Corbett, the last British Labour leader (3rd from right at back) holds aloft an "Always United" scarf (see Part VII:1).

IV: AS THEIR CHILDREN SAW THEM

1. Nicholas Bethell

by William Bethell

William Bethell is a chartered accountant who has spent most of his career in financial regulation. After stints at the FSA, JP Morgan and HSBC, he is currently head of compliance at Abu Dhabi Commercial Bank. His father, Nicholas, was a nominated member of the European Assembly from 1975 to 1979 and an elected member from 1979-94 and again in 1999-2003.

"The reasonable man adapts himself to the world: the unreasonable one persists in trying to adapt the world to himself. Therefore, all progress depends on the unreasonable man."

George Bernard Shaw

Nicholas was born in 1938 and aged two, shortly after the onset of the war, was evacuated to the USA. Reportedly, the convoy in which he travelled was hit hard by U-boat attacks. When he returned, his parents had separated, and he was sent off to boarding school, which he hated.

Cambridge followed Harrow, and then came National Service, which, for him, meant the Russian course at the Joint Services School for Linguists (JSSL), near St Andrews, where he met my mother. He became fluent in Russian, Polish (self-taught), French, Arabic, Persian and Latin. The Russian emigrés who taught him at the JSSL told horrific tales of Stalin's cruel and totalitarian regime, which led him to detest the Soviet system. These experiences made the man. Above all, in the aftermath of WWII, he was a man of peace.

When I was a boy, my dad was my hero. He fought for freedom of speech, human rights and justice, against malevolent forces, armed only with a dilapidated briefcase, a daisy wheel typewriter and an extraordinary gift for languages. I was also aware from an early age that his enemies did not eschew violence. The murder in 1978 of Georgi Markov, whose wife Annabel is my godmother, left no room for doubt that the stakes were high.

Our home was in Sussex Square, near Hyde Park. It was a large, imposing house. My brother James and I lived on the top floor, and Nicholas worked out of the ground floor dining room, dictating books, articles and letters, often in his silk pyjamas. Visitors would come and go. Foreign dignitaries, dissidents, journalists and shady characters with sideways glances. I am still haunted by the sight of an unspeakably gaunt and damaged Russian dissident arriving after several years in the Lubyanka. Who had done this to him?

The house had been acquired in 1972 with the proceeds of a libel action against Private Eye that was settled out of court. Auberon Waugh had implied that Nicholas had acted as a Soviet stooge when he had smuggled the manuscript of Solzhenitsyn's *Cancer Ward* from behind the Iron Curtain, translated it and had it published in the West. As if!

As a result of the Private Eye episode, Nicholas's ministerial career came to an abrupt halt. However, Mrs Thatcher put him forward as one of the nominated members of the European Assembly (the elected Parliament's forerunner) in 1975. This meant that the three of us would now be holidaying in Brussels, Strasbourg and Luxembourg, whilst our friends were in the Cotswolds or Cornwall. Whenever we went on Parliament business, there always seemed to be lots of parties, and non-stop chat about this great new venture that these erstwhile enemies had embarked upon. My pre-pubescent vocabulary was expanded to include such useful words as "plenary", "tripartite" and "reciprocity".

The 1980s were Nicholas's heyday. He was a relentless campaigner. If he started an argument, he would not let go until he had won, and didn't care whom he upset in the process. There was always some blowback, sometimes from unexpected sources. Somehow, Mrs Thatcher objected when he took Joshua Hassan, the chief minister of Gibraltar, to the Parliament, as this did not fit the government narrative at the time. The Labour group objected when he took Sir Bob Geldof to the Parliament to ask for more funds for Africa. They saw Saint Bob as "one of them" and couldn't understand why he was consorting with a Tory peer.

The Foreign Office had a fit when he brought two Soviet soldiers back from Afghanistan to highlight the war crimes being committed by the Soviets. Nicholas couldn't care a fig. He considered the Foreign Office to be populated almost entirely by faint hearts and appeasers. Mrs Thatcher, on the other hand, respected Nicholas's view that you had to present a strong front, especially to the Soviets. They despised weakness and saw conciliatory tones as a prelude to surrender. This meant that Nicholas and Mrs T had a solid working relationship, despite her increasing Euroscepticism, which led to heated debates, particularly about monetary union.

Nicholas was determined to drive the European project forward, as he saw it as the best way of guaranteeing that there would be no more conflict in Europe, and he remained convinced that the UK would join the euro one day. Despite their differences on economic policy, Mrs Thatcher would help Nicholas with his human rights campaigns, where possible. She received Yelena Bonner, Andrei Sakharov's wife, at 10 Downing Street, and when she met Mikhail Gorbachev in 1986 she started the conversation by demanding the release of Sakharov.

The European Parliament's Sakharov Prize was first awarded, in 1988, to Nelson Mandela. Nicholas had interviewed Mandela in Pollsmoor Prison in South Africa in 1984, at a time when a lot of Conservatives considered Mandela to be a Marxist and a terrorist. Nicholas explained to me over dinner that Mandela was the only man who could bring together the ANC, the Zulus (he had a strong relationship with Chief Buthelezi) and the Whites, and thus bring a peaceful end to apartheid. The prize was presented in Strasbourg to Mandela's grandson, Mandla, who was 14 at the time. I had the task of minding this tall but rather shy boy, making sure he was looked after during the trip and, when we parted, I presented him with a copy of the hit single "Free Nelson Mandela" by the Special AKA which I had purchased from Virgin Records in Marble Arch.

Nicholas did not mind taking extraordinary physical and financial risks. As a result of his anti-Soviet campaigns, he had been banned from visiting Russia since the early 1970s. This was an apt punishment, as he loved Russia and the Russian people. Finally, to his delight, he was allowed in during the glasnost era in early 1987. The three of us went with our old friend, Simon (now Lord) Wolfson, on a trip to Moscow and Leningrad. We visited Yelena Bonner in her flat in the Moscow suburbs and other prominent dissidents and refuseniks. We found it odd that, wherever we were, there always seemed to be a taxi waiting, and the drivers seemed to be unusually well dressed, with smart shoes and expensive watches...

As we were leaving Leningrad airport, a huge row broke out about currency controls, of all things. We were unable to change our unused roubles back into pounds, and we weren't allowed to take them out of the country. A standoff ensured as my father shouted in Russian at the officials, while the security guards fingered their AK-47s. Eventually, Nicholas settled the argument by throwing the roubles in the air, like confetti, whilst we looked on, in awe and terror. James, Simon and I were jolly pleased when we touched down at Heathrow. Nicholas took it all in his stride.

During the Gdansk shipyard strikes, Nicholas was arrested as he tried to get into Lech Walesa's compound. I heard the story unfold, with increasing concern, on the radio in my room at school. My mother was dead. Who was going to look after me? My schoolmates thought the whole thing was hilarious. Nicholas was released after a few hours. He described the incident in his memoirs as "irritating".

He bet the house on a legal action – Bethell v Sabena – designed to break the national airlines' cartel on European flights and bring down prices for consumers. He gave an interview that implied that, if he lost, his costs would mean that he would have to sell our home!

Needless to say, I had a few questions to ask when I next saw him. He laughed them off. Eventually, he won that fight, we kept our house, and we now have EasyJet, RyanAir and Tui. Some would say a mixed blessing.

At my 40th birthday party, Nicholas's sister, Sally, described our upbringing as "fascinating, and occasionally hair-raising" which is a fair assessment. Nicholas was a one-off, as a politician, a campaigner – and a father.

2. Bill Newton Dunn

by Tom Newton Dunn

Tom Newton Dunn is presenter and executive editor of TalkTV's flagship evening news programme, The News Desk. Previously, he was Times Radio's chief political commentator, and before that The Sun's political editor for 12 years. His father, Bill Newton Dunn sat in the European Parliament from 1979 to 1994, 1999 to 2014 and then again from 2019: he was the only British MEP elected in 1979 who was still a member when the UK left the EU in 2020. In 2000 he left the Conservative Party because of its increasing Euroscepticism and joined the Liberal Democrats.

Every political argument has opposing poles. The farthest left, the hardest right. The libertarian absolute, the totalitarian extreme. In Britain's eternal debate about its role in Europe, my father occupied the pro-European pole. He was the arch-federalist, the ultimate anti-nationalist, and the devout believer in the United States of Europe.

The Eurosceptics, who eventually morphed into the hard Brexiteers, were his mortal enemy. They eventually won (though only for now, he insists) but the war that Bill Newton Dunn and his tribe waged against them has lasted half a century to date and defined his entire political career. Thirty-one of those years for my father were spent in the European Parliament, making him England's longest serving MEP by the time it all ended. But politics for him began in Stockwell, not Brussels.

Being a Conservative in that part of south London in the mid-1970s could be a lonely business, because there weren't many of them. Bill chaired Stockwell Conservatives and used to team up with the chairman of Brixton Conservatives to knock on doors in some of their tougher patches for protection. His name was John Major. Both were looking for seats for the 1979 general election. My father got down to the last two in Putney and was narrowly beaten by a silver-tongued young QC, David Mellor. So Bill found a berth elsewhere.

A month later, the first direct elections to the European Parliament were held and Bill was voted in as the Tory MEP for Lincolnshire. I was five years old at the time, so have little memory of my dad doing anything else. Even then, I knew it was something important and that made me feel very proud. The older I grew, the more I engaged him over the dinner table about it all, and I'm fairly certain it was those precocious interrogations that gave me a taste for political journalism. After a brief conviction, aged around 10, that I would one day be prime minister, I soon came to an early realisation that I relished being a tomato thrower and not a tomato catcher like my father and other politicians. It's far more fun, and less hard.

Bill soon "went native" in Brussels, as Thatcher's No. 10 used to enjoy saying. My father and many of his generation born in the 1930s and 1940s felt a deep philosophical commitment to building a Europe that would never go to war with itself again. That only deepened once he was surrounded by an explosion of bonhomie of so many different cultures and languages crowding the Parliament's corridors and umpteen bars. That, plus working alongside an array of fascinating people (many of whom had held very high office in their home nations already), led him to believe Westminster, with its quaint traditions and unelected upper house, was the past and Brussels and Strasbourg the shiny future.

An early win for Bill in his new cause was to help persuade the European Parliament to propose majority voting in the Council of Ministers (effectively removing a national veto for many issues). In turn, the Council enforced it on a livid Margaret Thatcher. The prime minister hauled my father and other Tory MEPs into No.10

for a horrendous bollocking, which then turned into a two-way shouting match with Bill and several others. She never forgave them.

Thatcher and her friends were reported to have celebrated when my father and a few other Europhile Tory MEPs lost their seats in 1994. It was the tail end of the Major government, and true blue Lincolnshire went Labour red – the same way as hundreds of Tory constituencies up and down the land then did in the 1997 Blair landslide.

With the battle intensifying with his Eurosceptic "bastards", Major offered my father a peerage in the hope of bolstering his pro-European ranks in Westminster. My father turned it down, feeling it wasn't for him without a ministerial job to go with it, and preferring to bide his time for a return to Brussels.

He was re-elected as an MEP in 1999, on the same Tory ticket as arch-sceptic Roger Helmer. A decade later, neither man represented the Tories anymore. My father defected to the Lib Dems just 18 months later in 2000, citing the Conservatives' growing Euroscepticism and insisting – as many defectors have done before and since – that he "hadn't left his party, but his party had left him".

It was the pre-email age. I only learned of his personal bombshell when descending the steps of a Boeing 747 on my return to Heathrow from a romantic holiday in Cuba when I was finally able to check my mobile phone messages. The voicemail from my father was a vintage example of his characteristic sense of underplay: "Your father here. Hope you had a nice time in Cuba. I've defected to the Liberal Democrats. Your mother's well, toodle-pip for now".

And Roger Helmer? He defected to UKIP in 2012. I've often thought their opposing trajectories neatly summed up the civil war that was devouring their former party.

To tackle just that ever more vicious schism, David Cameron had promised the Brexit referendum, and it would become a reality if his government was re-elected in 2015. Actually, leaving the EU was only ever a fringe cause that was not believed in even by many Tory MPs who went on to become prominent Brexiteers. Many of them told me so. But as soon as Cameron made it a 50/50 realistic option, it began to develop as a popular bandwagon.

While never a strong Europhile or Europhobe myself (I was one of those middle of the roaders that once made up so much of the country), it was around then that I began to clash with my father over the onward march of ever closer European integration. Whether it was the right or wrong thing was not my beef with him. It was that I could quite painfully see its proponents were leaving the people behind. As it turned out, quite a significant few of those alienated voters lived in his patch of Lincolnshire.

Bill's second European Parliament innings again came to an end, again involuntarily, in May 2014 with an almost entire clear out of Lib Dems – who went from 12 MEPs down to one. As the junior coalition partner, Nick Clegg's party was deeply unpopular and its Westminster base was also destroyed a year later at the general election.

Aged 73, my father had had a good innings by then and had come to terms with hanging up his parliamentary pass – having promised my long-suffering mother (plus me and his two new grandsons) at the previous election that he wouldn't stand again. What is it with politicians and promises, eh? Because there was one more swansong to come. The much-depleted Lib Dems asked Bill to stand as a paper candidate in the Euro-elections in May 2019. In doing so, he became the only Brit (and possibly the only person in any of the member states) to contest all nine European elections between 1979 and 2019.

To his immense surprise, and at the grand age of 78, Bill was re-elected as a Lib Dem MEP for the East Midland region, alongside a Labour candidate and three from the Brexit Party. Not a single Tory MEP was returned in this once Tory bastion region in what became the party's worst national election for 100 years, as well as the death knell for Theresa May's premiership. It also made my father the only surviving MEP elected to the first European Parliament in 1979 who was still there 40 years later.

With the British people's decision to leave the EU long in place by then, the swansong would never last long. My father made one of the last speeches ever by a British MEP in the European Parliament on 29 January 2020. It was the Parliament's final plenary session before the United Kingdom formally left the European Union at 11pm Greenwich Mean Time two days later.

Tieless by then, as was the way of many in the Liberal group, he rose from his seat to tell the Brussels hemicycle of "his immense pride in helping to contribute to the uniting of Europe". He added:

> "We are all small nations in Europe now. We have to work with other Europeans to resist the superpowers – Russia, China, America and India. We're going to get a very bad time as we discover reality, and then I think we'll be back".

Will we? I can't see it – or not at least in the political short and middle term. But if we are, it wouldn't be the first time my father had caught a political tomato and returned it with vigour.

3. Stanley Johnson

by Rachel Johnson

Rachel Johnson started her journalistic career at the Financial Times as the paper's first female graduate trainee. She has also worked at the BBC and most national newspapers, with stints in Washington DC and Brussels. She hosts LBC radio on Sunday nights and a podcast called Rachel Johnson's Difficult Women and is the author of eight books, most recently "Rake's Progress", an account of her doomed attempt to become an MEP in the 2019 election. Stanley Johnson sat as a Conservative MEP from 1979 to 1984, having prior to that worked at the European Commission.

My father Stanley (born 1940) is a man of evergreen optimism and energy.

The Daily Mail's epithet for him became "omnipresent father of the PM" which does not begin to cover his lifetime contribution to animal welfare, pollution control, wildlife, the environment, Exmoor, and his equally unflagging service to his multitudinous family and friends, his six children and rugger team of grandchildren.

Right from the start, he saw Britain as being at the heart of Europe (if not quite the heart and soul of Europe, as he is at every event he attends). A gregarious multi-lingual internationalist who grew up on a primitive hill farm in Somerset with parents of French and Turkish origin, he was a natural first-footer when it came to Britain's participation and influence in what was then the EEC.

He was also one of this country's first Jolly Green Giants when it came to the environment, an early advocate for our natural world and all that is in it (possibly, I would add, with the exception of one species: homo sapiens. As children, when we would ask him over breakfast if he had to choose to save the last of a rare species of monkey, or all four of us, he would unhesitatingly nominate the monkey).

Britain's accession in 1973 thus provided him with the perfect platform for what he wanted to do – and the delivery system for how he wanted to do it.

Even though he'd read Classics at Oxford and only scraped Maths O level at Sherborne, and the Brussels bosses wanted a proper boffin, his chutzpah led him to pitch from London for a plum job in the Environment and Consumer Protection Service of the Commission. He got it. And so it was we all moved – Stanley, my mother Charlotte, plus their four children, to Brussels. He was 32.

His title – Head of the Division for the Prevention of Pollution and Nuisances – sounded dull to me compared to "diplomat" or "journalist" but what the job description lacked in glamour it made up in importance. My father was an A3 (two down from director-general); we lived in a succession of large *villas-avec-jardin* and he loved it.

The living was easy and the lunch-hours so long he would come home for lunch, a quick game of tennis with a fellow *fonctionnaire*, and then cycle back to the Berlaymont, often one-handed as he was dictating a thriller (he is the author of dozens of books and eleven novels) into his dictaphone on his way to and from the office.

He enrolled us (his children, Boris – then called Alexander, me, Leo and Joseph) in the European School, on the Avenue Vert Chasseur, to become *bons petits Européens* (with, as you might agree, not unmixed results).

But the lifestyle – the long lunches, the wild dinners, the weekends in the Ardennes – was not why he loved it. He believed and continues to believe that Britain in Europe was helping to do God's work. "Would the Member States, without the push from the Brussels Commission, have ever adopted such a mass of environmental legislation covering as it did a whole range of subjects – air, noise, water, chemicals, waste, nature protection etc? No, in my view, they certainly wouldn't have" he wrote in the second volume of his autobiography, *Stanley I Resume* (the first volume is called *Stanley I Presume* and both are *vaut le voyage*, though I speak as a loyal daughter). "Though individual countries might have developed their own legislation, it would never have been as coherent and comprehensive as that adopted at the European level. And, by definition, purely national legislation would not have been continent-wide."

Fast forward six years from our arrival in Brussels. As the Treaty of Rome had prescribed, in 1979 it was writ that the first European Parliament of 410 members was to be directly elected by universal suffrage. My father has always had political ambitions (a cover interview with Saga Magazine in 2019 after his son had become prime minister and first lord of the Treasury was headlined "It should have been ME!") and has never been backwards about coming forwards. He was duly selected to contest the seat for Hampshire East and the Isle of Wight for the Conservative Party.

He rented a Hansel-and-Gretel cottage in a dark wood owned by a local grandee, Lord Bessborough, to be in the constituency for the campaign. We would visit him on dreary weekend exeats to observe his lack of practical or domestic skills, i.e. chain-sawing off the branch he was sitting on up a tree, or putting the chicken for Sunday lunch in the oven in its plastic wrapping.

Polling day was a gala day for the Johnson household. We were all hauled out of our various boarding schools to "rally round". My father's campaign slogan was "A Strong Britain in a Strong Europe" (which he cleaves to, to this day). Rallying round meant standing gormlessly about, wearing rosettes, and poxing the place with "Vote Johnson" stickers before piling into the family car – a Fiat 125 – which actually caught fire on the motorway as we were en route to inspect my father's piles (still his favourite political joke) at Portsmouth Town Hall.

We arrived slightly singed, and very late, at the count, where my father was returned with the second largest majority in the country. Turnout in the UK that June was only around 30% (until the Brexit referendum, "Europe" was a subject of infinite boredom and zero salience electorally) but it was – another favourite Johnson phrase – a total success.

At that time, the Parliament gravy-trained pointlessly between Brussels for committee sessions, and plenaries in Strasbourg or Luxembourg. Once or twice, I accompanied my father for asparagus binges in auberges along the route des vins. He had a whale of a time, doing what he loved: saving seals from being clubbed on ice floes in Canada, or steering important directives on habitats or wildlife or animal welfare through Parliament.

At the beginning, MEPs' work was mainly advisory, but he reminds me now that Maastricht, the treaty that inter alia established the eurozone, also bequeathed the right of co-decision to the Parliament, which meant that MEPs actually got to legislate and do stuff. MEPs, in fact, had more power than MPs.

This is why, I suppose, as a young mother I returned to Brussels, and as relief from the hard yards of looking after three tiny children I worked in the European Parliament for the leader of the Tory MEPs, Edward McMillan-Scott. I shared an office with Kate (now Baroness) Fall, who went on to become David Cameron's self-proclaimed "gatekeeper" in Downing Street, and when my children came to lunch at the excellent subsidised canteen, I would take them up to my office afterwards so they could swivel in my chair and gaze out over the architectural wasteland of the Quartier Européen. Although Brussels was – and had been – getting a very bad press (I refer you to mythical tales of the exploding Berlaymont, bendy bananas, prawn cocktail crisps etc), my children were terribly impressed and thought the whole building – including the famous hemicycle – was my private domain. "Mummy's office is MUCH bigger than Daddy's" they would whisper to each other.

It also helps to explain why, in 2019, I put myself forward to be a candidate for the doomed Change UK party led by nine Remainer MPs, which famously fought every seat in the Euro-elections that year and failed to win a single one.

And then, come January 2020, the UK left the EU and we had no MEPs in Brussels or anywhere else. *Sic transit gloria mundi!*

My father still continues to campaign for all the causes and issues that he cares about more than life: pollution, animal welfare and the environment. He is determined to call out any government – even one led by his own son – if it falls short of its commitment to uphold or even improve on EU standards when it comes to the quality of air and water, as well as protecting nature and wildlife. "We may be on different sides of the Channel from our continental partners, but we live in the same bio-geographical region. It is as much in Europe's interest for the UK to have a strong and effective environmental policy as it is in ours" he says. He has started, and he will finish.

I am very proud of all he has done, and my futile gesture with and for Change UK was of course in part a daughterly tribute to him and his life's work.

It would take a writer of the comic genius of Spike Milligan to document the true and real story of the Johnsons' part in the rise and fall of the EU; it would take an analyst with the insight of Freud to ascertain whether Brexit was, at root, an Oedipal conflict that could only be resolved on a continental scale.

I might conclude by observing this. My father applied for and got a French passport, to retain mobility and residence rights in the European Union. "It's not a question of becoming French. If I understand correctly, I am French!" he explained. "My mother was born in France, her mother was completely French as was her grandfather." I hope the French take him to their hearts. After all, he was there at the start of the UK's marriage with the EU, just as I was part of its divorce, and I have no doubt he will continue to lobby and campaign on these causes till the end.

You can take Britain out of Europe, but you can't take Europe out of this Briton, my astonishing father – Stanley Johnson, former MEP. *Floreat Europa!*

4. Derek Enright

by Duncan Enright

Duncan Enright is a Labour & Cooperative cabinet member on Oxfordshire County Council and deputy leader of West Oxfordshire District Council, and was mayor of Witney in 2019-20. He is the owner of award-winning specialist medical publisher Evidence-based Networks Ltd, and director of LeaderShape Global Ltd. His father, Derek, was a Labour MEP from 1979-84 and also sat in the House of Commons from 1991 until his death in 1995.

Our five boxer puppies were born and raised in 1977 on pro-European propaganda.

For a decade we used oversupplied newspapers carrying the famous "The outcome is GOOD for Britain, GOOD for Europe" headline alongside an avuncular portrait of PM Harold Wilson as the lining for our lives. During the referendum my dad was the local organizer for "Yes to Europe", and despite delivering tens of thousands of the things, bales of newspapers sat in our garage for years – until my mum sold the house in 1999. They made good eco-friendly litter tray liners.

This was one of the first experiences I remember of European politics in the Enright household in Pontefract in the 1970s. My dad's enthusiasm for internationalism germinated in his youth, during the war, and flowered as a result of CND and other causes with an internationalist slant – nurtured by involvement in the

Young Christian Workers and the Justice and Peace Movement. Willy Brandt was an inspiration, and the global work of CAFOD and other agencies shaped his political growth. We all believed that socialism could not exist in one country alone, and the cause of justice and peace extended to our brothers and sisters in the developing world as much as the cold-war industrial and mining Yorkshire we inhabited.

It was natural that after a spell as a West Yorkshire metropolitan county councillor and chair of planning and transportation, Derek chose to expand his horizons and put his name forward to be the MEP in the first elected European Parliament. Initially he was unsuccessful for the nomination for Yorkshire West (which included Pontefract), but rather surprisingly he won selection for Leeds – the city seat in our largest nearby centre. The family didn't know what to make of it – we were ecstatic!

The nominations were handed in with great ceremony. The Labour Party fought patchily – diminished by in-fighting (largely triggered by a split over Europe but exploited by entryists), demoralized by the Winter of Discontent and the terrible general election loss. The pro-European Labour stalwarts carried the scarlet standard high, and Leeds voted Enright and Labour, after a hugely enjoyable campaign including hustings and car-cades through the city centre with blaring music. Our campaign theme was inspired by the George Cohan war propaganda anthem "Over There":

"Over there, over there,
There's a fight for your rights, Over there.
But Enright's coming, yes Enright's coming,
With red flags flying over there!"

It was an awful result for Labour. Liverpool, Leicester and large parts of London elected Tory MEPs. Once in Europe, though, the group of 18 Labour and SDLP MEPs became part of the largest group – the Socialist group – and were led by Barbara Castle.

The Enrights weren't sure what to make of Barbara. She had been the most frighteningly powerful voice in the No campaign in the referendum. Derek wasn't at all sure they would see eye to eye. In fact, they became as close as family, Barbara adopting Derek and the whole Enright clan, so that I became her bag carrier for many years at Labour conference. Barbara's view was that the British people had spoken in the referendum, and if they wanted her to battle for Britain inside the Parliament, then she would make damn sure Europe listened. That wasn't far from how Derek saw things. That small group of first MEPs laid a foundation for social Europe, union rights, international cooperation and development, and generally punched above their weight against Thatcher's regime at home.

One of the first actions of the new Parliament was to flex its muscles by voting down the budget of the whole European Community. Derek was firmly behind this – an unelected Commission was struggling with corruption, bloated with unaccountability, and needed to be brought to democratic heel. An unfortunate side effect was that it led to no expenses or salaries for MEPs being paid for the best part of a year until the impasse was resolved. Belated and heartfelt thanks to the manager of the Midland Bank, Pontefract – only he and his overdraft powers stood between the Enright family and destitution, though we children only learned of this later. MEPs' salaries were tied to Westminster rates, which left them among the most poorly paid in rather more expensive continental Europe. On the first day a taxi driver refused a tip from Derek on the grounds that his basic wage was somewhere close to double a UK MEP's.

In 1980 the family went on the first of a handful of trips to Strasbourg to visit the Parliament. We missed the first flight – a fate which befell Derek on more than one occasion. In those days there was fierce competition between the cities of mainland Europe to host the Parliament, and the mayor of Strasbourg entertained us royally in his Hôtel de Ville. This was when I first met Barbara, as we compared the various buffet items and settled on the chicken. Barbara always made sure her boys were well fed.

Summer holidays during the early 1980s were spent in Italy, as my father converted his fluent Latin and Ancient Greek into (never more than serviceable) Italian. His French was strong enough to give several speeches to local audiences. I remember these holidays as bliss – other children went too, and this was a relief as I could dump my three younger siblings and exercise a bit of teenage independence, one time sharing a decent stock of beer from a hotel fridge with a mate. The other MEPs were extremely impressive, and some were close friends such as Joyce Quin, Win Griffiths, Brian Key and Ken Collins. We hosted boisterous parties in Pontefract and I remember singing with John Hume. Interpreters were also part of the family, and Frances Edmonds was a favourite of Derek's. I recall spending a boozy Sunday lunchtime in the RAF Club, during a break in the Test Match at Headingley, with the hugely charismatic and talented left-arm spinner – her husband Phil Edmonds. International political stars included "Red" Heidi Wieczorek-Zeul and kind but cool Katharina Focke. On one occasion we were entertained by the local MEP, Vera Squarcialupi, an Italian Communist, in her ancestral home where the people who worked her land touched their forelocks as we passed.

Derek served on two committees and was extremely proud of their work. He boasted he was the only man on the Women's Committee, and whatever his input they laid the foundations of women's equality across Europe. His main love was the Aid, Trade and Development Committee. His passion was fair trade, and he played a significant part in the Lomé II treaty negotiations throughout which he championed trade rather than aid as a route to justice and peace. He continued this work after leaving the Parliament as European delegate to Guinea Bissau, where he controlled the largest aid budget but importantly expanded trade in goods and particularly fish – British fishermen helped build capacity and capability under his watch.

Derek was always aware of the need to promote Europe back home. His regular column in the Yorkshire Evening Post shared news of his work in an entertaining style that betrayed my mother's journalist influence and involvement. He even shared poems – now lost to posterity – which he would write during long sessions of the Parliament. Always with an eye to a good story, he introduced Tetley's Yorkshire Bitter to the Parliament bar, sharing a pint with continental colleagues in full media glare. His attempt to trump the French Golden Delicious apple with a homegrown variety was initially less successful, but became a hit when he couldn't find his samples as he scrabbled around with last minute packing for the press conference. He always did things at the last minute. In desperation, he spun a line that we children had eaten the lot, so delicious were they, and it became us, the hungry and thieving kids, who were in all the papers. Needless to say, the bag of apples was found under a pile of washing in the kitchen several days later. They still tasted pretty good.

Derek got on with pretty much everyone. Once he shared a taxi to the airport, at the last minute, with Dr Ian Paisley, the feisty Northern Irish politician and MEP. The two shared stories but became aware that in his haste to meet the flight the driver was breaking speed records. Dr Paisley leaned forward, tapped the driver on the shoulder, and said: "Young man, if you put your foot down any harder, we won't be needing that plane".

Despite the absences, most weeks and often during holidays, I remember my dad's time in the European Parliament as an exciting and happy one. My mum sometimes accompanied him, and we managed fine with grandparents in charge. The most alarming thing that happened was that my mum decided she needed to learn to drive; it is a miracle we are all alive to tell the tale. It was a great sadness for us when, at the height of Labour's civil war of the early 1980s, Derek was de-selected as an MEP along with other pro-Europeans. It seems politics at home matter more than what you achieve in Parliament. His collection of papers, probably including the poems, are now housed at the Bodleian Library in Oxford, a quirky record of that first elected European Parliament.

After his time as an MEP, Derek embarked on two more big adventures, alongside a period of frustrating lassitude. For two years he served as delegate (ambassador) for the EU in Guinea Bissau – one of the poorest countries in the world and a former Portuguese colony in West Africa. His commitment to international development and his deft political touch meant he built strong relationships in both the government and the diplomatic corps. Such was his reputation that he was awarded the highest honour of the country available to a foreigner, and at diplomatic meetings sat by the president in a place of seniority (bolstered by the significant funds and trade agreements garnered from Europe to build this nation just ten years after independence).

Derek saw his role as being to cement the bond between the developing nation of Guinea Bissau and its people, and the people of Europe, in a positive and inclusive way. To commemorate the 30th anniversary of the signing of the Treaty of Rome, in 1987, he decided that instead of a government and embassy event with cocktails and speeches, it would be better to include the nation in celebration. So the EU delegate sponsored a football tournament between the four top clubs. The prize was the Taca Schuman, the Schuman Cup, procured by Derek through friends who brought it from Lisbon. Five feet tall and splendid, it went on display to great admiration in a local shop window. The final is vividly described in his own words as "a very entertaining game" with "a carnival atmosphere".

After a period of enforced reflection and a return to Pontefract, he was selected to fight the Westminster by-election in Hemsworth after the death of George Buckley MP. Winning in style, he conducted a press conference in Latin alongside shadow minister Michael Meacher (Derek had been a classics teacher in the local comprehensive). This was merely a warning of things to come. In the Commons Derek caused a sensation when, during a debate on the unwelcome narrowness of the proposed national curriculum, he was dared by an opponent to back up his statement that bringing subjects to life in the classroom demanded unusual but impactful measures. He was invited to sing a Beatles song in Latin for the Chamber, as he had done in our classrooms in Yorkshire and indeed in the corridors in Brussels. Without hesitation he launched into a version of Yellow Submarine: "*Habitamus sub vitreo, sub vitreo, sub vitreo.*"

Doubtless he would have continued had he not been reminded of parliamentary protocol, which according to his good friend Geoff Lofthouse MP, the presiding deputy speaker, takes a dim view of MPs singing in Chamber.

To the regret of his many friends in Parliament and Yorkshire, Derek died before Labour achieved power in 1997. Geoff Hoon, a close friend and former Labour cabinet minister, writes movingly about Derek's death in St Thomas' Hospital, "looking out at a near perfect view of Parliament". Those final hospital visits were marked by laughter and reminiscence, including an impromptu visit by the shadow Treasury team led by Gordon Brown who tramped across Westminster Bridge "to see how Derek is" and spent a jolly but poignant half hour at his bedside. Geoff recounts a funny story by Derek, and recalls "I joined in the laughter but was actually closer to tears".

Sources

Geoff Hoon, *See How They Run*, Unicorn, 2021

B. Enright et al, *The Man Who Sang Yellow Submarine in Latin*, Pontefract Press, 1996

5. Roy Perry

by Caroline Nokes

Caroline Nokes is Conservative MP for Romsey and Southampton North and chair of the Women and Equalities Select Committee. As immigration minister she attended cabinet in 2018-19. Her father, Roy Perry, was Conservative MEP for Wight and Hampshire South from 1994-2004.

It would be fair to say I feel something of a fraud writing this, an account of an MEP's life from a child's perspective. I was hardly a child when my dad was elected to the European Parliament: 21 years old and about to graduate; but for girls at least imposter syndrome is nothing new.

I can still remember dad being chosen to fight Wight and Hampshire South in the 1994 European election. He was stunned that at the grand old age of 51 he had even been selected, notionally for a winnable seat, though the omens did not look great. The Tories were not exactly popular in 1994; his predecessor Richard Simmonds, a lovely man, was retiring through ill health; and the still relatively newly minted Liberal Democrats were making inroads across the south. His main contender was Mike Hancock, at one time the MP for Portsmouth South and infamous in many ways. I delighted in commenting, on my election to the Commons in 2010, that my dad was the last Tory to have beaten Hancock in an election! Of course, Flick Drummond also went on to do so in 2015, but by that time he was no longer a Liberal Democrat.

A lovely lady, Susan Burgess, confessed that during the selection process she had backed dad for no better reason than he was the same age as her, and that 51 was therefore not too old for a second career! And he proved that, serving as an MEP for two terms until rather unceremoniously dumped down the party list in 2004 for being too pro-European.

The 1994 election campaign was daunting for many reasons, not least the unpopularity of the Conservatives, who had been in government for 15 years, and that the massive geography of Wight and Hampshire South and the near half million electorate made it a challenging patch to cover. However, it was home (or very nearly). Not for us the slogging along the M4 to distant Swansea that my sister and I had endured when Roy was the candidate in the 1992 general election. The Euro constituency started just beyond Eastleigh, a mere 15 miles away, stretched up the M3 to Winchester, and all along the M27 to Havant. So you could get there relatively quickly, but once there, my goodness there were some doors to knock and miles to cover.

My best memories of the campaign came from the Isle of Wight. While one of the old boy's predecessors had commented that he had once seen the Isle of Wight from a cruise ship, dad took a very different attitude, and loved to go there. And the sun always shone on the island. To this day I think of the Isle of Wight, bathed in sunshine, with beautiful landscapes and beaches, and smile. Perhaps not so much when I was battling aggressive, snappy letter boxes with endless leaflets.

Election campaigns teach you many things: how to smile when a Yorkshire terrier is biting your ankle; the technique of dealing with vertical as opposed to horizontal letter boxes; and that low level ones are the ultimate curse. As a brand new graduate, it also teaches you to set your career ambitions higher than postman or woman – although in fairness it was not that European election that taught me that: any child of a politician learns it as soon as they are old enough to hold a stack of leaflets in one hand and roam off down a driveway on their own.

Dad always described himself as a "weekly boarder" in Brussels; God knows why, he had never been to boarding school. But it was a lifestyle adjustment for both him and mum. Nobody talks about the impact a politician has on their spouse, and arguably for MEPs it was much worse than it is for those of us in Westminster. But after 25 years of marriage, they were effectively separated during the week, and the weekends were spent at Tory fundraisers, local election campaigning or probably just sleeping off the effects of endless travel. A constituent once said to me "how privileged" my father was to have benefited from all that travel. I don't know how many weeks of his life he spent in departures at Heathrow or Brussels airport, or indeed arguing with Virgin Express about delayed flights and lost luggage. It makes my gripes about South Western Railway seem positively mild. But every child of an MEP surely discovered the acronym of the Belgian national airline Sabena: "Such A B***** Experience Never Again".

Finally, to reflect on the manner of dad's leaving, I recall the re-selection process ahead of the 2004 European election vividly. Having previously been number two on the South East list, he was unceremoniously dumped to number six – effectively de-selected. I can remember advising him then to just "tell them what they want to hear". Dad was pro-European, the Tory Party not so much and, full credit to him, he left with his integrity intact. He refused to take my advice. Little did I think that 15 years on I would find myself in an eerily similar position, chucked out of the Tory Party for refusing to sign up to what I regarded as a damaging No Deal Brexit.

I had always resented Europe for becoming the defining issue of the time, and I spent years in Parliament steadfastly refusing to talk about it. I had seen his moderate, pragmatic views force my father out of a role he loved, over bloody Europe. Little did I think I would ever follow in his footsteps. But as I tell people that I became a Tory in spite of my father, rather than because of him, it would be fair to say that I am clearly more than a chip off the old block.

V: THE NATIONS

1. Scotland

by Michael Russell

Michael Russell is professor in Scottish Culture and Governance at the University of Glasgow. He is also president of the SNP, having held senior positions in Scottish politics and government for many years, including as an MSP and Scottish government minister. He is the honorary president of the European Movement in Scotland.

Looking through the results of the nine sets of elections to the European Parliament held in Scotland between 1979 and 2019 is like looking through a series of snapshots of Scottish politics, with the fortunes of the respective parties and their constitutional viewpoints changing over those forty years in much the way that Scottish politics itself changed and diverged from the UK during a period which saw the re-establishment of a Scottish Parliament, a first independence referendum and four terms (so far) of nationalist government, currently in co-operation with the Green Party. Indeed, even now the EU and the European Parliament remain of importance in Scottish politics given that the issue of EU re-entry is a key part of the continuing intense constitutional debate.

In the first direct elections in 1979, the Conservatives took five of the eight Scottish seats. Yet so rapid was their fall that they could not secure even a single member in either 1989 or 1994 and were only saved by the introduction of proportional representation in

1999 (as also happened in the Scottish Parliament). In the 2019 European election, with the noise of Brexit all around, they managed to retain only a single member.

Labour quickly rose to dominance, taking five seats in 1984 but the party's decline thereafter was also precipitate, resulting in no members at all in that final ballot. The Liberal Democrats only secured representation once PR was introduced in 1999, and even then it was not continuous, with no member elected in 2014.

In contrast, the SNP, which in the doughty persona of Winnie Ewing had only just secured a place in 1979, thereafter never failed to have a member elected at any of the nine elections, something not matched by any other party. Winnie Ewing was the sole SNP representative until 1994 but thereafter there were two members returned at each election even though the overall number of seats allocated to Scotland dropped twice. At the final election in 2019 the party secured three of the six seats, having topped the poll for the third time in a row.

The change in party fortunes also points to a waning of initial Scottish Euroscepticism. Only two local authority areas in the entire UK voted against EC membership in the confirmatory referendum held in June 1975. Both were in Scotland and both were island groups – the Western Isles and Shetland. The negative vote in those areas was driven by a variety of factors including their remoteness from continental Europe, fishing (always a key European issue in Scotland) and, in the Western Isles, even religion. Scotland voted 58% to 42% to confirm UK membership compared to 68% in favour in England.

However, by the time of the 2016 Brexit referendum Scottish voters had become more persuaded of the benefits of EU membership, possibly by highly visible spending on infrastructure and perhaps also by a growing confidence in their own country. In 2016 every Scottish local authority area recorded a Remain vote (a unanimity not found in England, Wales or Northern Ireland) with the Scotland-wide outcome being 62% for Remain, compared to 53% for Leave south of the border.

Yet there are other stories which need to be told, ones which add a human dimension to the political statistics. Those are the stories of the 29 individuals who were elected as MEPs for parts, and then the whole, of Scotland and the work that they did for those who sent them to Brussels and – once a month – to Strasbourg.

The first direct elections in June 1979 took place on a constituency basis which in Scotland resulted in eight large (in some cases very large) areas each returning one member elected by first-past-the-post. That system remained in place until 1999 when the UK anticipated that a change to PR would be forced upon it if it did not introduce proportionality voluntarily.

Consequently, for the elections of that year Scotland became one of the 11 UK regions electing eight members by a list system. However, the number of MEPs allocated to Scotland fell to seven in 2004 and to six in 2014 (a decision made by the UK government without consultation with the Scottish Parliament) although Ireland – with a smaller population – actually increased its representation during that time.

Turnout in 1979 and at subsequent elections was very low, never rising above 40% across the country as a whole and falling to just below 25% in 1999. Partly as a result of this low turnout, some contests were close, particularly in the first round of elections.

The Conservative James Provan in the North East of Scotland won with only 33% of the vote and Winnie Ewing secured only one percent more in her hard fought battle in the Highlands and Islands against the Highland Liberal MP Russell Johnston, a result all the more surprising as she had lost her own Highland Westminster seat in the 1979 general election which took place only a month before the European vote.

In some areas, however, the results were more clear cut, with Labour's redoubtable Janey Buchan in Glasgow securing 49% of the vote and her fellow Labour MEP Ken Collins in Strathclyde East gaining just a fraction under 50%.

In Mid Scotland and Fife, the Conservative John Purvis, an international financial expert with family and farming roots in the area, was elected. He quickly set to work in Brussels as a member of the Economic and Monetary Affairs Committee, joining a subcommittee which laid the groundwork for the single market. UK Tory MEPs were in the greatest part enthusiasts for the development of the internal market and the alignment of standards across a wide range of goods; this was reflected in the role played by the then prime minister, Margaret Thatcher, in encouraging the development of the single market.

John Purvis was a good example both of the application that Scottish MEPs showed in a role which was little known or understood even by their own parties in Scotland, and of the vagaries of politics at home – as well as being, for all his political life, a keen exponent of European democratic and social values. He initially served for only a single term, losing in 1984 to Labour's Alex Falconer. However, he returned to the Parliament in 1999, having been elected as the second place nominee on the Tory party list, and this time served for two terms during which he was vice-chair of the Economic and Monetary Affairs Committee and was rapporteur in a number of significant inquiries.

Involvement in the detailed committee work of the Parliament and its development as an institution was seen by most Scottish MEPs as one of the prime purposes of participation. This was also possible because intensive individual constituency caseloads, the lot of most elected parliamentarians, were much less of a burden for MEPs, though most tried to establish and nurture links with local communities.

The most outstanding example of constructive and detailed engagement with the Parliament and its institutions by a Scottish MEP was Labour's David Martin. He sat as an MEP for 35 years until his defeat in 2019, making him the longest-serving UK member (and the second longest-serving of all the Parliament's members – see Part III.7). He took the Lothian seat at the second direct election in 1984, defeating the single-term Conservative, Ian Dalziel, and immediately threw himself into the work of the Parliament as well as the UK Labour and European Socialist groups. Rapporteur for the Parliament on the Maastricht and Amsterdam treaties, the youngest leader of the UK Labour delegation, a vice-president of the Parliament for a record 15 years and in 2002 the Socialist group candidate for president, he finally fell victim to the decline of Labour in Scotland when that party failed to secure a single seat in the 2019 election, obtaining only 9.3% of the vote – some two and half percentage points behind the Tories and five and half behind the Brexit Party.

Winnie Ewing of the SNP was a member of the UK delegation in the nominated European Parliament from 1975 while a Westminster MP, and then sat in the directly elected European Parliament from 1979 to 1999. Her EP career was second in length only to that of David Martin among Scottish MEPs. Ewing served as a member of the Lomé Committee which dealt with trade and aid involving 71 African, Caribbean and Pacific countries, and succeeded in bringing the Lomé Assembly to Scotland for the first time in 1985. She also secured European Objective One development status for the Highlands and Islands which resulted in significant new investment in infrastructure for her area. The French paper Le Monde was the first to call her "*Madame Ecosse*" given her visibility at home and abroad, and the name stuck. She did not seek re-election in 1999, preferring to join her third parliament as a founder member of the Scottish Parliament and – as the oldest member – opening the first session on 12 May 1999 with the words: "The Scottish Parliament, adjourned on the 25th day of March in the year 1707, is hereby reconvened".

Of the 29 elected Scottish members of the European Parliament, 10 served for only a single term, or part of a term, the shortest being that of the SNP's Heather Anderson, who replaced Alyn Smith for four days in late January 2020. The majority were active in areas of key importance to Scotland, the most common of which were fishing and agriculture though some, like Catherine Stihler (the youngest UK MEP when elected in 1999 as Catherine Taylor) combined that with other interests – in her case the economy, consumer rights and open access, the last of which led to her leaving the European Parliament before the final set of elections to work in that field.

Professor Sir Neil MacCormick, an SNP member elected in 1999, brought his experience as a distinguished legal academic to the task of membership of the Convention on the Future of Europe (as one of 16 participating MEPs nominated by the institution) which drafted the proposed (though eventually unratified) Constitutional Treaty on the European Union under the chairmanship of former French president Valéry Giscard d'Estaing.

Another Scottish MEP who pursued a professional interest to great effect was Ken Collins, the MEP for Strathclyde East from 1979 to 1999 and chair of the Environment Committee for two terms. A local authority planner by training, on retirement from the Parliament he became chair of the Scottish Environment Protection Agency, serving eight years in that post, bringing a wealth of high level European regulatory experience to the task.

Henry McCubbin, a one-term Labour member for the North East of Scotland, campaigned for increased safety in the offshore oil industry, the Piper Alpha Disaster of July 1988 having taking place the year before he was elected, whilst Bill Miller, a former Strathclyde Labour councillor, was active as a Labour whip and as a member of the Parliament's delegation to South East Asia and Korea.

Most Scottish MEPs were keen to work cross-party where possible to advance Scotland's interests and this "Team Scotland" approach was encouraged after devolution by successive Scottish governments, which used their presence at Scotland House in Brussels to provide briefings and opportunities for wider engagement with Scottish and European audiences. Some Labour members found it difficult to participate for a while after their party lost control of the Scottish Parliament, but such political sectarianism was eventually rare with the only MEP refusing to approach the matter positively being UKIP's David Coburn. Elected in 2014, Coburn publicly argued for Scotland House to close after Brexit and attended events there only to make his anti-EU views known and to condemn the Scottish government for its positive approach to the Parliament, Commission and Council of Ministers.

Unlike in Wales, hardline Brexit views never gained a foothold in the Scottish Parliament with no UKIP or Brexit Party representative ever elected, though at both the 2014 and 2019 European elections those views did garner sufficient support to take a seat. Coburn, a voluble former antiques dealer formerly based in London, was the lead Scottish UKIP candidate elected in 2014 (he was styled as "Scottish leader" of UKIP) but five years later he was not reselected by UKIP's successor, the Brexit Party, which placed a care home investor and property developer with no political experience in prime position for the unexpected 2019 poll. Louis Stedman-Bryce was notable as the first black candidate elected to parliamentary office in Scotland. However, on the left of his party, he eventually fell out with the Brexit leadership and, having withdrawn as the Glasgow East candidate for the 2019 Westminster general election, spent his last weeks in the European Parliament sitting as an independent.

Equalities issues were of growing concern to parties as they contended for election, the more so in that up until the 2019 election only five women had been elected as Scottish MEPs in 40 years, that total rising to 8 after the final poll. By 2019 most parties were trying at the very least to gender-balance their lists, though ensuring that equalities considerations counted in terms of securing winning places was still not as effective as it needed to be.

MEPs were usually experienced and time-served politicians, and the lure of politics at home remained strong for many, some of whom may have seen the post as a stepping stone to a domestic parliament, though it was never an easy or direct one.

Ian Duncan, the sole Tory elected from Scotland in 2014 and who had a background in fisheries research and European issues, was the Conservative candidate for Perth and North Perthshire in the 2017 Westminster election, failing to take the seat by only 21 votes. Nonetheless, only days later he was elevated to the House of Lords and became a UK government minister, being replaced as the Conservative MEP by another peer, Baroness Mobarik, former chair of the Scottish CBI, who agreed to retire temporarily from the House of Lords. The normal procedure of replacement by the next person on the list was not practised on this occasion (Baroness Mobarik having been third, not second on the 2014 Conservative list) resulting in threats of court action against the Scottish Conservative leadership by the person deliberately passed over.

Alyn Smith, who had been elected to Brussels for the SNP in 2004 to replace Sir Neil MacCormick, who retired after a single term to return to academic life, was elected as MP for Stirling in December 2019, thus having to resign his seat as MEPs may no longer serve simultaneously in two parliaments. In contrast, the other two SNP MEPs elected in 2019 had been MSPs, losing their seats at the 2016

Scottish Parliament election. One of them, Christian Allard, was a French citizen and former fish exporter who had served as a NE Scotland regional member at Holyrood and was also a local authority councillor in Aberdeen.

In all, seven of the 29 members elected over the four decades had either been members of other parliaments, or were subsequently elected to them, and a number of others had been local authority councillors. Two – George Lyon, a Liberal Democrat and former president of the Scottish National Farmers' Union who served one term from 2009, and Aileen McLeod, who was elected as an MEP in 2019 but had worked as an assistant to the SNP MEP Alyn Smith some years before – had also been ministers in the Scottish government. Lyon had held the junior finance brief in the Labour/Liberal coalition for its last two years, while McLeod was SNP environment and land reform minister from 2014 to 2016.

A number of members also sought to change constituencies or regions to seek re-election to the European Parliament after being defeated. This proved successful for James Provan, who lost in the North East in 1989 but returned as the member for the English constituency of South Downs West in 1994, subsequently serving two terms during which he was the Conservative whip.

Although the list system makes by-elections unnecessary, there was a European by-election in Scotland during the period before proportional representation. The NE Scotland European by-election resulted from the sudden death of Dr Allan Macartney, the then SNP deputy leader. It was held on 25 November 1998, and although the turnout only just topped 20% it resulted in a substantial victory for Ian Hudghton of the SNP, a local authority councillor in Angus, who took almost 50% of the vote in a six-way contest. He remained an MEP until retiring in 2019.

That final full election of 23 May 2019 had a turnout of almost 40%, making it one of the highest European polls experienced in Scotland. The UK government only finally conceded on 7 May 2019 that the election would have to take place, having hoped that the UK's formal departure from the EU would dispense with any need to participate. However, the planned exit date of 29 March 2019 (two years after the submission of the Article 50 letter) was not met and although the UK government, expecting a disastrous result, tried to find a way to avoid the poll, at the very final minute it had to concede that there was no alternative.

As anticipated, the Tories were humiliated, securing only 4 of the 73 UK seats and the newly formed Brexit Party gaining 29. In Scotland the SNP took 3 seats, and the Conservatives, Liberal Democrats and Brexit Party one each, though the Greens failed yet again to secure a place: they never succeeded in having an MEP elected in Scotland despite their constant presence in the Scottish Parliament.

The term of office of those elected at the end of May 2019 lasted longer than they and most commentators expected, the UK's final departure from the EU being delayed on several occasions and only taking effect on 31 January 2020.

Re-entry to the EU – and therefore a renewed Scottish involvement in the European Parliament – by means of negotiation after a successful independence referendum remains the policy of the SNP and Greens, with the Scottish Conservatives firmly opposed. Independence is also resisted by Labour and the Liberal Democrats but those parties' policy in Scotland on re-joining the EU is less clear, and they continue to take a more pro-EU and anti-Brexit line than their Westminster leadership.

It is therefore an open question as to whether the departure of Scottish members from the European Parliament on the 31 January 2020 marked the end of Scottish representation in that institution or merely a pause in their active and positive presence.

2. Wales

by Gareth Williams

Gareth Williams worked in the European Parliament's Socialist group in the early 1990s. He founded and managed for 15 years a Welsh-focused social research consultancy and for five years was a special adviser to the Welsh first minister.

Wales is a small nation and, as a constituent part of a member state, its representation in the European Parliament did not match that of member states with equivalent populations. Wales generally was represented by four MEPs although from 1994-2004, prior to enlargement to the Central and Eastern European nations, there were five.

Nevertheless, it would appear (at least to this not unbiased observer) that Wales punched above its weight in terms of its representation. Not only, in Glenys Kinnock, did it have one of the few MEPs genuinely to have a UK-wide profile (as well as being a distinguished co-chair of the EU-African, Caribbean and Pacific Parliamentary Assembly) but it also provided a leader of the European Parliamentary Labour Party (Wayne David), a leader of the Conservative group (Jonathan Evans), the youngest MEP elected in 1994 (Eluned Morgan), two vice-presidents of the EP (Allan Rogers and Win Griffiths), a chair of the delegation to the USA (Jonathan Evans), the Socialist group spokesperson on budgetary control at the time of the sacking of the European Commission (Eluned Morgan), a distinguished member of the Economic and Monetary Affairs Committee and the Special Committee on the Financial, Economic and Social Crisis (Kay Swinburne), and one of the longest-serving British MEPs (Jill Evans).

This chapter, based partly on responses to questions by the majority of the former MEPs alive at the time of the research, first gives a brief history of Welsh representation before considering MEPs' experience prior to their election, their achievements and their regrets, followed by their political and general careers after standing down from Parliament. It then draws some brief conclusions.

A brief history of Welsh representation

Despite the first direct elections to the European Parliament following hot on the heels of the 1979 general election which propelled Margaret Thatcher to power, in Wales Labour won three of the four seats (South Wales, South-East Wales and Mid & West Wales) relatively comfortably with Win Griffiths, Allan Rogers and Ann Clwyd comprising 15% of the British Labour group.

In North Wales, Beata Brookes won the seat for the Conservatives – and in the process became the only non-Labour politician to be elected to the EP from Wales during the years before proportional representation. She held the seat in 1984 (with Labour and the Alliance neck and neck on around 25% of the vote), while elsewhere Win Griffiths was re-elected in South Wales, with Llew Smith and David (Dai) Morris winning the South-East Wales and the Mid & West Wales seats in succession to Allan Rogers and Ann Clwyd, who had both been elected in the 1983 general election in the neighbouring Westminster seats of Rhondda and Cynon Valley.

At the third European election in 1989, Win Griffiths stood down, having been selected to fight the Bridgend constituency (though not yet having been elected to Westminster), and Wayne David was elected in his place in South Wales. David Morris and Llew Smith were comfortably re-elected, while in North Wales Joe Wilson took the seat from Beata Brookes by a small margin, giving Labour a monopoly on Welsh representation in the European Parliament.

As a result of the enlargement of the Parliament in 1994, Wales gained a fifth seat, with Eluned Morgan, at 27, winning the new seat of Mid & West Wales for Labour – a result which would have been surprising in any other European election year, but was not in the context of Labour winning 62 of the 84 seats in Great Britain. In North Wales, Joe Wilson was comfortably re-elected while in South Wales, Glenys Kinnock, Wayne David and David Morris piled up huge majorities in the new constituencies of South-East Wales, South Wales Central and South-West Wales, Llew Smith having stood down following his election to Westminster in Blaenau Gwent in 1992.

In Wales, as elsewhere in Great Britain, the introduction of proportional representation marked a fundamental *caesura* in electoral history. Whereas under first-past-the-post Labour had been totally dominant, the 1999 election saw an erosion of its position. This was the result not just of the electoral system but of a deeply divided Welsh Labour Party, following a contested leadership election in the run-up to the first elections to the National Assembly and poor results in those elections a month earlier. Labour's share of the vote – an incredible 56% in 1994 – fell to 32%, while Plaid Cymru came second, with nearly 30% compared to 17% at the previous European election.

The 1999 elections thus saw Glenys Kinnock and Eluned Morgan returned for Labour, Jill Evans, a former chair of Plaid Cymru, and Eurig Wyn taking Plaid's first ever seats and Jonathan Evans becoming Wales's second Conservative MEP. With enlargement to Central and Eastern Europe imminent, Wales lost a seat and reverted to four MEPs in 2004. As a result, Plaid Cymru lost its second seat (Eurig Wyn having decided to stand down), with the other three members being re-elected.

By contrast, 2009 – a low point for Labour support – saw major changes, with the Conservatives topping the poll, and Kay Swinburne elected in place of Jonathan Evans, who had stood down to run in the 2010 Westminster election. Both Glenys Kinnock and Eluned Morgan retired, after 15 years in Brussels, and Labour only won one seat, for Derek Vaughan. Plaid's Jill Evans retained her seat, while the UK Independence Party (UKIP) had a breakthrough by taking the fourth seat for John Bufton.

The 2014 elections again saw each of the four parties winning one seat apiece, with Derek Vaughan, Jill Evans and Kay Swinburne elected, and Nathan Gill taking a seat for UKIP, John Bufton having chosen to stand down.

In the wake of the 2016 referendum and in the somewhat bizarre circumstances of the 2019 European elections, Derek Vaughan stood down as did Kay Swinburne. Whereas the latter was replaced by Jackie Jones (with Labour trailing third on 16%, the worst performance of Welsh Labour in any election – although of a piece with results across the UK), the Conservatives failed to win a seat. The Brexit Party won two seats, James Wells joining Nathan Gill, with Jill Evans re-elected to the remaining seat.

Life before Brussels

It is striking that, for Labour, standing for the European Parliament was often a first step on the political ladder for neophytes. Indeed, in sharp contrast to the experience in many member states (though not the rest of the UK) not one of the 11 Labour MEPs had held electoral office above the level of a local authority, or even (with two exceptions) stood as parliamentary candidates, although several (such as Allan Rogers, Joe Wilson, Derek Vaughan) had fairly significant local authority experience.

By contrast, from the Conservatives Beata Brookes, though never having been elected, had stood in a series of parliamentary seats going back to the general election of 1955. Likewise, a generation later, Jonathan Evans, having stood in general elections in 1974, 1979, and 1987 was MP for Brecon and Radnor from 1992 to 1997 and a minister in the Major government before being elected to the European Parliament.

Though it was unsurprising, given the scant success Plaid Cymru had enjoyed in first-past-the-post elections, Jill Evans had not been elected to Westminster; she too was a prominent figure in her party, having been both chair and president of Plaid Cymru, as well as having significant local government experience, representing Wales on the EU's Committee of the Regions.

One common thread amongst the Labour members in the early years was the Workers' Educational Association (WEA), whose tutors had significant contacts across the Welsh Labour Party and trade unions. Allan Rogers was its Wales director when elected, and he had recruited both Win Griffiths and Llew Smith, as well as the future Labour Party leader, Neil Kinnock. Wayne David also worked for the WEA before being elected in 1994.

Life in Brussels

No Welsh MEPs attained the highest office in the Parliament – Henry Plumb having been the only Brit to become president – although two of the earliest intake, Allan Rogers and Win Griffiths, served as vice-presidents.

In terms of committees, while generalising from a small cohort such as the Welsh MEPs is perhaps dangerous, a few common threads emerge.

The Budgets and Budgetary Control committees, often seen as a somewhat dusty corner of the Parliament but of critical importance to holding the Commission to account, was an area where British MEPs commonly made a mark. Eluned Morgan was the Socialist group co-ordinator on the Budgetary Control Committee between 1999 and 2002. Derek Vaughan followed in her footsteps, as a full member throughout his two terms in Parliament, as well as being its first vice-chair from 2014 to 2019 and a member of the Budgets Committee from 2009 to 2014. In 2011, Derek held the key role of rapporteur for the 2012 budget.

Less surprising, given the legacy of heavy industry and de-industrialisation in Wales, the Regional Policy Committee often had a Welsh Labour member. Win Griffiths (1979–1989) and Wayne David (1989–1999) were members throughout their terms of office, with the former being the Socialist group co-ordinator, while Derek Vaughan was a member from 2014 to 2019. UKIP's John Bufton was also on this committee. Agriculture was a similar area of interest, with Eurig Wyn and Joe Wilson both focusing on this committee (with the latter being the deputy co-ordinator for the Socialist group).

Another committee which attracted a range of Welsh MEPs was Economic and Monetary Affairs. Allan Rogers' main focus was this committee, chaired at the time by Jacques Delors, while Jonathan Evans was the deputy co-ordinator for the EPP-ED group, leading on competition law. His successor Kay Swinburne (with a background in investment banking) was a highly respected member and coordinator for the ECR group on both this and the related Special Committee on the Economic, Financial and Social Crisis.

In addition to Glenys Kinnock's major role with developing countries, many Labour MEPs were engaged in this rather niche area. David Morris devoted much of his energy to international development and Derek Vaughan was a full member of the ACP delegation during his first term (2009-2014), while Allan Rogers as a vice-president of the Parliament deputised for President Simone Veil at a meeting of the ACP in Zaire. Win Griffiths similarly took part in a meeting of the ACP in Arusha as a substitute member. Plaid's Eurig Wyn was very active in the EU's international work, while from the opposite side of the political spectrum James Wells of the Brexit Party sat on the Development Committee during his brief period of office.

Unsurprisingly given the bonds of language, North America was another focus for the Welsh. Jonathan Evans chaired the US delegation while Joe Wilson was heavily involved with Canada, intervening to help resolve the so-called "Turbot War" between Canada and Spain in 1995.

Other members had interests across the spectrum of committees and delegations. Jill Evans' focus over her 21 years was successively on Employment and Social Affairs, Environment and Public Health, and Cultural Affairs and Education, while she also served as vice-chair of Women's Rights and Equal Opportunities from 1999 to 2004. Eluned Morgan during her final term was a member of the Energy, Industry and Science Committee and rapporteur on the EU's 2006 green paper on *A European Strategy for Sustainable, Competitive and Secure Energy* which helped drive forward European commitments to renewable energy.

Ann Clwyd was rapporteur on the International Year of the Disabled and played a key role in the accession negotiations with Portugal as co-chair of the relevant committee.

In terms of their political families, both Wayne David and Jonathan Evans led their delegations, giving them a significant role in the Socialist and EPP groups respectively. Jill Evans chaired the European Free Alliance group and was first vice-president of the Greens–EFA group in 2009-2014. In an earlier generation, Allan Rogers was the first secretary of the British Labour group, which gave him de facto a place on the Socialist group bureau. This he used to embed British Labour more into the group than might otherwise have been the case given the Labour leader, Barbara Castle's well-known antipathy to the EEC.

Achievements and regrets

Several former MEPs who contributed to this research, following Edith Piaf, did not feel they had any particular regrets. While any achievements or regrets were reflections of their individual contributions, a few themes emerged, covering both sides of this particular coin.

One related to the constant struggle which Labour MEPs had to connect with the mainstream of the Labour Party and to move it from the Euroscepticism of the early 1980s to the much more positive approach of the Blair government in its early days and then to sustain this engagement after the watershed of the Iraq War.

Allan Rogers felt he had made a positive contribution as BLG secretary and a vice-president of the Parliament in counteracting the most antagonistic elements of the anti-European majority in the small Labour representation in the first directly elected Parliament, and in establishing Labour's credibility within the Socialist group.

Similarly, Wayne David noted that as leader of the EPLP (and thus an ex officio member of the Labour Party's national executive committee) he helped build bridges between Labour MEPs and the Socialist group with the Labour Party in the UK, particularly after the debacle when some EPLP members opposed the totemic move by Tony Blair, after becoming leader of the opposition, to scrap the

Clause 4 commitment to common ownership from the party's constitution.

On the flip side, Wayne David, Win Griffiths and Ann Clwyd all expressed disappointment and frustration at the way divisions within the EPLP and between the EPLP and Westminster colleagues limited their ability to bring about pro-European change, while they and others from across the spectrum (Derek Vaughan, Jill Evans, Jacqui Jones) highlighted the broader failure to build sufficient support for the European ideal amongst the wider population. By contrast, James Wells felt that, for the Brexit Party, the final departure of the UK from the EU was "job done".

Another area of regret cited by both Ann Clwyd and Win Griffiths was the failure to persuade the government of Margaret Thatcher to sign up to the D'Avignon plan to restructure and hence retain a significant steel industry in the UK.

In terms of the achievements, a common thread relates to ensuring, in 1999, that Wales qualified for the highest level of regional funding (initially "Objective 1" and then "Convergence" status) and subsequently increasing the scale of EU aid. Wayne David worked closely with Labour ministers in the then Welsh Office and with Labour EU commissioner, Bruce Millan, to find a route for much of Wales to qualify (which involved redrawing the map of so-called "NUTS 2" regions in Wales) and to persuade the Treasury to ensure that the funding was passported to Wales, over and above the mechanism of the Barnett formula, which determines the level of public spending in Wales. Eluned Morgan and Derek Vaughan also believed they contributed to securing more significant funds for Wales in successive funding rounds (in each case using their involvement with the Budgets Committee as a mechanism).

Of the achievements noted by individual former MEPs, a few may perhaps be representative.

Eluned Morgan cited her role in helping to shape the energy green paper and persuading the Labour government to sign up to ambitious targets on renewables, as well as her role on the Budgetary Control Committee in securing greater accountability of the European Commission. Win Griffiths believed he had helped to secure UK commitment to the clean water directive, leading to a real improvement in the UK's bathing waters. Derek Vaughan referenced his role as budget rapporteur.

Joe Wilson considers he had "saved" the British sausage, by finding a seemingly innocent way to amend the draft Council directive on "Requirements for the production and placing on the market of minced meat and meat preparations" which might otherwise have required significant changes to the UK's traditional way of making sausages. He achieved this by working very closely with committee staff, whom he cultivated socially.

Jill Evans felt that she had played a role in raising Wales's profile internationally by consistently referring to Wales in her interventions in committee and in the chamber.

Life after the European Parliament

For many Welsh MEPs, particularly in the early years, a term or two as a European parliamentarian was, in effect, a step onto the political ladder back home, with the next rung being selection as a Westminster candidate. Five Labour MEPs (Allan Rogers, Ann Clwyd, Win Griffiths, Llew Smith and Wayne David) had subsequent careers as MPs, as did Conservative Jonathan Evans, who stood down to fight the Cardiff North seat in 2010. Of these, Wayne David was something of an outlier, as his ambition on standing down was to secure election to the new National Assembly for Wales in 1999, but he failed to win Rhondda and subsequently became the MP for Caerphilly.

Of the other Labour MEPs, Glenys Kinnock and Eluned Morgan continued their political careers after the European Parliament, Glenys being elevated to the House of Lords where she was a minister under Gordon Brown, and Eluned first being made a life peer and subsequently elected to the National Assembly (now Senedd Cymru) where she is currently minister for health and social services. By contrast, Joe Wilson and David Morris retired once they failed to secure winnable positions on the regional list after the introduction of proportional representation.

In terms of the non-Labour members, Jill Evans retired but is very active politically, while Eurig Wyn played an active part in local government in his home county of Gwynedd before his early death. Kay Swinburne resumed her career in the City, while both John Bufton and James Wells left politics. Nathan Gill is currently Welsh leader of Reform UK.

In closing

The experience and contribution of the Welsh MEPs can serve as an interesting case study of the less well-known British members over the 40 years the UK sent elected members to the European Parliament. Two points stand out.

Firstly, the introduction of proportional representation in 1999 was a watershed. Before then, Labour dominated the electoral scene in Wales even when its national standing was at its weakest; for ten years it enjoyed a monopoly of power. Indeed, it was not until 2009 that there were more non-Labour MEPs in Wales than the number of Welsh Labour MEPs recruited from the staff of the WEA.

From 1999, Labour struggled to reproduce its electoral success – even in terms of share of the vote – or to match its continued strong performance in general and Assembly/Senedd elections. In 2009 the Conservatives topped the poll and in 2019 the Brexit Party did the same. From 2009, Labour never won more than one of the four seats.

Secondly, for Labour members, particularly in the early days, election to the European Parliament was often an early step on a political ladder which led to Westminster. The five Labour MEPs who made this transition have together notched up more than 105 years in Westminster compared to 40 in the European Parliament.

This observation should not detract from some very real achievements in ensuring Wales enjoyed some of the benefits of EU membership. Unlike the UK as a whole, Wales was for more than 20 years a net beneficiary of the EU budget, thanks to the efforts of Welsh MEPs working with Welsh MPs and ministers in securing and retaining Objective 1/Convergence funding for West Wales and the Valleys, covering more than two thirds of the population of Wales.

The clean water directive, championed by Win Griffiths, brought huge improvements to the quality of bathing waters off Welsh coasts. The energy green paper, significantly influenced by Eluned Morgan as rapporteur, put a new emphasis on renewables, an area in which Wales has considerable potential. Welsh members (from both Labour and Plaid Cymru) played an important part in pushing forward the role of the EU as a partner with the developing world; and the presence of passionate and enthusiastic advocates of Wales (such as Jill Evans and Derek Vaughan) also raised Wales's profile on the international stage.

Moreover, Labour MEPs from Allan Rogers to Wayne David played a role in the transition of the Labour Party from the Euroscepticism of the early 1980s to the unapologetic pro-European stance of the 2000s – although Welsh Labour also contributed its share of Eurosceptics (Llew Smith and David Morris, for example) as of course did UKIP and Brexit Party members.

Plaid Cymru MEPs were strong advocates of European values and cooperation, while all three Conservative MEPs were pro-European, even as this became increasingly unfashionable in the Conservative Party.

In conclusion, the Welsh members helped to bring the benefits of the EU to Wales and to raise awareness of Wales in the European institutions. They did not, however, succeed in convincing a majority of the electorate in Wales that the benefits of EU membership were enough to vote for the UK to remain in the EU.

3. Northern Ireland

by Giada Lagana

Giada Lagana is a lecturer in Politics at Cardiff University, School of Law and Politics. She is the author of "The European Union and the Northern Ireland Peace Process" (2021) and president of the Irish Association for Contemporary European Studies.

The EP and the Northern Ireland peace process

The story of the important role that the European Union institutions played in restoring peace in Northern Ireland has been largely overlooked. Before the referendum in 2016, very few people either within or outside Northern Ireland had fully appreciated the role or the significance of the EU in the peace process. Political actors and local communities in Northern Ireland itself – the mainly Protestant unionist/loyalist community and the mainly Catholic nationalist/republican community – recognised and welcomed the EU's economic commitment. This was to them the only visible aspect of EU engagement in the region, which limited the story to how first the European Community and then the EU provided help in achieving political stability principally by economic means.

However, with the advent of the Brexit process, all European matters related to the peace process became politicised, triggering new discussions and debates. Moreover, new historical evidence showed how this was also the story of the enduring commitment of exceptional political actors: the Northern Ireland members of the European Parliament. They exemplified the ideal of European cooperation, notwithstanding their profound disagreements on the root causes of the Northern Ireland conflict. They worked together to pursue an integral social and economic plan for the region. In this way, they paved the way for a joint Anglo-Irish and communal approach to re-establishing peace and reconciliation in Northern Ireland.

"Discretion and subtlety" were the hallmarks of these MEPs' work. This was essential if their actions were to be tolerated by the UK and the Republic of Ireland governments, and by the unionist community. Furthermore, discretion and subtlety helped the subsequent European engagement in the peace process to co-exist with different and often contrasting political perspectives, allowing all the people of Northern Ireland to engage with peace initiatives and resources designed for their mutual benefit. Ultimately, these principles of mutual cooperation formed the basis of the 1998 Belfast/Good Friday Agreement (B/GFA). Their genesis is rooted in the policy-making structures of the European Parliament and has been filtered through the power-sharing institutions and North-South bodies on the island of Ireland.

The intertwining of personal and institutional interests took a specific form of cooperation in Europe for the Northern Ireland MEPs. The strategic preparatory work was laid down by John Hume. Hume was passionately pro-European. Deputy leader and later leader of the Social Democratic and Labour Party, his election to the EP in 1979 was roundly endorsed by the nationalist electorate, with 24.6% of the Northern Ireland constituency vote . However, even before he represented Northern Ireland in Strasbourg, Hume had begun to forge links with important actors within the Irish political elite. Moreover, his networking was not limited to an Irish context, as his role as political advisor to Ireland's EC commissioner for transport, trade and administration, Dick Burke, allowed him to build his knowledge and connections across a wider European space. His fluency in French also facilitated his engagement with key officials and representatives.

This is how Colm Larkin, an Irishman and a senior official of the European Commission, described Hume:

> "He was always alert to what was happening in the Commission and how it could relate to Northern Ireland ... He had a warm straightforward style and he was constantly being buttonholed by people. He would break off his conversation with you to talk to someone else. He was very well liked and respected and ended up with a very strong support network throughout Brussels and Strasbourg. ... I remember once when I was working with Peter Sutherland and there was a stand-off with President Delors. I found myself alone in the lift one morning with Pascal Lamy, Delors' formidable and overbearing *chef de cabinet*. He greeted me frostily. The last thing I wanted to do was to engage him on state aid, so I mentioned to him that I had just been with John Hume. The atmosphere was transformed. '*Ah Hume, c'est un chic type!*' he said and enthused about how Delors had worked with him as a fellow MEP in the Socialist Group."

Hume's combination of force of personality, conviction and ardent pro-Europeanism helped him win many allies in Europe after his election as an MEP. He sat with the then largest and most powerful political bloc in the EP – the Socialist group – and was promptly elected to its front bench, acting as the group's treasurer. This illustrates the esteem in which he was held, thanks to his networking amongst the leaders of the European left. He immediately began to lobby his new political colleagues to support his efforts to bring EP influence to bear on Northern Ireland. Within six months of becoming an MEP, he was able to table a resolution calling for an investigation into the ways in which the EC could help the region, with the support of his Northern Ireland colleagues, Ian Paisley and John Taylor.

Ian Paisley, leader of the Democratic Unionist Party, won the majority of unionist votes at 29.8% of the Northern Ireland constituency in 1979, by articulating a very different stance from Hume. He never positioned himself in any of the EP political groups. The fact that the foundation document of the EC was the Treaty of

Rome, and the Community had a Catholic majority population, allowed Paisley to portray this integrationist project as yet another "enemy of Protestant Ulster". He often described the EC as an instrument of the Vatican and was thrown out of the chamber for interrupting Pope John Paul II's address in 1988, shouting: "I renounce you as the anti-Christ".

Nevertheless, it is well known that, over time, working in the EP often influences the attitudes of its members. This process had a long-term socialisation effect on Paisley, who adapted a number of his newly acquired institutional interests to the new context. He famously declared: "I'm going to get all I can for Ulster, every grant we can possibly get our hands on. Then when we have milked the cow dry, we are going to shoot the cow". Hume perfectly understood this statement: as long as the focus was on economic benefits, he felt he could count on Paisley's support. The depth of the differences between Paisley and Hume, in their stances on Northern Ireland and their attitudes to the EU, makes all the greater their achievement in cooperating so effectively within the EP.

John Taylor, who had survived an assassination attempt by the IRA in 1972, represented the Ulster Unionist Party and served in the EP from 1979 to 1989. He sat with the European Democratic Group, alongside leading British Conservative MEPs such as Henry Plumb, James Scott-Hopkins and Diana Elles. This partly explains why, when expressing himself in plenary, Taylor invariably supported the UK government position. Always trailing the more voluble and charismatic Paisley in EP elections, he was not willing, however, to lose further unionist votes by allowing Paisley to gain sole credit for bringing home the European "milk". He declared in 1981, addressing an EP plenary session: "When it comes to the economic and social problems, the three Northern Ireland MEPs, irrespective of their political divisions, have a common love and concern for the future of their province". These comments were quite remarkable, showing how, within just two years of their election to the EP, these unionist MEPs were able to find common ground with Hume in lobbying the EC to support Northern Ireland. In Strasbourg and Brussels, away from the polarising pressures of the Northern Ireland conflict, the region's three MEPs stood together and always stressed their unity.

James (Jim) Nicholson followed John Taylor in 1989. Serving as an MEP in the European Conservatives and Reformists group until 2019, he was also the longest serving Northern Ireland MEP. Dynamic in his work within the EP, he recalls:

> "We, the Northern Ireland MEPs, had our differences but when European integration was driven forward after Jacques Delors became President of the European Commission, we knew we had to do more. The impact of the years of violence was felt most keenly in Belfast and Derry, in the small towns and border villages. As such, these were the focus of our efforts. Hume was very much at the forefront of this approach, but I have always found Paisley to be a force for good too".

The most tangible result of the MEPs' cooperation is the well-known, well-established PEACE funding package, which is specific to Northern Ireland. The package is an important validation and endorsement of the joint work of the Northern Ireland MEPs. It created a political space for new developments. It forced politicians and wider civil society groups to take on the responsibility for the allocation of EU resources. Indeed, local political parties came together to administer the new funding, alongside the voluntary and community sectors and other local actors. This exemplified the focus that Hume wanted to place on civil society and the need to address their needs first. It also embodied the concept of a "bottom-up" approach to peace building, which gave the people of Northern Ireland a part to play in their own peace process. Though political tensions continued to emerge, so successful was this new programme that the EU decided to renew it after the initial five-year plan (PEACE I), making only minor changes to the collaborative and locally led delivery mechanisms used the first time round. There were three iterations of the programme (labelled PEACE II, III and IV) running right through to 2020. Even when the UK voted to leave the EU during PEACE IV, agreement was made to continue funding cross-border reconciliation efforts on the island of Ireland until 2027 (PEACE Plus).

Lobbying to promote common, particularly economic interests generated a role for the EU in the Northern Ireland peace process. Hume perceived the "neutral arena" of the EP as a suitable context in which to develop such interests and gain additional political and economic support, to help resolve the Northern Ireland conflict. Despite their differences with Hume, unionist MEPs wanted to share in what Paisley called the "milk" of the EU "cow". Their collaborative input to relevant debates and initiatives within the EP are evidence of this. Unionists' interests also changed over time, particularly in response to changes in British policy on Northern Ireland, and London's greater cooperation with Dublin, especially after the signature of the 1985 Anglo-Irish Agreement and the ensuing institutionalisation of cross-border cooperation on the island of Ireland. Many years of legislating in common at the EU level had a socialising effect on the MEPs. They needed to positively engage in the governance of Northern Ireland to achieve any progress on that front, and this also meant positively engaging at the whole island level, as supported by the EU.

Changes in unionists' political attitudes show how they, like the nationalists, adapted their approach over time in response to the structure of decision-making within the EP. The European Parliament was also the only body serving the whole Union which was directly elected. This made the MEPs the only voice of the people of Northern Ireland in the EU institutions. In addition, the chance to exploit financial or political opportunities created new functional spaces, aiding unionist-nationalist and wider British-Irish cooperation. Both the UK and the Irish governments – implicitly or explicitly – supported this cooperative approach. The MEPs' policy proposals were articulated in Strasbourg and Brussels. The ensuing policy initiatives and programmes were implemented through specific ministerial decrees, administrative decisions and statutory changes made at the national level. The emphasis on subsidiarity under the Maastricht Treaty has furthered this long-standing principle.

After 2004, when John Hume stepped down, the duty to represent the nationalist community fell on the Sinn Féin candidates, Bairbre de Brún and Mary Lou McDonald. Diane Dodds (DUP) joined the EP in the subsequent 2009 election, thus establishing a new tradition of female political voices coming from Northern Ireland. Martina Anderson (Sinn Féin) and Naomi Long (Alliance Party) followed, having to deal, among other matters, with the limits of the power-sharing executive and the detrimental effects of the Brexit process. Times had changed, creating different challenges, and the new generations of MEPs had difficulty in employing the same common approach and networking abilities that had been used to such good effect by their predecessors.

The legacy of the first Northern Ireland MEPs' work survives in the PEACE programmes, in the institutional framework laid down by the Belfast/Good Friday Agreement, and the way in which the EU has learnt to respond to Northern Ireland local initiatives by facilitating these, and by trying to connect them to peace building developments. It is too often forgotten that the Northern Ireland Protocol, a measure agreed between the UK and the EU to mitigate any possible adverse effects of Brexit on the region, should be considered an integral part of the EU's enduring commitment to the Northern Ireland peace process. The processes of mutual cooperation described in this chapter are endogenous to the EU institutions – and particularly the European Parliament – and have significantly contributed to restoring peace and fostering reconciliation among the people of Northern Ireland.

VI: MAKING A DIFFERENCE

1. The environment

by Caroline Lucas

Caroline Lucas MP became the Green Party's first Member of Parliament when elected in 2010 to represent Brighton Pavilion, following eleven years in the European Parliament. She has also served as party leader and now chairs the all-party Parliamentary Group on Climate Change.

Elected Greens at last

One of my most vivid political memories is of the night in June when the 1989 European election results started to roll in. The Green bar on the BBC's election graph continued to grow inexorably until, by the end of the night, the Green Party of England and Wales had won a staggering 14.9% of the vote, with well over 2 million people voting Green. As the party's press officer at the time, I'd known we were going to do well, but a result of that scale surprised all of us. Yet in spite of winning more votes than any other Green Party in Europe, the UK's deeply unfair first-past-the-post electoral system meant that those votes weren't translated into seats, and we were unable to join our colleagues in the first formal Green group in the European Parliament.

Ten years later, following the change to a more proportional voting system, I was press officer no longer, but instead top of the Greens' candidate list in the South East region – and along with my colleague in London, Jean Lambert, became one of the first two Green MEPs elected in the UK.

It felt like some kind of justice had finally been done. Indeed, 1999 saw Green parties achieve our best results across the EU since 1984, with a total of 38 Green MEPs elected. Together with 10 MEPs from the European Free Alliance (regionalists and democratic nationalists, including the SNP and Plaid Cymru), we formed the Greens/EFA group, becoming the fourth largest political group in the Parliament.

It was a high point for Green politics. In the same year, German Michaele Schreyer became the first Green EU commissioner, with responsibility for budget and anti-fraud issues. Around this time, Green parties were also in government in five EU member states: Italy, Finland, France, Germany and Belgium. The political consequences were considerable: five Green environment ministers had a decisive impact on the negotiations on the Kyoto Protocol on climate change, as well as on EU environmental legislation more generally, including the effective moratorium on genetically modified organisms.

The excitement of working alongside successful Green parties from across the EU was enormous, and it gave our whole party a sense of greater confidence and credibility – undercut only by the British media's total lack of interest in any serious political developments at EU level.

I wasn't the only candidate from a new party elected from the South East, however. I shared that privilege with Nigel Farage, from the right-wing anti-EU UK Independence Party, UKIP, formed six years earlier. For some, his election was an argument against a more proportional voting system. But rigging an electoral system simply because you don't like the results it throws up has always seemed wrong to me. Better to seek to understand the factors that led to those results and seek to address them at root. The British establishment's signal failure to do that was arguably a key factor in the Brexit vote seventeen years later.

Compromise is not a dirty word

The European Parliament could not have been more different to Westminster – collaborative, collegiate and with almost a third of MEPs being women. For me, it's a difference summed up in the contrasting approaches to the idea of compromise. In Brussels, it wasn't the dirty word it tends to be in British politics, with the associations of "selling out" and weakness. On the contrary, compromise was regarded as a noble endeavour to find sufficient common ground between the different parties to enable an agreement that all could live with. It was refreshing and constructive.

Not only that, but it felt that, as a member of the European Parliament, I could have far greater influence over policy than I ever would as a backbencher at Westminster. Indeed "backbencher" in the European Parliament wasn't really a meaningful concept, since all MEPs have the chance to pilot legislation through the system, from initial Council proposal through to enactment as European law. How different from Westminster where, unless you happen to strike incredibly lucky in the annual ballot for a private member's bill, your chances of personally bringing in legislation are pretty close to zero.

But if the British media hadn't cottoned on to the growing significance of the European Parliament in policy making, the same was not true for the swelling numbers of representatives from industry lobby groups, who increasingly roamed the corridors of Brussels and Strasbourg seeking to influence legislative outcomes.

NGOs and civil society also played a strong role in this process, and suddenly I found myself being sought out as someone to be intensively lobbied and briefed. With real power in the European institutions, the Greens were regarded as influential and effective partners in the struggle for more ambitious environmental policy in a way that still wasn't the case at Westminster.

Environmental policy

European environmental policy is an area of co-decision, not just consultation, between the Parliament, Council and Commission, which meant that as a member of the powerful Environment Committee, I could have real influence over policy outcomes. And as rapporteur for a couple of high profile legislative dossiers, I was proud to have the chance to make a real difference.

Take illegal logging and deforestation, for example. Tackling them had long been one of my priorities, so I jumped at the opportunity to be Parliament's rapporteur on the somewhat tortuously titled "Proposal for a regulation laying down the obligations for operators who place timber and timber products on the market". Since anywhere between 20 and 40 per cent of global industrial wood production is estimated to come from illegal sources, and up to 20% was finding its way into the EU, this was a key moment to try to achieve a full EU ban on trading in illegally logged timber.

The initial Council common position stopped short of such a ban, only requiring those operators first placing timber on the EU market to implement a system of "due diligence" instead. However, after much lobbying from Green politicians, environment NGOs, and a much stronger position from the Parliament in favour of prohibition, the Council eventually agreed to a ban. While the final outcome didn't cover everything I wanted – for example, printed matter is excluded from its scope, a worrying loophole that is likely only to grow in size – it was nevertheless a globally significant breakthrough to have the EU shut down its market in illegally harvested timber. And Parliament had been crucial in that result.

Another important contribution to environmental legislation was the REACH directive (Registration, Evaluation and Authorisation of Chemicals) where Green MEPs played a prominent role in fighting for tougher control of chemicals in the EU, alongside a reduction in cruel and outdated animal testing. In the face of intensive lobbying from the chemical industry to water down the proposed law, we launched a campaign in 2005 to underline the dangers inherent in everyday chemicals, mobilising civil society including the Women's Institute, many of whose members arrived in Brussels on a bus from the UK to take the issue directly to decision makers. The compromise finally adopted by the EU, while falling sort of the level of protection we wanted, nonetheless represented a big step forward in the protection of consumers and the environment from toxic substances.

In spite of progress in the EU on environment issues which affected everyone in the UK, particularly as a result of the influence of the substantial bloc of Green MEPs, there was still no recognition at home of work being done in Brussels and Strasbourg. Journalists were simply not interested. I vividly remember meeting BBC producers and literally begging the weekly Radio 4 Westminster Hour programme to feature interviews with MEPs, as well as MPs, even just for one week in every four. It didn't happen. The impact that the lack of knowledge of the work of MEPs had on the Brexit vote should be the subject of another book – suffice to say that it was significant.

But what's the EU for?

During my first term as an MEP, the Greens/EFA group became very active in the debate on European integration, despite differences between national parties. The Green Party of England and Wales, along with the Swedish Greens and those from Ireland, were the strongest critics of ever greater integration, arguing that there were dangers of a lack of democratic legitimacy. Nonetheless, Green members were very active in the Convention, at which the Charter of Fundamental Rights was drafted and then, later, in the European Convention, which led to the draft constitution for the EU.

My own work focused on trying to answer the question that I felt simply wasn't being addressed: what was the EU actually for? As I wrote in a pamphlet at the time, all too often it felt as if the EU was being done *to* people, rather than *with* them. There had never been the opportunity in the UK to debate fully its role and purpose beyond its function as a single market. It was clear that it needed to become democratic and transparent, more accessible and accountable.

As an MEP, I was confronted on an almost daily basis with the fact that the original Big Idea – to bring peace to post-war Europe by binding its nations together in an ambitious free trade project – was no longer enough to sustain public support for the EU. And I was convinced that a new Big Idea – based on putting sustainability and social justice at the heart of the EU – could revitalise its institutions and re-inspire the public enthusiasm that had been eroded by the EU's drive towards "economism" – the idea that the overriding goals of European integration are purely economic, and its progress should be measured simply in terms of economic growth and the removal of trade barriers.

Looking back with the benefit of hindsight, following the tragic act of self-harm which was Brexit, I can only wish that this national debate had been held with greater passion and conviction.

2. Human rights and civil liberties

by Claude Moraes

Claude Moraes OBE was a Labour MEP for London from 1999-2020. He served as chair of the Committee on Justice and Home Affairs, first vice-president of the Socialist group and deputy leader of the EPLP.

When I left the European Parliament on the day of Brexit, it came with the obvious mix of emotions. I left as the last UK vice-president of a political group and chair of a committee, but the one nagging feeling that I probably shared with other Labour MEPs who had strong legislative track records was that our achievements and the contribution that UK MEPs and officials had made in the EU had never really been acknowledged back home.

In the words of a former Labour MEP who chaired the Budgets Committee, often making significant decisions that were seldom known in the UK: "Claude, nobody at home really knows what we do, but we have to get on with it, and it's a privilege". We can argue why that is the case, but the regular onslaught on the EU in the media ensured that the MEPs who engaged in the EP, as opposed to those who did no work or came to destroy it in recent years, were lumped together. And we were all diminished in the public eye.

Yet over those years – particularly after the 2009 Lisbon Treaty – it was surprising how, in influential parliamentary positions,

Labour MEPs made a genuine difference as the Parliament assumed equal (co-decision) legislative power with the Council, as well as enhanced regulatory and soft power.

To understand the change the Lisbon Treaty brought to my own job in 2009, just as I became a coordinator on the Committee on Civil Liberties, Justice and Home Affairs – known colloquially as LIBE – and then chair from 2014 until 2019, is to explain how the treaty transformed the way that critical agreements with other countries on justice and home affairs would be decided. Furthermore, it made LIBE one of the leading legislative committees in the Parliament.

Before 2009, the EP had only limited powers over international agreements. After 2009 I developed a detailed role in agreements from anti-terrorism to digital policy and the refugee crisis. This was because the Commission would be the lead negotiator, rather than the Council. Agreements in Council were to be adopted by QMV (qualified majority voting) and, crucially, the European Parliament could henceforth exercise a veto over the outcome via the consent procedure. It placed me in the middle of ten years of formal and soft power within the Committee on Civil Liberties, Justice and Home Affairs.

And what an area of work! The LIBE committee by 2020 was the most prolific legislative committee, with competence for a range of issues which touched on the identity and political direction of some member states. These issues included the refugee crisis of the 2010s; migration and free movement; visa policy; Schengen; security and anti-terrorism; the rule of law (Hungary, Poland); data protection and privacy; governance of the internet (Facebook, Cambridge Analytica and election interference); and anti-discrimination law. Migration and refugee issues were having broad impacts in the rise of the far right and in putting pressure on centre parties across the EU.

How did that work in practice? A snapshot which illustrated where MEPs could stand in the hierarchy of EU decision making, and where my committee stood, was the Justice and Home Affairs Council at the end of the Romanian presidency in 2016. At that moment, security and anti-terrorism was one of the top priorities. While a dominant theme since 9/11, attacks within the EU had kept this issue at the forefront – the 2004 Madrid train bombings; the

2005 London bombings; the 2015 Charlie Hebdo terrorism; the 2016 suicide bombings in Brussels; the 2015 Thalys train attack, and in November of that year the single most deadly terrorist attack in French history when 90 were killed at the Bataclan theatre and dozens more at other Paris locations. Meanwhile, security policy was the responsibility of the LIBE committee.

At the close of this 2016 Justice and Home Affairs Council, three people spoke at the closing press conference: the director of Europol (arguably the EU's most respected agency), the EU commissioner for security, and myself as chair of the LIBE committee. It wasn't by coincidence that an EP chair was there at what was a Council meeting. My committee had just revamped the Europol accountability rules (creating the JSPG, the Joint Policy Scrutiny Group) and Europol was accountable to our committee. We had also invited national parliaments to the Europol scrutiny process including UK peers and MPs.

Looking back to that press conference, another curiosity was that the three individuals were all British (Sir Rob Wainwright, Sir Julian King and myself). I recall us looking at each other and having the conversation – people in the UK should know that it was UK officials and politicians who were at the forefront of what was also a UK priority. An added irony was that British officials and a British MEP were working on this while our country was in the process of leaving the EU.

Meanwhile, LIBE was leading on international anti-terrorism agreements such as Passenger Name Records (PNR) and the Terrorist Finance Tracking Programme (often called Swift or TFTP) with the US. I regularly had to scrutinise and lead on key security inter-governmental agreements like the Prüm Convention which enhanced cross-border cooperation, and EU databases such as the Schengen, Eurodac (fingerprinting) and Europol intelligence databases, ensuring that any action respected the data protection and fundamental rights of Europeans.

The Parliament, and I as committee chair, were directly involved in those international negotiations with the Commission. These were new post-Lisbon powers which we used with some seriousness. The task involved constant attention on EP resolutions and meetings with the Commission and Council.

Surprisingly, such was the European Parliament's role in the vexed question of data protection over the use of intelligence to fight terrorists, it put me into face-to-face meetings with several interior ministers, including the French interior minister Bernard Cazeneuve, over the Schengen databases, and with British home secretary Theresa May over PNR.

I regularly spoke at Justice and Home Affairs Councils (that is, with national ministers) over five years, even outliving some interior and justice ministers who were subject to rapid turnover in some member states, particularly speaking up for Europol and for data standards in the use of intelligence databases.

Direct meetings took place with the US treasury secretary on Swift and the director of the CIA on EU intelligence sharing. These were Obama-era meetings but, even during the Trump presidency, I had meetings with his national security adviser. This all illustrated Parliament's changed role in international agreements.

The "Lisbonisation" of the Committee on Civil Liberties, Justice and Home Affairs, with its responsibility for rapidly growing areas of work like digital and privacy, meant a huge and significant workload from 2009. As coordinator I presented the view of my Socialist group but, from 2014, would regularly chair the legislative trilogues – the detailed, often hours-long, negotiations between Parliament, Commission and Council in the co-decision legislative process.

One example was the GDPR (General Data Protection Regulation) – to date one of the largest pieces of legislation to come from the EU. While sometimes criticised, the GDPR is the first and only international privacy regulation. I chaired its first and some subsequent trilogues.

The Civil Liberties, Justice and Home Affairs Committee took a leading role in digital matters. In 2013, while its coordinator for the Socialist group, I was the rapporteur for the European Parliament inquiry into mass surveillance following Edward Snowden's revelations. The report, "US NSA Surveillance Programmes and their impact on EU citizens' fundamental rights and transatlantic cooperation in JHA", looked at critical issues such as encryption, governance of the internet and cybercrime, and was referred to at the time as the Parliament's "European Digital Bill of Rights".

Such issues became dominant and I chaired the high-profile Parliament inquiry into Facebook in 2018, opening with a special evidence session questioning Mark Zuckerberg, fresh from giving evidence to Congress though having avoided the UK. With major economic, tax and monopoly interests for Facebook in the EU, it was certain he would appear before our inquiry which examined electoral interference, misuse of personal data and the implications of the Cambridge Analytica affair. Some lessons learned are informing today's EU digital legislation, such as on artificial intelligence and the Digital Services Act. Such inquiries were good examples of the Parliament's increasing "soft power".

LIBE's international agreements competence extended to trade, where I led the EP's data adequacy agreements which formed integral parts of the EU's trade agreements with Japan and South Korea. Similarly, as the UK MEP on the EP Brexit steering committee, I worked on the EU/UK data adequacy agreement, which has still not been completed. Adequacy is a status granted by the European Commission to countries outside the EEA which provide a level of personal data protection comparable to that provided in European law. The EP has a formal role in granting adequacy with the Commission.

One major EU and global crisis was over refugees in the 2010s. Large numbers of refugees were making dangerous journeys from Africa and Syria. I was the rapporteur for the Asylum Support Agency in 2011, but as chair I convened the Asylum Support Group which brought together the rapporteurs for the "asylum package" – the directives (Reception, Returns, EASO, Resettlement) which made up the EU's response to the crisis. The package brought together complex legislation and an increased budget for member states like Greece, Italy, Germany and Sweden which were hosting the most refugees.

We were also responsible for Frontex, the EU agency based in Warsaw, which had naval assets in the Mediterranean charged with rescuing refugees. The committee was immersed in this humanitarian and political issue, and I led delegations to Libya, Lebanon, trafficking routes like Niger, as well as the EU "hotspots" Greece and Italy, to which migrants were also being pushed back from countries like Hungary. I had regular meetings with the home affairs ministers of Greece and Italy and the Commission as our role grew.

While one crisis was happening, another not unrelated one was over the rule of law. The committee was responsible for compliance with the EU treaties. In 2018 I was appointed standing rapporteur for the European Parliament consent procedure on the Commission's decision to directly invoke article 7 of the EU treaties for the first time into alleged rule of law breaches by the Polish government. I led "rule of law" delegations to Poland and Slovakia (where the murder of investigative journalist Ján Kuciak suggested alleged official involvement) and was immersed in the Hungarian breaches. These were highly sensitive issues which were becoming an existential crisis for the EU – namely, when is a member state acting outside the fundamental rights framework of the EU, and if so, what sanctions will be implemented?

One example was the committee's competence in criminal law. In 2019, alongside the chair of the Budget Control Committee, I negotiated with the Council and held sensitive hearings to fulfil the Parliament's mandate to appoint the EU's first European chief public prosecutor. I asked for the remit of the prosecutor's office to be extended to serious organised crime and people trafficking. With the Economic and Monetary Affairs Committee, I similarly chaired trilogues on the anti-money laundering directive.

Like many MEPs I've had the chance to legislate on issues close to my heart – on the race equality directive and on the protection of seasonal workers directive, bread and butter legislation which will hopefully stand the test of time.

At the time of writing though, another small piece of work is always in my mind. Russia has brutally invaded Ukraine and the whole question of its position in relation to the EU has been magnified. Some years ago, I was the rapporteur for the Ukraine visa waiver (one of many incremental attempts by the EU to reach out to Ukraine). In the grand scheme of things, it was a tiny regulation, but it facilitated a visit to Ukraine to understand the country. Today I know these initiatives were absolutely right. It is in these relatively small pieces of work that an active MEP could and can feel they are truly privileged and making a difference.

3. German reunification

by Alan Donnelly

Alan Donnelly is the founder and executive chairman of Sovereign Strategy. He was an MEP from 1989 to 99, and was secretary and then, in 1997-99, leader of the European Parliamentary Labour Party (EPLP). He was an official of the GMB union prior to his election to the European Parliament.

First elected to the European Parliament in June 1989 (aged just 31), I was learning the ropes as a member of the Economic and Monetary Committee, dealing with the internal market legislation and stage one of EMU: the creation of the committee of central bank governors. This was my first report as a rapporteur.

Out of the blue, I was invited by the Socialist group president, Jean-Pierre Cot to join him at a private dinner with the Commission president, Jacques Delors. Delors, as a French socialist, favoured parliamentary oversight of the EMU process and handed me a piece of paper with a compromise amendment, proposing that the chair of the central bankers' committee would have to appear before Parliament annually: exactly what the committee report wanted to achieve. This was in itself a big win for the EP, but it also became clear later that it was part of Delors' plan to have the future European Central Bank subject to parliamentary scrutiny.

It was that encounter with Jacques Delors in November 1989 which set in place a trusted relationship between one of Europe's iconic political leaders and a young British political novice – which turned out to be fortuitous given the work to come on German reunification.

From the fall of the Berlin Wall on 9 November 1989, through the historic addresses by Mitterrand and Kohl to the European Parliament on 22 November and the first meeting of the Temporary Committee on German Unification in March 1990, there was a real sense of history in the making. The leaders in the European Parliament knew that the process required both proper democratic legitimacy and oversight, but it also required the EP to deliver for the families in the German Democratic Republic (East Germany) while preventing any weakening of the European Community's ability to deliver for its existing citizens.

This was brought home to me when I took my place as the new committee rapporteur in the committee room for our first meeting. Among the twenty members we had the formidable Simone Veil, former president of the EP; Leo Tindemans, a former Belgian prime minister; Claude Cheysson and Fernando Morán, former foreign ministers of France and Spain respectively; and Rüdiger von Wechmar, West Germany's former ambassador to the UK and the UN.

The EP had also selected a team of its most experienced civil servants, able to advise the committee on all the complex matters including agriculture, competition, environment, transport, research and development, social cohesion and the interim customs rules to open up essential trade.

All of us recognised that the committee had to move efficiently and with speed, because hanging over the process was the risk that the Volkskammer – the East German parliament – might vote for immediate unification, which was foreseen in the West German basic law, its constitution, an act that would have thrown the EC into chaos. Indeed, on 23 August the Volkskammer declared accession and the extension of the German basic law to the GDR. We kept in regular contact with the interim leaders in the new East German government as well as leaders in the Volkskammer to demonstrate that we were pushing forward with the legal instruments for unification.

Through this process, we also wanted to send a strong message to other countries in Central and Eastern Europe that the EP looked forward to welcoming them into the European family provided, of course, they respected the *acquis communautaire*.

I had two first class advisers throughout the process, Francis Jacobs, from the Economic and Monetary Committee, and Gerhard Stahl, from the Socialist group secretariat. Together with the easy access to Delors and almost daily contact with Carlos Trojan, the Commission deputy secretary-general, this was critical, as the unification process was about to speed up significantly.

With the Deutschmark having been adopted from 1 July in the GDR, the Temporary Committee's interim report was approved by Parliament on 12 July 1990. The report stressed that the special measures and derogations for the GDR could not undermine the economic and social cohesion of the EC and, equally important, unification had to be a catalyst for deeper European integration.

Due to the pressure from events in the two Germanys, the Commission wanted to speed up the adoption of the secondary legislation needed for GDR integration. On 12 July, the EP adopted a further resolution giving the Temporary Committee unprecedented responsibility for the unification legislative package. We naturally had to work closely with the standing committees to incorporate their expert views. Two meetings were held of the Conference of Presidents (involving chairs of the political groups) and the Temporary Committee on 17 July and 29 August to take forward this transfer of competence.

The EP decided not to treat the integration of the GDR into the EC as an accession, a process that would have required the approval of national parliaments. However the EP successfully demanded that the other institutions should agree to a new procedure that would guarantee the European Parliament could have an impact on the shape of all legislation regardless of the legal base, and allowing two readings on all key secondary legislation.

With unification taking place on 3 October, at the Temporary Committee meetings in early October we conducted the first readings of the transitional measures, on the basis of the amendments proposed by the standing committees and, together with the legislative report, the Temporary Committee's second interim report was adopted on 24 October by Parliament.

To secure the second reading, Commissioner Martin Bangemann was obliged to make formal commitments, both to the Temporary Committee and the plenary in November, that any further modifications to the transitional arrangements beyond those of a technical nature would require normal legislative consideration. The final report of the Temporary Committee was approved in the plenary on 21 November, allowing the integration legislation to take effect.

The other pressing issue was the representation of the new Länder (the former East German regions) in the EP. Some wanted all German MEPs to resign and have a new election, but this idea was rejected. We discussed this question extensively, formally and informally within Parliament. A consensus emerged in favour of appointing observers for the rest of the current mandate until 1994.

Much has been written about how this was finalised and what algorithm was used to determine the number. In reality, I met with Elmar Brok MEP, a long-serving German EPP member of the Temporary Committee, for dinner in Strasbourg the evening before I had to put a recommendation to the committee. We agreed to recommend that 18 observers be appointed for the rest of the mandate – a sensible political compromise. It was a huge honour to be present when the observers eventually took their seats in Parliament, giving genuine legitimacy to an historic process.

There is no question that the smooth integration of the GDR into the EU was the most exceptional model of inter-institutional cooperation and cross-party cooperation. I also believe this played a significant role in convincing member state governments and the Commission that it was time to move to a proper co-decision process involving the EP as a full partner. The European Parliament had truly come of age.

4. Aid to democracy and human rights

by David Blackman

David Blackman is an expert on ancient maritime history and since 2002 has been a senior research fellow at the Centre for the Study of Ancient Documents at the University of Oxford. His career has also included 20 years at the European Parliament, where he was successively deputy general secretary of the Socialist group and then headed the Parliament's division monitoring developments in Central and Eastern Europe and running the aid and co-operation programme for the newly democratic parliaments.

Following the momentous fall of the Berlin Wall in November 1989 the European Parliament adopted an historic resolution in July 1990 on "additional priority tasks for the European Community (EC) as a result of the changed political situation in central and eastern Europe and the improved economic performance in the EC".

The centre-right European Democratic Group (EDG), which had become close to the movements for change across the region, proposed a paragraph on "the creation of a European Fund for the support of democracy". The Socialist group felt that the funds were likely to pass to political parties, but it also proposed to provide aid to the parliaments which had been democratically elected.

The European Democracy Fund proposed by the Conservative Edward McMillan-Scott MEP, spokesman for the EDG on foreign affairs, led to a specific line in the 1991 EC budget for the promotion of civil society and democratisation in the newly democratic states of Central and Eastern Europe. He had been following developments in that region and, as group spokesman on the key committee (and later group leader), he was able to play the key role in this initiative. British MEPs of all parties supported the eastward enlargement of the EC as well as the democracy initiative and links being developed by their political groups with parties in the countries concerned.

After some internal disagreements, the European Parliament voted 5 million ECU (some £3.592m) from 1992 for this purpose. Then in summer 1990 Parliament created a new unit "to monitor relations with central and eastern Europe". This small division, headed by the present author, concentrated on research, as well as briefing delegations, committees and individual MEPs. The work included training courses and information visits for parliamentary officials from the newly democratic central and east European parliaments.

This "European Democracy Initiative" was initially focused on the EC's new PHARE (Poland and Hungary Assistance for the Restructuring of the Economy) and TACIS (Technical Assistance to the Commonwealth of Independent States) programmes. A precondition for applications was to have partners in both the Community and at least one Central or East European country.

It also covered support for democracy building in Latin America and other parts of the world, particularly the African, Caribbean and Pacific (ACP) countries. Notably, the initiative remains the only EU programme to operate worldwide in territories without needing the host country's consent.

The initiative was based on five objectives (later adopted as the Copenhagen criteria in 1993 to formalise the EC's enlargement process): to "promote democracy, human rights, the rule of law, free media and a social market economy".

The key words in the May 1992 Parliament resolution are in its opening paragraph:

"the establishment of a 'European Democracy Initiative' to provide financial aid through the Community budget on a non-party basis, principally through parliamentary institutions and to nongovernmental organisations and non-profit groups, for general civic education and to stabilize and reinforce democratic principles in non-EC countries; also, to assist the development of human rights in such countries; in addition, to develop the concept of civil society in countries where human rights, multi-party systems, the rule of law and economic freedom have been lacking; such funds shall not be disbursed to any group, organisation or other, contrary to the European Parliament's declarations on racism, xenophobia, women's rights or religious freedom."

Applications were processed by the Commission's staff and reviewed by an advisory group with representatives of the Parliament, the Commission and the Council of Europe. Initially 52 projects were approved: ten under the heading "parliamentary practice"; 11 under "promoting and monitoring human rights"; five under "independent media"; ten under "development of NGOs and representative structures"; eight under "local democracy and participation"; and eight under "education and analysis". A dedicated office outside the EU institutions was set up in Brussels to administer the programmes while regional offices were opened in Prague, Moscow and Warsaw. A 1994 reform provided a better geographical spread, and by 1996 the Initiative extended to the EU's MEDA programme covering the Southern Mediterranean and wider Middle East.

In May 1997 the Parliament, with the Commission and the German Bundestag, supported a conference in Berlin on "Parliamentary Development Programmes: Evaluation and beyond"; and in October 1997 it hosted a conference in Brussels on "An Evaluation of Programmes to Strengthen Democracy in Central and Eastern Europe and the New Independent States". By then some 1,200 pro-democracy programmes were in operation, primarily in the EU's "neighbourhood". Later the programme was given worldwide scope and extended to "difficult" territories elsewhere, such as China, Cuba and Russia.

As the current author noted in 1995, "the implications of the linkage now established between the different European Community programmes, with a virtually worldwide coverage, should not be underestimated". These developments gave the European Parliament a leading role in today's increasingly close inter-parliamentary structures, as the European Union enlarged to 28 (now 27) countries, with a neighbourhood policy to 16 of its closest eastern and southern partners.

A key development was the formalisation in 2003 of COSAC, a standing conference of all the EU's national parliaments and the European Parliament, which also hosts its secretariat. COSAC formulates policy directions, and its secretariat provides a clearing house and data base of EU legislation as it is applied across member states.

In 2004 the Euro-Mediterranean Parliamentary Assembly (EMPA) started work. With 240 members, 120 from the 10 largely Arab countries – uniquely including Israel – and 45 MEPs plus 75 EU national parliament representatives, EMPA meets twice a year in full sessions, with its work deliberated by five sub-committees.

During his time as vice-president of the European Parliament, from 2004-2014, Edward McMillan-Scott remained responsible for all the European Parliament's activities and staff bodies involved in democracy and human rights, working closely with its foreign affairs, development and human rights committees.

As of 2022, what became the European Instrument for Democracy and Human Rights (EIDHR) is the world's largest such dedicated programme, with an annual budget of €1 billion and worldwide reach. However, its influence has also reached into all aspects of the European Parliament's evolution as the world's emblematic democratically elected international assembly, as envisaged by its founders in the aftermath of the Second World War.

VII: FAREWELL AND CONCLUSIONS

1. The farewell

by Rory Palmer

Rory Palmer was a Labour MEP for the East Midlands from 2017-2020, sitting on the Environment and Public Health, Employment and Social Affairs & International Development committees. He was previously the deputy city mayor of Leicester. He now works for a social justice charity.

I first took my seat in the European Parliament in October 2017. Theresa May had triggered Article 50 that March; thus the UK at that point was set to leave the EU on 29 March 2019.

As one of the UK's last MEPs and one of its youngest, I had a front row seat during the turbulent political events following the 2016 referendum. I was in Brussels and Strasbourg in the years, months, weeks, days and hours leading up to our 2020 exit. Those historic political events framed a personal journey for each of the UK's MEPs, staff and officials in Brussels.

Events unfolded in unforeseen ways: high-wire votes in the Commons; a change of prime minister; two general elections; European elections and Brexit dates that came and went. Against this eventful backdrop, UK MEPs continued to fulfil our responsibilities.

I had been appointed shadow rapporteur for the Socialist group on a major piece of environmental and public health legislation. I approached this work – meeting stakeholders, coordinating votes ahead of committee meetings, negotiating with the Commission and Council – knowing that it was highly unlikely I would be there for the final vote on this dossier.

In May 2019 the UK unexpectedly took part in the European elections, after which it remained business as usual. Labour's Seb Dance was elected vice-president of the Environment Committee; Claude Moraes as a vice-president of the Socialist group; Liberal Democrat Martin Horwood as a vice-president of the Renew group. Some thought this approach stoic, some that it reflected a false hope that events would change course. Above all, it was a sense of responsibility, knowing the exit was drawing closer, but doing the job we had been elected to do.

From May 2019 to January 2020, MEPs continued their work across committees as rapporteurs, shadow rapporteurs or political coordinators. The Leave MEPs – including the large new Brexit Party grouping – stayed true to their playbook, turning their backs during the EU anthem at the formal opening of the new parliamentary session.

Westminster events took more dramatic turns. Three planned dates for the UK's exit (29 March, 12 April and 31 October 2019) came and went, each time causing MEPs to pack, and then unpack, their various offices. Following the December 2019 general election, it was inevitable that this time we would pack up our offices for good.

Away from the headlines, we continued our parliamentary work whilst supporting our staff who, like MEPs, were facing imminent redundancy, as well as starting to tackle the practical realities of leaving. We packed, made final speeches, downed farewell coffees and beers with colleagues.

The UK left the EU at midnight (Brussels time) on Friday 31 January 2020. The Parliament was sitting in Brussels that week. It became impossible to walk anywhere without bumping into someone offering a sympathetic hug or a farewell handshake.

On the Wednesday, Parliament sat for a final debate on the Withdrawal Agreement, with a profound sadness hanging over Brussels. There were moving speeches from the Brexit process principals, Commission president Ursula von der Leyen (quoting George Eliot) and chief negotiator Michel Barnier. The dignity of the moment was only broken by Nigel Farage, for whom this was a moment of jubilant triumph, one last hurrah in Brussels.

The rendition of Auld Lang Syne in Parliament's hemicycle generated emotional footage for the evening's news. An emotional moment for many, planned by German Green MEP Terry Reintke. One Brexiteer MEP told me that even they were moved.

Following that final vote, UK MEPs were invited to a private reception hosted by Parliament's president, the late David Sassoli. The respective leaders of the UK parties made speeches and we each collected a framed certificate. The European Parliament was determined to ensure this was a dignified farewell, with the formal events choreographed to avoid opportunities for Brexiteer gloating.

For many, those final days were a surreal merging of the political, the practical and the personal. We packed, did TV interviews and said farewells, while Labour MEPs met for an emotional final meeting of the European Parliamentary Labour Party.

Many of the final images feature the "United in Diversity, UK-EU friendship" football scarves I designed and commissioned as farewell gifts for friends and colleagues. I wasn't expecting the attention they drew as people queued at my door asking where they could get one, as its design had so captured the mood. One side carries the EU's motto, "United in Diversity" and the dates 1973-2020, the reverse reads "Always United" a nod to our ongoing bonds of friendship and partnership beyond Brexit. Several MEPs wore their scarves to the final session where the Withdrawal Agreement was endorsed. One was deposited in the official EU museum, the House of European History.

Then it was time to head home. A final walk around the building, pausing at the hemicycle to note that the UK flag was still in place at the front of the chamber. I left a note wishing good luck to the next occupant of my office.

These were moments of historic political drama, but also deeply personal. For some colleagues, this final week represented the end not just of lengthy political careers but also a shuddering milestone as our country left a bloc and political project to which they had devoted many decades.

Some stayed in Brussels for the precise moment of the UK's departure, gathering to sing Auld Lang Syne at Place Jo Cox. As I left on the Friday morning, the European press at the Eurostar terminal carried front-page pictures from that final vote, many featuring the iconic scarves.

A few weeks before, a senior EU official who was a leading player in the Brexit negotiations told me that in politics there can be no room for sentimentality. Working alongside MEPs and others through this period, where political events shaped so many personal stories at such a historic moment, I'm not so sure.

2. Conclusions

by David Harley and Dianne Hayter

What remains from our British MEPs, now that they have gone and Britain is no longer a member of the EU? What did they leave behind before "the waves closed over them", to borrow Christopher Tugendhat's evocative phrase?

Europe and the Parliament itself had been transformed out of all recognition since the first directly elected MEPs arrived in Strasbourg on that fine summer evening in July 1979 for their inaugural plenary session. Many British MEPs actively participated in this transformation. Collectively, as is underlined in contributions to this volume, the MEPs were mostly held in high esteem among fellow MEPs from other countries. Taken individually, some chalked up significant achievements, while others came and went without making such an impression. Taking the 41-year period as a whole, the great majority assiduously attended and took an active part in their committees, political groups and national delegations and in debates in plenary session; they voted through reams of new legislation, held the Commission to account, represented the interests of their constituents, sought to maintain contact with their respective political parties and with the British government, and gave the lie to the accusation that EU decisions were taken by unelected bureaucrats. Indeed, most played a positive part in the unique multifaceted political ecosystem that was the European Parliament, in all its complexity and strangeness, and were directly involved in the enactment of laws and regulations to the benefit of millions of citizens in the member states, including the UK.

The MEPs' input into the European project coincided with, and helped shape, a series of tumultuous events in post-war Europe, including the break-up of the Soviet Union, the reunification of Germany and the refashioning of the entire continent following the return of democracy in Central and Eastern Europe. These years saw the launch of the single market (where the UK provided support and leadership) and the single currency (where the UK opted to remain outside). Throughout this period the EP was gradually increasing its legislative powers and competences, again with British MEPs (Christopher Prout, David Martin, Richard Corbett, Andrew Duff) in the front line of this ongoing institutional battle.

From roughly 2009 onwards, however, the political pendulum began to swing backwards, with the emergence of a second group of British MEPs, composed of UKIP and Eurosceptic Conservative members, whose goal was Britain's withdrawal from the EU. In the 2014 and 2019 elections, UKIP and its successor the Brexit Party won the highest number of seats among British parties. UKIP members used their allowances, and their status as MEPs, to build a platform in the media while making little or no contribution to the core legislative work of an MEP.

The final ten years thus produced two distinct tendencies among the UK MEPs, mirroring the growing division in the country, particularly once David Cameron had let the referendum genie out of the bottle with his Bloomberg speech in January 2013. Even though the majority of MEPs continued their work, that image of division and the two faces of contemporary Britain, remains part of the legacy unwittingly left behind. Britain's departure on 31 January 2020 was however the defining moment of our MEPs' remaining time in office.

Despite this epilogue, their collective legacy from earlier times is altogether more positive. That anti-climatic last goodbye should not overshadow some singular achievements in the preceding decades, nor those years in the late 1990s when Brits held the leadership of the largest political group with Pauline Green, the post of

Parliament secretary-general with Julian Priestley, and when the UK prime minister was the dominant player in the European Council. The Conservative MEPs for their part were securely embedded in the influential EPP family, and in January 2002 Graham Watson was elected chair of the ALDE group. The tentacles of British influence were extending in all directions. These were years of optimism for Britain in Europe and for British MEPs in the European Parliament.

Sowing the seeds of peace and reconciliation in Northern Ireland was perhaps the greatest of all the achievements by our MEPs, although in a category of its own and not open to members from the UK mainland. The role played by the European Parliament, through its MEPs from Northern Ireland, was decisive as a model of conflict resolution and has been largely overlooked. John Hume, together with the unionists Ian Paisley, John Taylor and Jim Nicholson, and with the backing of the EP across all groups and nationalities, devised and promoted cross-community cooperation in small towns and villages in the border area, funded by the EU on a proposal by the EP. The Parliament's culture of seeking compromise and consensus across national, ideological and sectarian divisions was essential to this historic success. The painstaking groundwork, which led to the Good Friday Agreement, could possibly not have happened anywhere else.

At committee level, British chairs of key committees such as Ken Collins (Environment), Malcolm Harbour (Internal Market) and Claude Moraes (Civil Liberties, Justice and Home Affairs) had a determinant influence on issues of vital importance to the wellbeing of European citizens and the European economy – and to the promotion of British interests. Of the many achievements by individual MEPs, Caroline Lucas's success in securing an EU ban on imports of timber from illegal logging despite Council opposition, thereby achieving a global breakthrough in the fight against deforestation, is a striking example of what could be achieved by a tenacious backbencher. The EP provided individual MEPs with a real opportunity to make their name on issues closest to their heart, rather than acting as lobby fodder. Year after year, Scottish and Welsh MEPs and those from deprived English regions made full use of Parliament's final say on the EU budget to maintain significant levels of EU spending in their home nations and constituencies.

On a less positive note, the respect in which British MEPs were held inside the EP was rarely replicated in London. Externally, relations with Whitehall and Westminster, and for Labour and Tory members with their parties back home, were often difficult and distant. While the MEPs felt undervalued and unappreciated, MPs from the two largest parties saw them as upstarts and occasional rivals. The relationship was not helped by the rejection of requests for MEPs to be given access to the facilities of the Houses of Parliament (as was the case in the German Bundestag, for example).

It should have been possible for the main parties to embrace their MEPs more fully. Prior to direct elections, as both Christopher Tugendhat and George Robertson note, the dual mandate meant the Assembly members were embedded in the Westminster parliamentary party structures. Little thought was given to the new situation with MEPs, despite one of the present authors writing in 1977 about the MEPs' relationship with the national party, asking "are they just to be tacked on at conference as a few more ex officio delegates?" She suggested at the least that they should "sit on NEC sub committees" or perhaps sit in the Lords (or not, as she noted, since that was due for abolition) or in the Commons without voting rights, though that alone might not be sufficient.

In fact, for both Labour and Conservatives, a more hands-off approach developed, leading to decisions in London being transmitted to Brussels rather than developed in a consensual way and, in particular, with little party acknowledgement of the MEPs' work and value, and a disregard for the political and democratic role they were playing in the European Parliament. Neither party showcased their leading MEPs nor sought to draw on their wide and deep involvement in European policies.

This dialogue of the deaf between Brussels and London (going wider than just at the intra-party level) hampered relations during much of the period of Britain's membership. From the MEPs' perspective a major stumbling block was the level of ignorance – at the highest level of the British government – of how the EU worked and of the European Parliament's place in that institutional architecture. Ivan Rogers, a distinguished former UK permanent representative, describes the Whitehall vision of the EU as "a world largely beyond their ken".

Looking through Westminster eyes, the European Parliament was a strange animal, with a shortage of political big beasts. Many openly expressed the view that it was not "a real parliament", because it didn't deal with a government as in Westminster.

MEPs might be good at the detail of legislation, went the line from London, but charisma and communication skills let alone passion and drama seemed in short supply. The problem of relations between the European and UK parliaments was never resolved, not helped by Labour and Tory MEPs often not finding the time, in addition to their travel to and from Brussels and Strasbourg, to visit London to liaise with their respective parties and contribute to discussions on European policy. The MEPs might reply that they were rarely asked, and never listened to.

The MEPs also had to cope with a generally hostile media, the tabloids bordering on the xenophobic, and (unequalled elsewhere in Europe) in their hostility to the European project. The idea of a political system based on respect for differences and compromise and decisions being reached through a deliberative process was the antithesis of politics as perceived by sections of the UK media. In the words of Tim Bale, professor of politics at Sussex University: "Democracy isn't just about an election every five years. It's a continual process of back and forth, listening, calibrating and adjusting". Furthermore, the media's lack of coverage of the positive work undertaken, alongside its focus on Nigel Farage (who appeared more often on BBC1's Question Time, for example, than any other politician – 4 times in 2013 alone) served to undermine any sense of a working, democratic and responsible parliament. No wonder the legacy of MEPs in terms of their image in the media or in Westminster is unworthy of their efforts.

Several contributors pay a warm tribute to the active 351 women and men who took part in this unique political and European adventure. Ivan Rogers' words are particularly poignant: "The EU as a whole benefitted from the expertise, the wisdom, the breadth, the temperament, the professionalism, the humour but even the healthy scepticism of so many British MEPs over decades. Those contributions won't be forgotten, and the imprint ... is indelible". The leading German politician David McAllister touches on the human side of life as an MEP in alluding to "the changes in the debate culture" resulting from the departure of British MEPs, and "the absence of a certain humour and wit that I can only describe as quintessentially British".

As actors in an important period in recent European history, Britain's MEPs deserve a better judgement of their record than to be dismissed as a mere footnote. Have they left a lasting legacy? The work they did – the reports adopted in late-night sittings, the crucial cross-party agreements patiently negotiated – and the good they did will live on long after their departure.

Most of them deserve to be remembered in a positive light. But history is often unfair: only time will tell. What is clear is that the unique, international European Union became not just an economic or free market bloc, but a democratic grouping, seeking to promote human, citizen, environmental, consumer and workers' rights across 28 nations and beyond. As these stories tell, such success owes much to the UK MEPs; taken as a whole, the record of their achievements is indisputably significant and will endure, even if Britain has since chosen another path.

ANNEXES

1. The 351

by Joshua Stratford

Joshua Stratford is a student of British Politics and Legislative Studies at the University of Hull and worked on this book during his year as a parliamentary intern with Dianne Hayter. He has been a member of the British Youth Parliament.

From the first direct elections in 1979 until the UK's withdrawal from the EU in 2020, the UK voted in 351 members of the European Parliament. Until now, there has been no consolidated list of these MEPs, and this is provided in Annex 2 below. Here we summarise some of the main characteristics of "the 351".

Throughout the nine parliamentary terms, this group of politicians collectively represented 21 different national political parties. They held a range of positions within the EP including president, vice-presidents, leaders of European political groups and parties, chairs and vice-chairs of parliamentary committees, rapporteurs, bureau members and quaestors. With changes in the British political landscape and the switch to proportional representation, the makeup of this group changed dramatically.

Gender

Of the 351, 96 were female (27.4%) and 255 male. As with the political representation, the balance changed over time.

In the first term (1979-1984), only 10 of the 81 were female (12.3%). This figure increased to 12 women (14.8%) in the second term (1984-1989) and stayed at 12 in the third term, until the 1994 election when it increased to 16 (18.4%). In the fifth term (1999-2004) there was a rise of 6, up to 22 women. In the sixth term (2004-2009), the number dipped to 20 (25.6%). In the seventh parliamentary term (2009-2014) it rose to 25 (34.7%). In 2014-2019 it rose to 26 (35.6%) and in the ninth and final term, it reached 30 (41.1%).

However, it should be noted that the number of UK MEPs changed over these years. The first 3 terms saw 81; there were 87 in the fourth and fifth terms, 78 in the sixth, 72 in the seventh and 73 in the eighth and ninth.

Gender by party

In the Conservative group, 20.1% across the 41 years were female, 24 out of 119, with 95 men. The Labour Party had fewer MEPs in total (107), although a higher percentage of women: 26.1% (28 MEPs) alongside 79 men.

Of UKIP's 33 MEPs, 9 were women (27.2%).

For the Liberal Democrats, of their 32 MEPs 17 were women – thus of the largest four political parties, it was the only one to have a (slight) majority of women (53.2%).

Out of the 10 Green Party MEPs, 7 were women: at 70% female representation the highest percentage of women out of parties with MEPs in double digits. The SNP had 8 MEPs, of whom 3 were female and 5 male, putting their female representatives at 37.5%. The DUP had 3 MEPs in total, one of whom was a woman. Sinn Féin had 2 MEPs, both female. The BNP likewise only had 2 MEPs, both male.

The Brexit Party had 29 MEPs: 13 women and 16 men, so women comprising 44.8%. Plaid Cymru had 2 MEPs, one of whom was female. The Alliance Party only had one MEP, who was female. The UUP had 2 male MEPs, and the SDLP had one.

National party leadership

The larger and more established political parties had more formal structures within their delegations: the smaller the party the less likely they needed any formal structure. Here we list the leaders of the party delegations, in chronological order:

Labour (BLG/EPLP) had 12 leaders: Barbara Castle, Alf Lomas, David Martin, Barry Seal, Glyn Ford, Pauline Green, Wayne David, Alan Donnelly, Simon Murphy, Gary Titley, Glenis Willmott and Richard Corbett.

The Conservatives had 14 leaders: James Scott-Hopkins, Henry Plumb, Christopher Prout, Tom Spencer, Edward McMillan-Scott, Jonathan Evans, Timothy Kirkhope, Giles Chichester, Philip Bushill-Matthews, Martin Callanan, Richard Ashworth, Syed Kamall, Ashley Fox and Geoffrey Van Orden.

There were 5 Liberal Democrat leaders: Graham Watson, Diana Wallis (2002-04 and 2006-07), Chris Davies, Andrew Duff and Fiona Hall.

Within the UKIP delegation, many were leaders of the national party whilst MEPs: Michael Holmes, Jeffrey Titford, Roger Knapman, Nigel Farage, Diane James, Paul Nuttall and Gerard Batten.

Length of time served

The longest serving British MEP was David Martin, winning a seat in 7 elections, and serving 35 years, making him the second longest serving MEP across the EU.

The shortest serving was Heather Anderson: just 4 days. She was fifth on the SNP list for the 2019 election. However only 3 seats were won by the SNP. Alyn Smith (first on the list) had stepped down on his election to the Commons and the fourth placed Margaret Ferrier had also become an MP, leaving the EP seat vacant for Anderson. She took her seat on the 27 January 2020, 4 days before the UK left the EU.

Family

There have always been families with multiple members involved in politics, not least Boris Johnson's father Stanley, who was an MEP from 1979-1984. Similarly, Jacob Rees-Mogg's sister, Annunziata, served from 2019-2020. There are four examples of UK MEPs having family members who also sat in the European Parliament. Peter and Christopher Beazley (father and son) both sat in the second and third parliamentary terms. Caroline and Robert Jackson (spouses) were MEPs: Robert only sat in the first parliamentary term whereas Caroline sat from the second through to the sixth term. Edward and Elaine Kellett-Bowman (spouses) both served in the first parliamentary term though Elaine only served that one term whereas Edward continued for another three terms. Diana and James Elles were mother and son: Diana served in the first two terms, whereas James sat from the second until the eighth term.

Political careers

Many MEPs not only had careers in the European Parliament, but also held positions in other political institutions.

(i) House of Commons

32 MEPs held seats in the Commons prior to becoming an MEP, 18 of whom were Conservative MPs: Robert Atkins, John Bowis, Nirj Deva, Den Dover, Basil de Ferranti, David Harris, Elaine Kellett-Bowman, Timothy Kirkhope, Roger Knapman, Harmar Nicholls, Emma Nicholson (who sat as a Liberal Democrat for the last two years as an MP), Tom Normanton, Brandon Rhys-Williams, James Scott-Hopkins, James Spicer, John Taylor, Ian Twinn and Ann Widdecombe.

8 MEPs were previously Labour MPs: Barbara Castle, Bob Cryer, Les Huckfield, Robert Kilroy-Silk, Stan Newens, Siôn Simon, John Tomlinson and Phillip Whitehead.

Three Liberal Democrats (not counting Emma Nicholson) were MPs before becoming MEPs: Chris Davies, Martin Horwood and Liz Lynne. Both UUP MEPs had previously sat in the Commons:

Jim Nicholson and John Taylor. Winnie Ewing was the only SNP member who held a seat in the Commons before becoming an MEP.

33 MEPs won seats in the Commons after being MEPs, 16 of whom were Labour: Roland Boyes, Richard Caborn, Ann Clwyd, Tony Cunningham, Bob Cryer, Wayne David, Anneliese Dodds, Derek Enright, Win Griffiths, Mark Hendrick, Geoff Hoon, Afzal Khan, Joyce Quin, Allan Rogers, Llew Smith and George Stevenson.

Their Conservative equivalents were David Curry, Sheila Faith, Vicky Ford, Eric Forth, Robert Goodwill, Christopher Heaton-Harris, Robert Jackson, Andrew Lewer, John Marshall, Anne McIntosh, Neil Parish and Theresa Villiers.

Both Nick Clegg and Chris Huhne of the Liberal Democrats and Caroline Lucas of the Green Party became MPs after their terms as MEPs. The SNP's Alyn Smith made the same move, while the SDLP's John Hume was both an MP and MEP from 1983 to 2004.

(ii) House of Lords

10 MEPs were already in the Lords before being elected to the European Parliament: Conservatives were Nicholas Bethell, Diana Elles, Richard Inglewood (Richard Fletcher-Vane), William Legge, Alexander Macmillan, Nosheena Mobarik, Harmar Nicholls and Charles Strachey. The other two were Liberal Democrats: Sarah Ludford and Emma Nicholson.

29 MEPs went to the Lords after becoming MEPs although Shelagh Roberts in 1992 died before taking her seat. At least one ex-MEP (Bill Newton Dunn) declined the offer of a peerage.

13 sat as Conservatives: Richard Balfe, Martin Callanan, Ian Duncan, Jacqueline Foster, Daniel Hannan, Gloria Hooper, Syed Kamall, Timothy Kirkhope, Anne McIntosh, Henry Plumb (who took his seat whilst still an MEP), Christopher Prout, Patricia Rawlings and Charles Wellesley (Duke of Wellington).

11 Labour MEPs joined the Lords: Angela Billingham, Michael Cashman, Barbara Castle, Christine Crawley, Lyndon Harrison, Wajid Khan, Glenys Kinnock, Eluned Morgan, Joyce Quin, John Tomlinson and Peter Truscott.

2 Liberal Democrats (Sharon Bowles and Robin Teverson), the DUP's Ian Paisley, and Brexit Party's Claire Fox moved to the Lords (the latter sitting as a non-affiliated peer).

8 MEPs held seats in both the Lords and Commons: Barbara Castle, Timothy Kirkhope, Anne McIntosh, Harmar Nicholls, Emma Nicholson, Ian Paisley, Joyce Quin and John Taylor (UUP).

(iii) Hereditary lords

There are six exceptions to those on the list of those appointed to the Lords, as they inherited their positions in the Lords rather than through being appointed. The first was Nicholas William Bethell, the 4th Baron Bethell, who inherited the Barony after the passing of his cousin in 1967. He sat in the Lords until the House of Lords Act 1999.

William Richard Fletcher-Vane, usually called Richard Inglewood, inherited his peerage in 1989 after the passing of his father. With the House of Lords Act, Richard was one of the 92 hereditary peers to retain his seat.

The third hereditary peer was William Legge, usually known as William Dartmouth; styled Viscount Lewisham from 1962-1997, he then inherited the title of 10th Earl of Dartmouth along with his father's seat and sat in the Lords as a Conservative. Like Nicholas Bethell, William Legge only sat in the Lords until 1999.

Alexander Daniel Alan Macmillan inherited his peerage from his grandfather Harold Macmillan in 1986, thereby becoming the 2nd Earl of Stockton. As with the previous peers, Alexander Macmillan lost his seat in 1999.

Charles Towneley Strachey inherited the family title at the age of 16, becoming the 4th Baron O'Hagan after the passing of his grandfather in 1961. However, he did not take his seat in the Lords until late 1967. He also lost his seat in 1999.

Charles Wellesley, now the Duke of Wellington, also inherited his seat in the Lords. From 1972-2014 he was formally known (when not as Charles Wellesley) under his hereditary title of the Marquess of Douro, becoming the ninth Duke of Wellington on the death of his father in 2014, though did not take his seat in the Lords until 2015 in a by-election.

(iv) Regional representatives

Four MEPs also served in the Scottish Parliament: Christian Allard, Winnie Ewing, George Lyon and Aileen McLeod.

Of the Northern Irish MEPs, seven served in the devolved body as MLAs: Jim Allister, Martina Anderson, Bairbre de Brún, Diane Dodds, John Hume, Naomi Long and John Taylor.

Two MEPs served in the Senedd: Nathan Gill and Eluned Morgan.

Age of MEPs and deaths while serving

Overall, the most common age range at election was 50-59, representing one third of those elected from 1979 to 2019. The age range of 40-49 was second most common, followed by 60-69 and 30-39. At any election there were only ever 1 or 2 elected who were aged 18-29, similar to the 70+ range. However, the 2019 election had four MEPs at 70+.

Six MEPs died during their parliamentary terms: Terry Pitt (1987), Basil de Ferranti (1988), Kenneth Stewart (1996), Allan Macartney (1998), Phillip Whitehead (2005) and Philip Bradbourn (2014).

Party switches, changes of allegiance, whip suspensions

The first instance of an MEP switching parties was in December 1983 when Michael Gallagher left the Labour Party and (in January 1984) joined the Social Democratic Party – the only change of party in the first three terms of the Parliament. Although there were no party moves in the second term, in late January 1987 John Taylor of the Ulster Unionist Party changed his European group allegiance, quitting the European Democrats for the European Right group.

The next occurrence was in October 1998 when James Moorhouse was the first to switch from the Conservatives to the Liberal Democrats. In December 1998 Ken Coates and Hugh Kerr left the Socialist group for the European United Left/Nordic Green Left. Ken Coates stayed as an independent whereas Hugh Kerr joined the Scottish Socialist Party.

In January 1999, both Brendan Donnelly and John Stevens left the Conservative Party and formed the Pro-Euro Conservative Party. On the 3 January 1999, Tom Spencer had the Conservative whip suspended.

The next move was in 2000 when Bill Newton Dunn left the Conservatives for the Liberal Democrats. All the earlier MEPs who had switched party had either not run for re-election or were defeated. However, in 2004 Newton Dunn successfully ran as a Liberal Democrat. Richard Balfe, having sat as a Labour MEP since 1979, had the whip withdrawn in 2002 and joined the Conservative Party. He stood down as an MEP at the next election, in 2004, and now sits in the House of Lords.

Only a month into the sixth parliamentary term, Ashley Mote left UKIP to become an independent and went on to become vice-chair of the Identity, Tradition and Sovereignty group. In October 2004 Robert Kilroy-Silk withdrew from the UKIP whip but remained as an independent member of the party. Despite this, he unsuccessfully attempted to gain leadership of the party. In January 2005, just a few months after his failed attempt, he left UKIP and created the Veritas party. However, he saw out his term as an Independent MEP.

Roger Helmer was suspended from the Conservative whip from May 2005 to September 2006, though remaining a non-attached member until 2009 when he joined the European Conservatives and Reformists with the rest of the Conservatives.

In March 2007, Jim Allister left the DUP and sat as an independent until he founded the Traditional Unionist Voice Party. The next switch was in November 2007 when Saj Karim left the Conservatives for the Liberal Democrats. Then in July 2009 Edward McMillan-Scott had the Conservative whip withdrawn and sat as a non-attached member until September when he was expelled from the party. His thoughts on this journey are described below.

In 2010 Nikki Sinclaire was expelled from UKIP. David Campbell Bannerman left UKIP for the Conservative Party in May 2011 whilst Roger Helmer moved from the Conservatives to UKIP in March 2012.

Andrew Brons left the BNP in October 2012 and stayed as a non-attached member until the end of his parliamentary term when he did not seek re-election. Mike Nattrass left UKIP in September 2013 and launched the Independence from Europe Party.

The biggest movement between parties happened in the eighth parliamentary term (2014-19) when 20 people left UKIP and one member was expelled, 13 joining the Brexit Party: Tim Aker, Jonathan Arnott, Jonathan Bullock, David Coburn, Jane Collins, Bill Etheridge, Nigel Farage, Ray Finch, Nathan Gill, Diane James, Paul Nuttall, Margot Parker and Julia Reid. Most sat as independents between their transition, though Tim Aker joined the Thurrock Independents in the interim as did Bill Etheridge for the Libertarian Party, and thence the Brexit Party.

Five of the previous UKIP MEPs stayed as independents: Janice Atkinson, Louise Bours, James Carver, William Dartmouth (William Legge) and Steven Woolfe. Amjad Bashir joined the Conservatives and Patrick O'Flynn the SDP (a very different party to the SDP that Michael Gallagher had joined, this second incarnation having been formed after the first SDP merged with the Liberal Party). In the same term, Richard Ashworth and Julie Girling left the Conservative Party, Ashworth joining the newly formed Change UK Party and Girling staying as an independent.

Although the last parliamentary term lasted less than a year, six people changed party – all from the Brexit Party. Lance Forman, Lucy Harris, John Longworth and Annunziata Rees-Mogg, joined the Conservatives. Andrew Kerr and Louis Stedman-Bryce remained as independents.

One mover's tale: Edward McMillan-Scott

One thread in this book is the change – for both the Conservative and Labour parties – of their stance towards Europe, and thus the EP, and how this impacted on the MEPs who were largely powerless in the central councils of their respective parties. Thus, in the Conservative case, the move of some Conservative MEPs to the Lib Dems reflected – as they saw it – the party itself moving from its pro-EU stance, while for Labour (as with the Conservatives) the national party acted to select or promote candidates closer to the prevailing policy.

Edward McMillan-Scott is one example of a respected, experienced MEP being so washed aside by the Conservative tide that he then followed others out of the fold and into Liberal Democrat arms. He was helped in this move – traumatic for any politician in our tribal politics – by following James Moorhouse and Bill Newton Dunn, but he did not go without a fight. Until Boris Johnson withdrew the whip from a swathe of long-serving MPs, McMillan-Scott's move was one of the most senior in recent times. He finally was to serve 30 years in the Parliament, including 15 as an EP vice-president and four as the Conservative MEPs' leader (1997-2001).

However, as he witnessed what he described as the "hard right" emerging in the Conservatives, evidenced by leader William Hague's Harrogate speech in 2001, which he believes was influenced by Daniel Hannan, he and Timothy Kirkhope (who remains in the Tory party) met with Hague to share their concerns about the anti-EU drift and indeed the role of Hannan. Within the MEP group, there was already a block of 8 or 9 (including Martin Callanan and Chris Heaton-Harris) who were asserting their Eurosceptic views, reflected in the party's reluctance to become full EPP members. Hague instructed McMillan-Scott and James Moorhouse to re-negotiate the party's relationship with the EPP despite the views of the majority of Tory MEPs. The right, however, wanted complete withdrawal from the EPP – later promised by Cameron as he sought the party leadership and which he later implemented – to the consternation of those like McMillan-Scott. This issue was especially sensitive as it happened around the time Christopher Prout, who had brought the Conservatives into the EPP, died.

McMillan-Scott himself, well regarded by his peers, stood for the position of vice-president of the Parliament against a candidate of the Conservatives' new political group, the ECR (to the consternation of Timothy Kirkhope, who then lost the anticipated leadership of the ECR) and thus promptly lost the whip. He then sat first as a non-attached member but later – having been approached by Nick Clegg – joined the Liberal Democrats.

Even today, McMillan-Scott has no regrets about his own move, only about the direction taken by his erstwhile party. Like other MEPs whose views became at variance with their party's but who had little influence on domestic politics, he had to take a plunge into a former opposing political home. That this happened more in the European Parliament than in the Commons is largely because of the overwhelming role Europe played in the Conservatives' recent history, but also because of the semi-detached nature of MEPs' position within their national parties.

Both main parties failed to accord MEPs a proper role, even when they were senior, experienced and respected politicians playing a key role in the European Parliament. This semi-detached approach to the EP and its work may also have contributed to certain popular perceptions in the UK of the Parliament and the EU in general which ultimately led to Brexit.

2 List of all elected UK MEPs 1979-2020

by Joshua Stratford

Showing party affiliation, date of birth/death and years in the EP.
Note: party affiliation is at the time of first election. Party switching, rather rare for much of the period, became common with the arrival of large numbers of Brexiteers in the later years. The issue of party switching is discussed in detail in Annex 1 above.

Adam, Gordon, Labour Party, 28.3.1934-; 1979-June 1999, December 1999-2004
Agnew, Stuart, UKIP, 30.8.1949-; 2009-2019
Ainslie, Scott John, Green Party, 27.12.1968-; 2019-2020
Aker, Tim, UKIP, 23.5.1985-; 2014-2019
Allard, Christian, SNP, 31.3.1964-; 2019-2020
Allister, Jim, DUP, 2.4.1953-; 2004-2009
Anderson, Heather, SNP, 31.1.1959-; 2020-2020
Anderson, Lucy, Labour Party, 2.6.1965-; 2014-2019
Anderson, Martina, Sinn Féin, 16.4.1962-; 2012-2020
Andreasen, Marta, UKIP, 26.11.1954-; 2009-2014
Arnott, Jonathan, UKIP, 12.1.1981-; 2014-2019
Ashworth, Richard, Conservative Party, 17.9.1947-; 2004-2019
Atkins, Robert, Conservative Party, 5.2.1946-; 1999-2014
Atkinson, Janice, UKIP, 31.8.1962-; 2014-2019
Attwooll, Elspeth, Liberal Democrat, 1.2.1943-; 1999-2009

Balfe, Richard, Labour Party, 14.5.1944-; 1979-2004
Balfour, Neil, Conservative Party, 12.8.1944-; 1979-1983

ANNEX 2

Barton, Roger, Labour Party, 6.1.1945-; 1989-1999
Bashir, Amjad Mahmood, Conservative Party, 17.9.1952-; 2014-2019
Batten, Gerard, UKIP, 27.3.1954-; 2004-2019
Battersby, Robert, Conservative Party, 14.12.1924-30.9.2002, 1979-1989
Bearder, Catherine Zena, Liberal Democrat, 14.1.1949-; 2009-2020
Beazley, Christopher, Conservative Party, 5.9.1952-; 1984-1994, 1999-2009
Beazley, Peter, Conservative Party, 9.6.1922-23.12.2004, 1979-1994
Bennion, Phil, Liberal Democrat, 7.10.1954-; 2012-2014, 2019-2020
Bethell, Nicholas, Conservative Party, 19.7.1938-8.9.2007, 1979-1994, 1999-2003
Billingham, Angela, Labour Party, 31.7.1939-; 1994-1999
Bird, John, Labour Party, 6.2.1926-18.11.1997, 1987-1994
Bloom, Godfrey, UKIP, 22.11.1949-; 2004-2014
Booth, Graham, UKIP, 29.3.1940-14.12.2011, 2002-2008
Bours, Louise, UKIP, 23.12.1968-; 2014-2019
Bowe, David, Labour, 19.7.1955-; 1989-2004
Bowis, John, Conservative, 2.8.1945-; 1999-2014
Bowles, Sharon, Liberal Democrat, 12.6.1953-; 2005-2014
Boyes, Roland, Labour Party, 12.2.1937-16.6.2006, 1979-1984
Bradbourn, Philip Charles, Conservative Party, 9.8.1951-19.12.2014, 1999-2014
Brannen, Paul, Labour Party, 13.9.1962-; 2014-2019
Brons, Andrew Henry William, BNP, 3.6.1947-; 2009-2014
Brookes, Beata, Conservative Party, 21.1.1930-17.8.2015, 1979-1989
Brophy, Jane, Liberal Democrat, 27.8.1963-; 2019-2020
Buchan, Janey, Labour Party, 30.4.1926-14.1.2012, 1979-1994
Bufton, John, UKIP, 31.8.1962-; 2009-2014
Bull, David, Brexit Party, 9.5.1969-; 2019-2020
Bullock, Jonathan, UKIP, 3.3.1963-; 2017-2020
Bunting, Judith Ann, Liberal Democrat, 27.11.1960-; 2019-2020
Bushill-Matthews, Philip, Conservative Party, 15.1.1943-; 1999-2009

Caborn, Richard, Labour Party, 6.10.1943-; 1979-1984
Callanan, Martin, Conservative Party, 8.8.1961-; 1999-2014
Campbell Bannerman, David, UKIP, 28.5.1960-; 2009-2019
Carver, James Bruce, UKIP, 15.08.1969-; 2014-2019
Cashman, Michael, Labour Party, 17.12.1950-; 1999-2014
Cassidy, Bryan, Conservative Party, 17.2.1934-; 1984-1999
Castle, Barbara, Labour Party, 6.10.1910-3.5.2002, 1979-1989
Catherwood, Fred, Conservative Party, 30.1.1925-30.11.2014, 1979-1994
Chichester, Giles, Conservative Party, 29.7.1946-; 1994-2014
Chowns, Ellie, Green Party, 7.3.1975-; 2019-2020
Clark, Derek Roland, UKIP, 10.10.1933-; 2004-2014
Clegg, Nick, Liberal Democrat, 7.1.1967-; 1999-2004
Clwyd, Ann, Labour Party, 21.3.1937-; 1979-1984
Coates, Ken, Labour Party, 16.9.1930-27.6.2010, 1989-1999
Coburn, David, UKIP, 11.2.1959-; 2014-2019
Collins, Jane, UKIP, 17.2.1962-; 2014-2019
Collins, Ken, Labour Party, 12.8.1939-; 1979-1999

Colman, Trever, UKIP, 27.8.1941-22.3.2022, 2008-2014
Corbett, Richard, Labour Party, 6.1.1955-; 1996-2009, 2014-2020
Corrie, John, Conservative Party, 29.7.1935-; 1994-2004
Cottrell, Richard, Conservative Party, 11.7.1943-; 1979-1989
Crampton, Peter, Labour Party, 10.6.1932-12.7.2011, 1989-1999
Crawley, Christine, Labour Party, 9.1.1950-; 1984-1999
Cryer, Bob, Labour Party, 3.12.1934-12.4.1994, 1984-1989
Cunningham, Tony, Labour Party, 16.9.1952-; 1994-1999
Curry, David Maurice, Conservative Party, 13.6.1944-; 1979-1989

Dalton, Daniel Anthony Thomas, Conservative Party, 31.1.1974-; 2015-2019
Daly, Margaret, Conservative Party, 26.1.1938-; 1984-1994
Dalziel, Ian, Conservative Party, 21.6.1947-; 1979-1984
Dance, Seb, Labour Party, 1.12.81-; 2014-2020
Dartmouth, William, UKIP, 23.9.1949-; 2009-2019
Daubney, Martin, Brexit Party, 22.6.1970-; 2019-2020
David, Wayne, Labour Party, 1.7.1957-; 1989-1999
Davies, Chris, Liberal Democrat, 7.7.1954-; 1999-2014, 2019-2020
de Brún, Bairbre, Sinn Féin, 10.1.1954-; 2004-2012
de Camborne Lucy, Belinda, Brexit Party, 15.10.1976-; 2019-2020
de Courcy-Ling, John, Conservative Party, 14.10.1933-10.11.2005, 1979-1989
de Ferranti, Basil, Conservative Party, 2.7.1930-24.9.1988, 1979-1988
Deva, Nirj, Conservative Party, 11.5.1948-; 1999-2019
Dhamija, Dinesh, Liberal Democrat Party, 28.3.1950-; 2019-2020
Dodds, Anneliese, Labour Party, 16.3.1978-; 2014-2017
Dodds, Diane, DUP, 16.08.1958-; 2009-2020
Donnelly, Alan, Labour Party, 16.7.1957-; 1989-2000
Donnelly, Brendan, Conservative Party, 25.8.1950-; 1994-1999
Dover, Densmore, Conservative Party, 4.4.1938-; 1999-2009
Dowding, Gina, Green Party, 15.07.1962-; 2019-2020
Duff, Andrew, Liberal Democrat, 25.12.1950-; 1999-2014
Duncan, Ian, Conservative Party, 13.2.1973, 2014-2017

Elles, Diana, Conservative Party, 19.7.1921-17.10.2009, 1979-1989
Elles, James, Conservative Party, 3.9.1949-; 1984-2014
Elliott, Michael, Labour Party, 3.6.1932-; 1984-1999
Enright, Derek, Labour Party, 2.8.1935-31.10.1995, 1979-1984
Etheridge, William 'Bill' Milroy, UKIP, 18.3.1970-; 2014-2019
Evans, Jill, Plaid Cymru, 8.5.1959-; 1999-2020
Evans, Jonathan, Conservative Party, 2.6.1950-; 1999-2009
Evans, Robert, Labour & Co-operative Party, 23.10.1956-; 1994-2009
Ewing, Winifred, SNP, 10.7.1929-; 1979-1999
Faith, Irene Sheila, Conservative Party, 3.6.1928-28.9.2014, 1984-1989
Falconer, Alex, Labour Party, 1.04.1940-12.8.2012, 1984-1999
Farage, Nigel, UKIP, 3.4.1964-; 1999-2020
Fergusson, Adam, Conservative Party, 10.7.1932-; 1979-1984
Finch, Raymond, UKIP, 2.6.1963-; 2014-2019

Flack, John, Conservative Party, 3.1.1957-; 2017-2019
Fletcher-Vane, Richard (Lord Inglewood), Conservative Party, 31.7.1951-; 1989-1994, 1999-2004
Ford, Glyn, Labour Party, 28.1.1950-; 1984-2009
Ford, Victoria 'Vicky' Grace, Conservative Party, 21.9.1967-; 2009-2017
Forman, Lance Philip, Brexit Party, 13.10.1962-; 2019-2020
Forster, Norvela Felicia, Conservative Party, 25.7.1931-30.4.1993, 1979-1984
Forth, Eric, Conservative Party, 9.9.1944-17.5.2006, 1979-1984
Foster, Jacqueline, Conservative Party, 30.12.1947-; 1999-2019
Fox, Ashley, Conservative Party, 15.11.1969-; 2009-2019
Fox, Claire, Brexit Party, 5.6.1960-; 2019-2020

Gallagher, Michael, Labour Party, 1.7.1943-10.6.2015, 1979-1984
Gibson, Barbara, Liberal Democrat, 25.8.1962-; 2019-2020
Gill, Nathan, UKIP, 6.7.1973, 2014-2020
Gill, Neena, Labour Party, 24.12.1956-; 1999-2009, 2014-2020
Girling, Julie McCulloch, Conservative Party, 21.12.1956-; 2009-2019
Glancy, James Alexander, Brexit Party, 25.8.1982-; 2019-2020
Goodwill, Robert, Conservative Party, 31.12.1956-; 1999-2004
Green, Pauline, Labour & Co-operative Party, 8.12.1948-; 1989-1999
Griffin, Nick, BNP, 1.3.1959-; 2009-2014
Griffin, Theresa, Labour Party, 11.12.1962-; 2014-2020
Griffiths, Win, Labour Party, 11.2.1943-; 1979-1989

Habib, Benyamin Naeem, Brexit Party, 7.6.1965-; 2019-2020
Hall, Fiona Jane, Liberal Democrat, 15.7.1955-; 2004-2014
Hallam, David, Labour Party, 13.6.1948-; 1994-1999
Hannan, Daniel, Conservative Party, 1.9.1971-; 1999-2020
Harbour, Malcolm, Conservative Party, 19.2.1947-; 1999-2014
Hardstaff, Veronica, Labour Party, 23.10.1941-; 1994-1999
Harris, David, Conservative Party, 1.11.1937-; 1979-1984
Harris, Lucy Elizabeth, Brexit Party, 19.10.1990-; 2019-2020
Harrison, Lyndon, Labour Party, 28.9.1947-; 1989-1999
Heaton-Harris, Christopher, Conservative Party, 28.11.1967-; 1999-2009
Heaver, Michael, Brexit Party, 22.9.1989-; 2019-2020
Helmer, Roger, Conservative, 25.1.1944-; 1999-2017
Hendrick, Mark, Labour & Co-operative Party, 2.11.1958-; 1994-1999
Hindley, Michael, Labour Party, 11.4.1947-; 1984-1999
Holmes, Michael, UKIP, 6.6.1938-; 1999-2002
Honeyball, Mary, Labour Party, 12.11.1952-; 2000-2019
Hook, Antony, Liberal Democrat, 10.4.1980-; 2019-2020
Hookem, Mike, UKIP, 9.10.1953-; 2014-2019
Hoon, Geoffrey, Labour Party, 6.12.1953-; 1984-1994
Hooper, Gloria, Conservative Party, 25.5.1939-; 1979-1984
Hopper, William Joseph, Conservative Party, 9.8.1929-; 1979-1984
Hord, Brian Howard, Conservative Party, 20.6.1934-30.8.2015, 1979-1984
Horwood, Martin, Liberal Democrat, 12.10.1962-; 2019-2020

Howarth, John, Labour Party, 31.10.1958-; 2017-2020
Howell, Paul Frederick, Conservative Party, 17.1.1951-20.9.2008, 1979-1994
Howitt, Richard, Labour Party, 5.4.1961-; 1994-2016
Huckfield, Leslie, Labour Party, 704.1942-; 1984-1989
Hudghton, Ian Stewart, SNP, 19.09.1951-; 1998-2019
Hughes, Stephen, Labour Party, 19.8.1952-; 1984-2014
Huhne, Christopher, Liberal Democrat, 2.7.1954-; 1999-2005
Hume, John, SDLP, 18.1.1937-3.9.2020, 1979-2004
Hutton, Alasdair Henry, Conservative Party, 19.5.1940-; 1979-1989

Jackson, Caroline, Conservative Party, 5.11.1946-; 1984-2009
Jackson, Christopher, Conservative Party, 24.5.1935-13.12.2019, 1979-1994
Jackson, Robert, Conservative Party, 24.9.1946-; 1979-1984
James, Diane Martine, UKIP, 20.11.1959-; 2014-2019
Johnson, Stanley, Conservative Party, 18.8.1940-; 1979-1984
Jones, Jacqueline 'Jackie', Labour Party, 10.2.1966-; 2019-2020
Jordan, Christina Sheila, Brexit Party, 19.6.1962-; 2019-2020

Kamall, Syed, Conservative Party, 15.2.1967-; 2005-2019
Karim, Sajjad, Conservative Party, 11.7.1970-; 2004-2019
Kellett-Bowman, Edward, Conservative Party, 25.2.1931-; 1979-1984,1988-1999
Kellett-Bowman, Elaine, Conservative Party, 8.7.1923-4.3.2014, 1979-1984
Kerr, Andrew, Brexit Party, 23.9.1958-; 2019-2020
Kerr, Hugh, Labour Party, 9.7.1944-; 1994-1999
Key, Brian Michael, Labour Party, 20.9.1947-20.1.2016, 1979-1984
Khan, Mohammed Afzal, Labour Party, 5.4.1958-; 2014-2017
Khan, Wajid, Labour Party, 15.10.1979-; 2017-2019
Khanbhai, Bashir, Conservative Party, 22.9.1945-16.04.2020, 1999-2004
Kilby, Michael Leopold, Conservative Party, 3.9.1924-9.9.2008, 1984-1989
Kilroy-Silk, Robert, UKIP, 19.5.1942-; 2004-2009
Kinnock, Glenys, Labour Party, 7.7.1944-; 1994-2009
Kirkhope, Timothy, Conservative Party, 29.4.1945-; 1999-2016
Kirton-Darling, Judith 'Jude', Labour Party, 2.6.1977-; 2014-2020
Knapman, Roger Maurice, UKIP, 20.2.1944-; 2004-2009

Lambert, Jean, Green Party, 1.6.1950-; 1999-2019
Lewer, Andrew Lain, Conservative Party, 18.7.1971-; 2014-2017
Lomas, Alf, Labour Party, 30.4.1928-6.1.2021, 1979-1999
Long, Naomi Rachel, Alliance Party, 13.12.1971-; 2019-2020
Longworth, John, Brexit Party, 14.5.1958-; 2019-2020
Lowe, Rupert James Graham, Brexit Party, 31.10.1957-; 2019-2020
Lucas, Caroline, Green Party, 9.12.1960-; 1999-2010
Ludford, Sarah, Liberal Democrat, 14.3.1951-; 1999-2014
Lynne, Elizabeth "Liz", Liberal Democrat, 22.1.1948-; 1999-2012
Lyon, George, Liberal Democrat, 16.7.1956-; 2009-2014

Macartney, Allan, SNP, 17.2.1941-25.8.1998, 1994-1998

ANNEX 2

MacCormick, Donald Neil, SNP, 27.5.1941-5.4.2009, 1999-2004
Macmillan, Alexander Daniel, Conservative Party, 10.10.1943-; 1999-2004
Magid, Magid, Green Party, 26.6.1989-; 2019-2020
Marshall, John, Conservative Party, 19.8.1940-; 1979-1989
Martin, David, Labour Party, 26.8.1954-; 1984-2019
Mather, Graham, Conservative Party, 23.10.1954-; 1994-1999
Matthews, Rupert Oliver, Conservative Party, 5.12.1961-; 2017-2019
Mayer, Alex, Labour Party, 2.6.1981-; 2016-2019
McAvan, Linda, Labour Party, 2.12.1962-; 1998-2019
McCarthy, Arlene, Labour Party, 10.10.1960-; 1994-2014
McClarkin, Emma, Conservative Party, 9.10.1978-; 2009-2019
McCubbin, Henry, Labour Party, 15.7.1942-; 1989-1994
McGowan, Michael, Labour Party, 19.5.1940-; 1984-1999
McIntosh, Anne, Conservative Party, 20.9.1954-; 1989-1999
McIntyre, Anthea, Conservative Party, 29.6.1954-; 2011-2020
McLeod, Aileen, SNP, 24.8.1971-; 2019-2020
McMahon, Hugh, Labour Party, 17.6.1938-; 1984-1999
McMillan-Scott, Edward, Conservative Party, 15.8.1949-; 1984-2014
McNally, Eryl, Labour Party, 11.4.1942-; 1994-2004
Megahy, Thomas, Labour Party, 16.7.1929-5.10.2008, 1979-1999
Miller, Bill, Labour Party, 22.7.1954-; 1994-2004
Mobarik, Nosheena Shaheen, Conservative Party, 16.10.1957-; 2017-2020
Mohammed, Shaffaq, Liberal Democrat, 21.7.1972-; 2019-2020
Monteith, Brian, Brexit Party, 8.1.1958-; 2019-2020
Moody, Clare, Labour Party, 30.10.1965-; 2014-2019
Moorhouse, Cecil James Olaf, Conservative Party, 1.6.1924-6.1.2014, 1979-1999
Moraes, Claude, Labour Party, 22.10.1965-; 1999-2020
Moreland, Robert John, Conservative Party, 21.8.1941-; 1979-1984
Morgan, Eluned, Labour Party, 16.2.1967-; 1994-2009
Morris, David, Labour Party, 28.1.1930-24.1.2007, 1984-1999
Mote, Ashley, UKIP, 25.1.1936-30.3.2020, 2004-2009
Mummery, June Alison, Brexit Party, 1963/1964?-; 2019-2020
Murphy, Simon, Labour Party, 24.2.1962-; 1994-2004

Nattrass, Mike Henry, UKIP, 14.12.1945-; 2004-2014
Needle, Clive, Labour Party, 22.9.1956-; 1994-1999
Nethsingha, Lucy Kathleen, Liberal Democrat, 6.2.1973-; 2019-2020
Newens, Stan, Labour & Co-operative Party, 4.2.1930-2.3.2021, 1984-1999
Newman, Eddy, Labour Party, 14.5.1953-; 1984-1999
Newton Dunn, Bill, Conservative Party, 3.10.1941-; 1979-1994, 1999-2014, 2019-2020
Nicholls, Harmar, Conservative Party, 1.11.19-15.9.2000, 1979-1984
Nicholson, David, Conservative Party, 2009.1922-19.7.1996, 1979-1984
Nicholson, Emma, Liberal Democrat, 16.10.1941-; 1999-2009
Nicholson, Jim, UUP, 29.1.1945-; 1989-2019
Normanton, Tom, Conservative Party, 12.3.1917-6.8.1997, 1979-1989
Nuttall, Paul Andrew, UKIP, 30.11.1976-; 2009-2019

Oddy, Christine, Labour Party, 20.9.1955-27.7.2014, 1989-1999
O'Flynn, Patrick James, UKIP, 29.8.1965-; 2014-2019
O'Toole, Barbara "Mo" Maria, Labour Party, 24.2.1960-; 1999-2004
Overgaard-Nielsen, Henrik Eyser, Brexit Party, 8.2.1959-; 2019-2020

Paisley, Ian, DUP, 6.4.1926-12.9.2014, 1979-2004
Palmer, Rory, Labour Party, 19.11.1981-; 2017-2020
Parish, Neil, Conservative Party, 26.5.1956-; 1999-2009
Parker, Margot, UKIP, 24.7.1943-; 2014-2019
Patten, Matthew, Brexit Party, 21.5.1962-; 2019-2020
Patterson, George "Ben" Benjamin, Conservative Party, 21.4.1939-; 1979-1994
Pearce, Andrew, Conservative Party, 1.12.1937-; 1979-1989
Perry, Roy, Conservative Party, 12.2.1943-; 1994-2004
Phillips, Alexandra Louise Rosenfield, Green Party, 9.7.1985-; 2019-2020
Phillips, Alexandra Lesley, Brexit Party, 26.12.1983-; 2019-2020
Pitt, Terry, Labour Party, 2.3.1937-3.10.1986, 1984-1986
Plumb, Henry, Conservative Party, 27.3.1925-15.4.2022, 1979-1999
Pollack, Anita, Labour Party, 3.6.1946-; 1989-1999
Porritt, Luisa Manon, Liberal Democrat, 23.5.1987-; 2019-2020
Prag, Derek, Conservative Party, 6.8.1923-20.01.2010, 1979-1994
Price, Peter, Conservative, 19.2.1942-; 1979-1994
Procter, John Michael, Conservative Party, 7.11.1966-; 2016-2019
Prout, Christopher, Conservative Party, 1.1.1942-12.7.2009; 1979-1994
Provan, James Lyal Clark, Conservative Party, 19.12.1936-; 1979-1989, 1994-2004
Pugh, "Jake" Edward Francis, Brexit Party, 20.10.1960-; 2019-2020
Purvis, John Robert, Conservative Party, 6.7.1938-20.3.2022, 1979-1984, 1999-2009

Quin, Joyce, Labour Party, 26.11.1944-; 1979-1989

Rawlings, Patricia, Conservative Party, 27.1.1939-; 1989-1994
Read, Mel, Labour Party, 8.1.1939-; 1989-2004
Rees-Mogg, Annunziata, Brexit Party, 25.3.1979-; 2019-2020
Reid, Julia, UKIP, 16.7.1952-; 2014-2019
Rhys-Williams, Brandon Meredith, Conservative Party, 14.11.1927-18.5.1988, 1979-1984
Ritchie, Sheila E., Liberal Democrats, 18.5.1957-; 2019-2020
Roberts, Shelagh, Conservative Party, 13.10.1924-16.1.1992, 1979-1989
Rogers, Allan, Labour Party, 24.10.1932-; 1979-1984
Rowett, Catherine Joanna, Green Party, 29.12.1956-; 2019-2020
Rowland, Robert Andrew, Brexit Party, 28.2.1966-23.1.2021, 2019-2020

Scott Cato, Molly, Green Party, 21.5.1963-; 2014-2020
Scott-Hopkins, James, Conservative Party, 29.11.1921-11.3.1995, 1979-1994
Seal, Barry, Labour Party, 28.10.1937-; 1979-1999
Seligman, Madron, Conservative Party, 10.11.1918-9.7.2002, 1979-1994
Seymour, Jill, UKIP, 8.5.1958-; 2014-2019
Sherlock, Alexander, Conservative Party, 14.2.1922-18.2.1999, 1979-1989

Simmonds, Richard J., Conservative Party, 2.8.1944-; 1979-1994
Simon, Siôn, Labour Party, 23.12.1968-; 2014-2019
Simpson, Anthony, Conservative Party, 28.10.1935-14.8.2022; 1979-1994
Simpson, Brian, Labour Party, 6.2.1953-; 1989-2004, 2006-2014
Sinclaire, Nicole, "Nikki", UKIP, 26.7.1968-; 2009-2014
Skinner, Peter, Labour Party, 1.6.1959-; 1994-2014
Smith, Alex, Labour Party, 2.12.1943-; 1989-1999
Smith, Alyn, SNP, 15.9.1973-; 2004-2019
Smith, Llewellyn 'Llew', Labour Party, 16.4.1944-26.5.2021, 1984-1994
Spencer, Tom, Conservative Party, 10.4.1948-; 1979-1984, 1989-1999
Spicer, James Wilton, Conservative Party, 4.10.1925-21.3.2015, 1979-1984
Spiers, Shaun, Labour & Co-operative Party, 23.4.1962-; 1994-1999
Stedman-Bryce, Louis, Brexit Party, 00.12.1974-; 2019-2020
Stevens, John, Conservative Party, 23.5.1955-; 1989-1999
Stevenson, George, Labour Party, 30.8.1938-; 1984-1994
Stevenson, Struan John Stirton, Conservative Party, 4.4.1948-; 1999-2014
Stewart, Kenneth, Labour Party, 28.6.1925-2.9.1996, 1984-1996
Stewart-Clark, John "Jack", Conservative Party, 17.9.1929-; 1979-1999
Stihler, Catherine, Labour Party, 30.7.1973-; 1999-2019
Strachey, Charles Towneley, Conservative Party, 6.9.1945-; 1979-1994
Sturdy, Robert, Conservative Party, 22.6.1944-; 1994-2014
Sumberg, David Anthony Gerald, Conservative Party, 2.6.1941-; 1999-2009
Swinburne, Jacqueline Kay, Conservative Party, 8.6.1967-; 2009-2019

Tannock, Charles, Conservative Party, 25.9.1957-; 1999-2019
Tappin, Michael, Labour Party, 22.12.1946-; 1994-1999
Taylor, John David, UUP, 24.12.1937-; 1979-1989
Taylor, John Mark, Conservative Party, 19.8.1941-28.5.2017, 1979-1984
Taylor, Keith Richard, Brexit Party, 1.8.1953-; 2010-2019
Taylor, Rebecca, Liberal Democrat, 10.8.1975-; 2012-2014
Tennant, John David Edward, Brexit Party, 25.12.1986-; 2019-2020
Teverson, Robin, Liberal Democrat, 31.3.1952-; 1994-1999
Thomas, David, Labour Party, 12.1.1955-; 1994-1999
Tice, Richard, Brexit Party, 13.9.1964-; 2019-2020
Titford, Jeffrey William, UKIP, 24.10.1933-; 1999-2009
Titley, Gary, Labour Party, 19.1.1950-; 1989-2009
Tomlinson, John, Labour & Co-operative, 1.8.1939-; 1984-1999
Tongue, Carole, Labour Party, 14.10.1955-; 1984-1999
Truscott, Peter, Labour Party, 20.3.1959-; 1994-1999
Tuckman, Frederick Augustus, Conservative Party, 9.6.1922-6.7.2017, 1979-1989
Turner, Amédée, Conservative Party, 26.3.1929-13.9.2021, 1979-1994
Twinn, Ian, Conservative Party, 26.4.1950-; 2003-2004
Tyrrell, Alan Rupert, Conservative Party, 27.6.1933-23.10.2014, 1979-1984

Van Orden, Geoffrey, Conservative Party, 10.4.1945-; 1999-2020
Vanneck, Peter, Conservative Party, 7.1.1922-2.8.1999, 1979-1989
Vaughan, Derek, Labour Party, 2.5.1961-; 2009-2019

Villiers, Theresa, Conservative Party, 5.3.1968-; 1999-2005
Voaden, Caroline Jane, Liberal Democrat, 22.11.1968-; 2019-2020
von Wiese, Irina Stephanie, Liberal Democrat, 11.9.1967-; 2019-2020

Waddington, Susan, Labour Party, 23.8.1944-; 1994-1999
Wallis, Diana, Liberal Democrat, 28.6.1954-; 1999-2012
Ward, Julie, Labour Party, 7.3.1957-; 2014-2020
Warner, Frederick, Conservative Party, 2.5.1918-30.9.1995, 1979-1984
Watson, Graham, Liberal Democrat, 23.3.1956-; 1994-2014
Watts, Mark, Labour Party, 11.6.1964-; 1994-2004
Wellesley, Charles (Marquess of Douro, Duke of Wellington), Conservative Party, 19.8.1945-; 1979-1989
Wells, James, Brexit Party, 00.00.00, 2019-2020
Welsh, Michael, Conservative Party, 22.5.1942-; 1979-1994
West, Norman, Labour Party, 26.11.1935-7.9.2009, 1984-1998
White, Ian, Labour Party, 8.4.1945-27.6.2021, 1989-1999
Whitehead, Phillip, Labour Party, 30.5.1937-31.12.2005, 1994-2005
Whittaker, John, UKIP, 7.6.1945-; 2004-2009
Widdecombe, Ann, Brexit Party, 4.10.1947-; 2019-2020
Willmott, Glenis, Labour Party, 4.3.1951-; 2006-2017
Wilson, Joe, Labour Party, 6.7.1937-; 1989-1999
Wise, Thomas Harold, UKIP, 13.5.1948-; 2004-2009
Woolfe, Steven Marcus, UKIP, 6.10.1967-; 2014-2019
Wyn, Eurig, Plaid Cymru, 10.10.1944-25.6.2019, 1999-2004
Wynn, Terry, Labour Party, 27.6.1946-; 1989-2006

Yannakoudakis, Marina, Conservative Party, 16.4.1956-; 2009-2014

Index of Names

Note: all British MEPs 1979-2020 are additionally listed in Annex 2 above.
P = page in photo sections.

Adams, Gerry 140
Aker, Tim 293
Alexander, Danny 66
Alfonsín, Raoúl 147
Allard, Christian 228, 291
Allister, Jim 291-2
Almunia, Joaquin 86
Anderson, Donald 93
Anderson, Heather 225, 287
Anderson, Martina 247, 291
Andreasen, Marta 29, 181
Andreotti, Giulio 157
Arndt, Rudi 46
Arnott, Jonathan 293
Ashdown, Paddy 181
Ashworth, Richard 34, 287, 293
Atkins, Robert 29, 288
Atkinson, Janice 293
Attwooll, Elisabeth 59-60

Bainbridge, Timothy 136
Balfe, Richard 49, 289, 292
Balfour, Neil 135
Bangemann, Martin 58, 66, 266
Barnier, Michel 192, 275
Barón, Enrique 144, 148
Barroso, José Manuel 66, 79-80, 96, 183
Barrot, Jacques 183

Bartenstein, Martin 191
Barton, Roger 49
Bashir, Amjad 29, 33, 293
Batten, Gerard 287
Bearder, Catherine 60-2, 66, 112
Beazley, Christopher 288
Beazley, Peter 288
Beckett, Margaret 7, 48, 162
Bell-Cross, Lorin 68
Benn, Tony 40
Bennion, Phil 60, 62
Berlinguer, Enrico 5
Bethell, Nicholas 11, 146, 194-8, 289-90, P1
Bethell, William 194
Billingham, Angela 289
Blackman, David 267
Blair, Cherie 174
Blair, Tony 29, 48-50, 59, 69-70, 76, 84-91, 95, 114-6, 162-4, 180-1, 186, 236
Bolkestein, Frits 190
Bond, Martyn 65
Bonner, Yelena 196-7
Borrell, Josep 173
Bours, Louise 293
Bowe, David 49
Bowis, John 28, 288
Bowles, Sharon 15, 60, 81, 112, 290, P7
Boyes, Roland 6, 289
Bradbourn, Philip 291
Brandt, Willy 5-6, 210
Brittan, Leon 105, 107, 129
Brok, Elmar 154, 266

Brons, Andrew 293
Brookes, Beata 231, 233
Brophy, Jane 62
Brown, Gordon 30, 155, 188, 215, 238
Buchan, Janey 45, 223
Buckley, George 214
Budd, Colin 87
Bufton, John 233-4, 239
Bullock, Jonathan 293
Bunting, Judith 62
Burke, Dick 242
Bushill-Matthews, Philip 287
Buthelezi, Chief 196
Byers, Steve 94

Caborn, Richard 289
Callaghan, James 5, 121
Callanan, Martin 28, 188, 287, 289, 294
Cameron, David 7, 30-4, 54, 74, 79-80, 110-1, 152, 186-8, 192, 201, 278, 294
Campbell Bannerman, David 28, 33, 292
Carswell, Douglas 74, 187
Carver, James 293
Cashman, Michael 98, 117, 289
Castle, Barbara 5, 40-5, 47, 101, 121-5, 160, 174, 210-1, 287-90, P1, P3
Castle, Ted 122
Catherwood, Fred 106, 150
Cheysson, Claude 264
Chichester, Giles 29, 58, 287
Chirac, Jacques 5, 87, 162, 183
Churchill, Winston 19, 63, 98
Ciolos, Dacian 66
Clarke, Ken 15, 29, 31
Clegg, Nick 59-60, 64-5, 89, 117, 289, 294
Cleverly, James 72
Clinton, Bill 140
Clwyd, Ann 231, 236-8, 289
Coates, Ken 49, 291
Coburn, David 226, 293
Cockfield, Arthur 145
Collins, Jane 293
Collins, Ken 15, 126-32, 212, 223, 226, 279, P13
Cook, Robin 88, 164
Corbett, Richard 15, 54-6, 89, 98, 112, 175-9, 278, 287, P16
Corbyn, Jeremy 12, 55, 177-8
Cot, Jean-Pierre 94, 161, 263
Cox, Pat 66, 158, 166

Crampton, Peter 49
Crawley, Christine 289
Crick, Michael 72, 180
Cryer, Bob 43, 288-9
Cunningham, Tony 289
Curry, David 289

Dalziel, Ian 224
Dance, Seb 55, 274
Dartmouth, William (William Legge) 290, 293
David, Wayne 46, 48-50, 56, 230-2, 234, 236-8, 240
Davies, Chris 59-62, 66, 287-8
de Brun, Bairbre 246, 291
de Ferranti, Basil 5, 133-7, 288, 291, P4
de Gaulle, Charles 20
De Vries, Gijs 66
Delors, Jacques 24, 66, 94, 102, 104, 106, 115-6, 136, 141, 156-7, 235, 243, 245, 263-5
Deva, Nirj 28, 288
Dhamija, Dinesh 62
Dodds, Anneliese 289
Dodds, Diane 246, 291
Donnelly, Alan 10, 15, 49, 56, 161, 263-6, 287, P10
Donnelly, Brendan 149, 292, P11
Douro, Marquess of, see Wellesley, Charles
Dover, Den 28, 288
Drummond, Flick 217
Duff, Andrew 59-60, 66, 81, 89, 112, 278, 287, P11
Duncan Smith, Iain 29
Duncan, Ian 227, 289

Edmonds, Frances 212
Edmonds, Phil 212
Elles, Diana 150, 244, 288-9
Elles, James 288
Elliot, Michael 49
Enright, Derek 209-15, 289, P2
Enright, Duncan 209
Erhard, Ludwig 96
Etheridge, Bill 293
Evans, Jill 231-3, 235-8, 240
Evans, Jonathan 10, 230, 232-3, 235-6, 238, 287
Evans, Robert 49

Ewing, Winnie 106, 222-3, 225, 289, 291, P3

Faith, Sheila 289
Falconer, Alex 49, 224
Fall, Kate 207
Farage, Kirsten 183
Farage, Nigel 13, 16, 70, 72-5, 103, 116-7, 180-4, 188, 252, 275, 281, 287, 293, P15
Ferrier, Margaret 287
Fieldhouse, Tom 12-3, 17
Finch, Ray 293
Fletcher-Vane, Richard (Lord Inglewood) 289-90
Foot, Michael 44
Ford, Glyn 47, 50-1, 56, 161, 287
Ford, Vicky 81, 97, 112, 117, 289
Forman, Lance 36, 293
Forth, Eric 23, 289
Foster, Jacqueline 289
Foulkes, George 93
Fox, Ashley 80, 287
Fox, Claire 290
Fuller, Annabelle 183

Gaitskell, Hugh 20
Gallagher, Michael 43, 291, 293
Galland, Yves 66
Gebhardt, Evelyne 191
Geldof, Bob 196
Giannini, Rita 165
Gibson, Barbara 62
Gill, Nathan 233, 239, 291, 293
Gill, Neena 10, 97, 112
Girling, Julie 34, 83, 293
Giscard d'Estaing, Valéry 66, 104, 115, 167, 225
Gladwyn, Lord (Gladwyn Jebb) 57
Glinne, Ernest 5
Goldsmith, James 69-70, P15
González, Felipe 86, 163
Goodwill, Robert 289
Gove, Michael 33
Gow, David 154
Green, Pauline 7, 14, 47-8, 56, 71, 106, 160-4, 278, 287, P5
Griffin, Nick 182
Griffiths, Win 212, 230-1, 234-5, 237-8, 240, 289
Gundelach, Finn 123

Hague, William 28-9, 152, 186, 189, 294
Hain, Peter 115
Hall, Fiona 60, 66, 287
Hallam, David 49
Hancock, Mike 216
Hannan, Daniel 11, 28, 30, 33, 35, 70, 185-8, 289, 294, P14
Harbour, Malcolm 15, 81, 112, 189-92, 279, P13
Hardstaff, Veronica 11
Harley, David 15, P9
Harris, David 288
Harris, Lucy 36, 293
Harrison, Lyndon 289
Hassan, Joshua 196
Hattersley, Roy 162
Hayter, Dianne 35, 47, P8
Heaney, Seamus 139, 143
Heath, Edward 19-22, 134
Heaton-Harris, Chris 28, 70, 289, 294, P14
Heffer, Eric 40
Helmer, Roger 70, 81, 201, 292, P14
Henderson, Doug 163
Hendrick, Mark 289
Heseltine, Michael 150
Hill, Jonathan 80
Hindley, Michael 49
Holmes, Michael 72, 181, 287
Hook, Anthony 62
Hoon, Geoff 10, 94, 214, 289, P3
Hooper, Gloria 289
Horwood, Martin 61-2, 64, 274, 288
Howard, Michael 29, 186
Howe, Geoffrey 15, 26, 44, 144
Huckfield, Les 43, 288
Hudghton, Ian 228
Huggett, Richard 58
Hughes, Stephen 49
Huhne, Chris 59-60, 89, 289
Hume, John 11, 106, 139-43, 164, 212, 242-6, 279, 289, 291, P5
Hurd, Douglas 87

Jackson, Caroline 101-2, 288
Jackson, Robert 288
Jacobs, Francis 135, 265
James, Diane 287, 293
Jenkins, Roy 66, 98, 100

John Paul II, Pope 147, 244
Johnson, Boris 33, 35-6, 76, 93, 184, 187, 205, 288, 294
Johnson, Rachel 204
Johnson, Richard 39
Johnson, Stanley 204-8, 288, P2
Johnston, Russell 57-8, 223
Jones Parry, Emyr 145
Jospin, Lionel 87, 162
Juncker, Jean-Claude 90

Kamall, Syed 82, 287, 289, P7
Karim, Saj 292
Kaufman, Gerald 92
Kellett-Bowman, Edward 288, P2
Kellett-Bowman, Elaine 23, 288
Kennedy, Charles 64
Kerr, Andrew 293
Kerr, Hugh 49, 291
Kerr, John 67, 104, 107, 116
Key, Brian 212
Khan, Afzal 289
Khan, Wajid 97, 289
Kilroy-Silk, Robert 75, 181, 288, 292
King, Julian 259
Kinnock, Glenys 117, 169-174, 230, 232, 238, 289, P7
Kinnock, Neil 39, 44, 46-7, 92, 155-6, 234
Kirk, Peter 21
Kirkhope, Timothy 23, 27-30, 97, 112, 188, 287-90, 294
Knapman, Roger 287-8
Kohl, Helmut 105, 146, 151, 157, 162, 264
Kok, Wim 86

Lagana, Giada 241
Laitenberger, Johannes 79
Lambert, Jean 252
Lamy, Pascal 243
Larkin, Colm 243
Le Pen, Jean-Marie 144
Le Pen, Marine 182
Letwin, Oliver 31-3
Lewer, Andrew 289
Lexden, Alistair 133
Liddle, Roger 84
Lidington, David 79
Lofthouse, Geoffrey 214
Lomas, Alf 44-7, 49, 287
Long, Naomi 61, 247, 291

Longworth, John 36, 293
Lucas, Caroline 117, 279, 289, P10
Ludford, Sarah 59-60, 289
Lynne, Liz 59-60, 288
Lyon, George 60, 228, 291

Macartney, Allan 228, 291
MacCormick, Neil 225, 227
Machel, Graça 172
Macmillan, Alexander 289-90
Macmillan, Harold 19-20, 290
Major, John 10, 26-7, 85, 94, 104, 150-1, 157, 200-1
Mandela, Mandla 197
Mandela, Nelson 146-7, 172, 196-7
Mandelson, Peter 50, 67
Marchenko, Anatoli 146
Mardell, Mark 177
Markov, Georgi and Annabel 195
Marshall, John 161, 289
Martin, David 14, 106, 112, 154-9, 224-5, 278, 287, P6
Martin, Simone 141
Maxwell, Gordon 42
May, Theresa 34, 63, 67, 154, 177, 184, 187, 202, 260, 273
McAllister, David 282
McAvan, Linda 11
McCarthy, Arlene 117
McCreevy, Charlie 115, 191
McCubbin, Henry 226
McDonald, Mary Lou 246
McGowan, Mike 49
McIntosh, Anne 289-90
McIntyre, Anthea 35
McLeod, Aileen 228, 291
McMahon, Hugh 49
McMillan-Scott, Edward 10, 14, 28, 31, 59, 61, 117, 207, 268, 270, 287, 292-5, P12
McNally, Eryl 49
Meacher, Michael 214
Megahy, Tom 49
Mellor, David 200
Menon, Anand 116
Merritt, Giles 165
Miliband, Ed 53
Millan, Bruce 105, 156, 171, 237
Miller, Bill 226
Mitterrand, François 157, 264
Mobarik, Nosheena 35, 227, 289

Mohammed, Shaffaq 62
Montgomerie, Tim 75
Moore, Richard 58
Moorhouse, James 28, 59, 291, 294
Moraes, Claude 15, 112, 117, 257, 274, 279, P10
Morgan, Eluned 11, 173-4, 230-2, 234-5, 237-8, 240, 289, 291
Morris, David 49, 231-2, 235, 238, 240
Mote, Ashley 181, 292
Murphy, Simon 51-2, 54, 56, 287
Mussolini, Alessandra 182

Napolitano, Giorgio 88, 94
Nattrass, Mike 293
Neave, Airey 19
Needle, Clive 49
Nethsingha, Lucy 61-2
Newens, Stan 49, 288
Newton Dunn, Bill 23, 28, 59, 61-2, 199-203, 289, 292, 294, P6
Newton Dunn, Tom 199, P6
Nicholls, Harmar 23, 288-90
Nicholson, David 5, 101
Nicholson, Emma 59-60, 288-90
Nicholson, James 245, 279, 289
Nokes, Caroline 216
Normanton, Tom 23, 288
Nuttall, Paul 287, 293

O'Flynn, Patrick 293
Oddy, Christine 49
Oliver, Craig 67

Paisley, Ian 105, 141, 147, 213, 243-6, 279, 290, P5
Palmer, Rory 273
Parish, Neil 29, 117, 289
Parker, George 114
Parker, Margot 293
Patten, Chris 105, 150
Patterson, Ben 23, 28-9, 135, P2-3
Paxman, Jeremy 177
Perry, Roy 216-8, P2
Pitt, Terry 291
Plumb, Henry 14, 23-4, 42, 101, 144-50, 172, 234, 244, 287, 289, P9
Pollack, Anita 121, P1
Porritt, Luisa 62
Pounder, Rafton 21

Powell, Charles 137
Priestley, Julian 15, 158, 162, 279, P9
Prout, Christopher 15, 25, 149-53, 278, 287, 289, 294, P4
Purvis, John 28, 223-4

Quin, Joyce 11, 129, 212, 289-90

Ramsay, Robert 145
Rawlings, Patricia 289
Read, Mel 10
Reagan, Ronald 124
Reckless, Mark 74
Rees-Mogg, Annunziata 36, 288, 293
Reid, Alec 140
Reid, Julia 293
Reintke, Terry 275
Rhys-Williams, Brandon 23, 288
Ritchie, Sheila 62
Roberts, Shelagh 289
Robertson, George 71, 92, 280, P8
Rocard, Michel 48, 88
Rogalla, Dieter 136
Rogers, Allan 230-1, 233
Rogers, Ivan 14, 106, 281
Russell, Michael 221

Sainsbury, David 66
Sanders, Adrian 58
Santer, Jacques 108, 164
Sassoli, David 275
Schreyer, Michaele 252
Schröder, Gerhard 86, 162
Schulz, Martin P9
Schüssel, Wolfgang 191
Scott-Hopkins, James 5, 23, 101, 244, 287-8
Seal, Barry 44, 46-7, 49-50, 55-6, 287
Seligman, Madron 23, P3
Simon, Siôn 288
Sinclaire, Nikki 181, 183, 292
Sked, Alan 181
Smith, Alex 49
Smith, Alyn 97, 225, 227-8, 287, 289
Smith, Chris 131
Smith, John 7, 48, 161, P8
Smith, Llew 169, 231-2, 238, 240
Solzhenitsyn, Aleksandr 195
Soyinka, Wole 173
Spicer, Jim 23, 288

Spiers, Shaun 49
Squarcialupi, Vera 212
Stahl, Gerhard 265
Stedman-Bryce, Louis 227, 293
Steel, David 64
Stevens, John 28, 292
Stevenson, George 289
Stewart, Ken 43, 49, 291
Stewart-Clark, Jack P3
Stihler, Catherine 225
Strachey, Charles 289-90
Stratford, Joshua 285
Straw, Jack 52, 69, 76, 180
Stuart, Gisela 116
Suttie, Alison 66
Swinburne, Kay 80, 112, 231-3, 235, 239

Tannock, Charles 97, 112
Taylor, John 141, 243-5, 279, 288-91
Taylor, Rebecca 60
Teasdale, Anthony 15
Teverson, Robin 58, 65, 290
Thatcher, Margaret 5, 21-2, 24-6, 94, 98, 137, 146-7, 151, 195-6, 200-1, 224, 237
Thomas, David 49
Thorning-Schmidt, Helle 102
Tindemans, Leo 146, 264
Titford, Jeffrey 72, 181, 287
Titley, Gary 45, 52, 56, 161, 287
Tomlinson, John 45, 288-9
Trimble, David 140
Trojan, Carlos 265
Trump, Donald 183, 260
Truscott, Peter 289
Tugendhat, Christopher 71, 100, 280
Turner, Amédée 151
Twinn, Ian 288

Van Orden, Geoffrey 35, 97, 112, 287

Van Rompuy, Herman 54, 73, 112, 176, 183
Vanneck, Peter 101
Vaughan, Derek 232-5, 237-8, 240
Veil, Simone 6, 66, 101, 235, 264
Verhofstadt, Guy 66
Villiers, Theresa 117, 289
Voaden, Caroline 62, 66
von der Leyen, Ursula 55, 274
von Wiese, Irina 62, 97
von Wogau, Karl 136

Waddington, Sue 49
Wainwright, Rob 259
Walker-Smith, Derek 21
Wall, Stephen 88
Wallis, Diana 59-60, 66, 287
Warner, Fred 101
Watson, Graham 15, 57, 66, 165-8, 279, 287, P12
Waugh, Auberon 195
Webster, Sharon 173
Wellesley, Charles (Marquess of Douro, Duke of Wellington) 5, 289-90
Wells, James 233, 235, 237, 239
West, Norman 49
White, Ian 49
Whitehead, Phillip 53, 288, 291
Widdecombe, Ann 288
Wilding, Peter 67
Williams, Gareth 230
Williamson, David 105, 144
Willmott, Glenis 53-4, 56, 112, 287
Wilson, Harold 21, 39, 209
Wilson, Joe 49, 231-5, 238
Wise, Tom 181
Wolfson, Simon 197
Woolfe, Steven 293
Wulf-Matthies, Monika 174